Microsoft® Word 6.0 For Windows

Microsoft® Word 6.0 For Windows®

Sarah E. Hutchinson

Glen J. Coulthard

THE IRWIN ADVANTAGE SERIES FOR COMPUTER EDUCATION

IRWIN

Chicago • Bogotá • Boston • Buenos Aires • Caracas
London • Madrid • Mexico City • Sydney • Toronto

Book Team
Sponsoring editor: *Paul Ducham/Garrett Glanz*
Project editor: *Jane Lightell*
Production supervisor: *Pat Frederickson*
Manager, graphic and desktop services: *Kim Meriwether*
Designer: *Laurie Entringer*
Compositor: *Douglas & Gayle, Limited*
Typeface: *11/13 Bodoni Book*
Printer: *WebCrafters*

Times Mirror
Higher Education Group

ISBN 0-256-20228-1

Printed in the United States of America
2 3 4 5 6 7 8 9 0 WC 2 1 0 9 8 7 6

Contents

SESSION 1

MICROSOFT WORD 6.0 FOR WINDOWS
Fundamentals

SESSION 2

MICROSOFT WORD 6.0 FOR WINDOWS
Formatting Commands

SESSION 3

MICROSOFT WORD 6.0 FOR WINDOWS
Editing and Proofing Tools

SESSION 4

MICROSOFT WORD 6.0 FOR WINDOWS
Printing and Document Management

SESSION 5

MICROSOFT WORD 6.0 FOR WINDOWS
Increasing Your Productivity

APPENDIX

USING THIS GUIDE

Welcome to the Irwin Advantage Series! This tutorial is one in a series of learning guides that lead you through the most popular microcomputer software programs available. The following features are incorporated into each session of our guides to ensure that your learning experience is as productive and enjoyable as possible:

- Each session begins with a real-world ***case study*** that introduces you to a fictitious person or company and describes their immediate problem or opportunity. During the session, you obtain the knowledge and skills necessary to define and solve the problem or take advantage of the opportunity. At the end of the session, you are invited to solve problems directly related to the case scenario.

- ***Concepts, skills, and procedures*** are grouped into session topics and are presented in a logical and structured manner.

- ***In Addition boxes*** are placed strategically throughout the guide to provide information about topics related to the current discussion, but beyond the scope of the text.

- Commands and procedures are introduced using ***hands-on examples in a step-by-step format***, and students are encouraged to perform the steps along with the guide.

- Each session concludes with ***short answer questions and hands-on exercises***. These exercises are integrated with the session's objectives; they were not added as an afterthought. The exercises are comprehensive and meaningful, and they provide students with an opportunity to practice the session material. For maximum benefit, students should complete all the exercises at the end of each session.

- For each of the learning guides, an instructor's resource kit is available with suggested answers to the questions, exercises, and case problems appearing at the end of each session. In addition, the resource kit provides a test bank of additional questions and exercises.

The exercises and examples in this guide use several standard conventions to indicate menu options, keystroke combinations, and command instructions.

MENU INSTRUCTIONS

In Windows, all Menu bar options and pull-down menu commands have an underlined or highlighted letter in each option. When you need to execute a command from the Menu bar—the row of menu choices across the top of the screen—the tutorial's instruction line separates the Menu bar option from the command with a comma. Notice also that the word "CHOOSE" is always used for menu commands. For example, the command for quitting Windows is shown as:

CHOOSE: File, Exit

This instruction tells you to choose the File option on the Menu bar and then to choose the Exit command from the File pull-down menu. The actual steps for choosing a menu command are discussed later in this guide.

KEYSTROKES AND KEYSTROKE COMBINATIONS

When two keys must be pressed together, the tutorial's instruction line shows the keys joined with a plus (+) sign. For example, you can execute a command from the Windows Menu bar by holding down ALT and then pressing the key with the underlined or highlighted letter of the desired command.

To illustrate this type of keystroke combination, the following statement shows how to access the File menu option:

PRESS: ALT+`f`

In this instruction, you press the ALT key first and then hold it down while you press `f`. Once both keys have been pressed, they are then immediately released.

COMMAND INSTRUCTIONS

This guide indicates with a special typeface data that you are required to type in yourself. For example:

TYPE: `Income Statement`

When you are required to enter unique information, such as the current date or your name, the instruction appears in italics. The following instruction directs you to type your name in place of the actual words: "your name."

TYPE: *your name*

Instructions that use general directions rather than a specific option or command name appear italicized in the regular typeface.

SELECT: *a different pattern for the chart*

ADVANTAGE DISKETTE

The Advantage Diskette provided with this guide or by your instructor contains the files that you use in each session and in the hands-on exercises. ***This diskette is extremely important to your success with the guide.*** If you are using this guide in a self-study program, we suggest that you make a copy of the Advantage Diskette using the DOS DISKCOPY command. When the guide asks you to insert the Advantage Diskette, you insert and work with the copied diskette instead. By following this procedure, you will be able to work through the guide again at a later date using a fresh copy of the Advantage Diskette. For more information on using the DISKCOPY command, please refer to your DOS manual.

ACKNOWLEDGMENTS

This series of learning guides is the direct result of the teamwork and heart of many people. We sincerely thank the reviewers, instructors, and students who have shared their comments and suggestions with us over the past few years. We do read them! With their valuable feedback, our guides have evolved into the product you see before you. We also appreciate the efforts of the instructors and students from Vernon's Continuing Education division of Okanagan University College who classroom-tested our guides to ensure accuracy, relevancy, and completeness.

We also give many thanks to Tom Casson and Kim Meriwether from Richard D. Irwin for their skillful coordination and production of this text. You and your respective teams were a pleasure to work with. Special recognition goes to Stacey Sawyer for her original design work on the series and for being just so talented! Finally, to the many others who weren't directly involved in this project but who have stood by us the whole way, we appreciate your patience and understanding.

WRITE TO US

We welcome your response to this book, for we are trying to make it as useful a learning tool as possible. Write to us in care of Thomas Casson, Publisher, Richard D. Irwin, 1333 Burr Ridge Parkway, Burr Ridge, IL 60521. Thank you.

Sarah E. Hutchinson

Glen J. Coulthard

Microsoft Word 6.0

Fundamentals

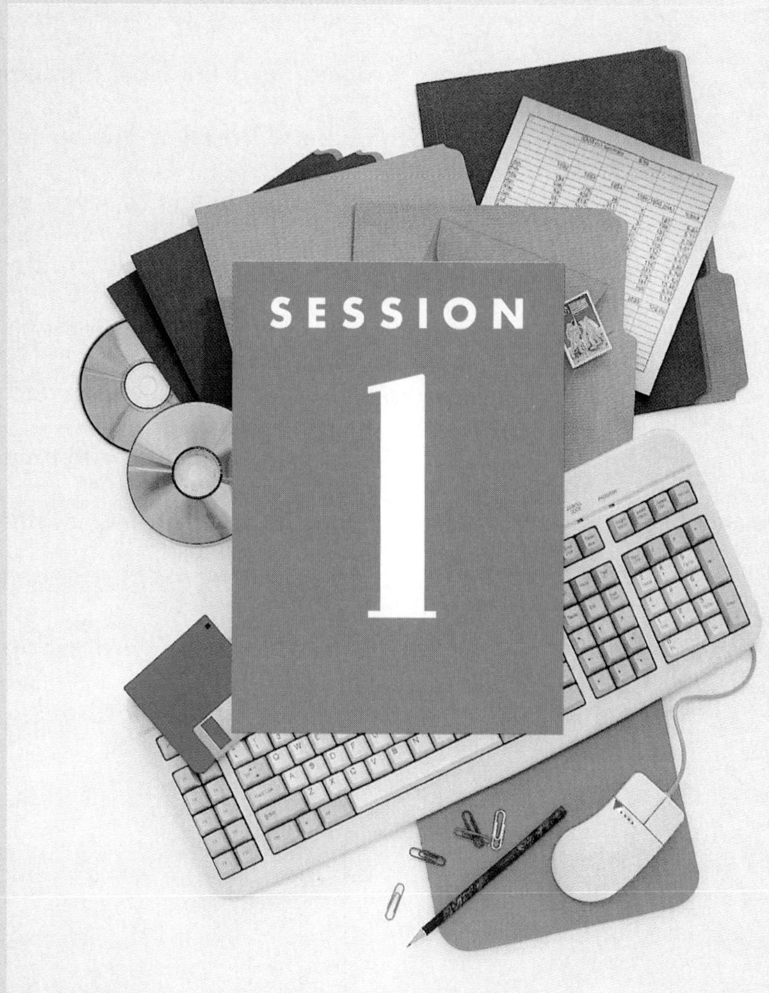

SESSION OUTLINE

Word Processing with Microcomputers
The Windows Advantage
Features of Microsoft Word 6.0
Working with Word
Starting Word
The Guided Tour
Getting Help
Creating a Document
Using the Undo Command
Saving and Closing a Document
Beginning a New Document
Opening an Existing Document
Leaving Word
Summary
Key Terms
Exercises

INTRODUCTION

Word processing is the most popular application for microcomputers. Whether you write term papers, business plans, or letters, a word processing software package lets you easily create, edit, format, and permanently store documents. Nowadays you are expected to use a computer and word processor to create your work—handwritten correspondence just isn't acceptable in formal business and educational environments. In this session, you explore the features and benefits of word processing using Windows and Microsoft Word 6.0.

CASE STUDY

THE EXPERT HANDYMAN, INC.

George Perrera has lived in Irvine, California, for over 25 years. Sometimes he feels as if he knows everyone in town. His phone rarely stops ringing because he is *the* person to call when you need a household handyman. George has been working as a handyman for over ten years now, but one year ago he gave his business a name: The Expert HandyMan. Hoping to spend less time performing administrative tasks like creating invoices, George bought a computer for his business.

George operates his company out of his basement at 1990 Jillson Street. To generate new business, he relies on word-of-mouth advertising and the occasional newsletter. He currently performs an average of eight house calls per day and always seems to have more business than he can comfortably handle himself.

Now let's focus on the problem. Invoices, invoices, invoices! With all this business, George generates eight invoices a day, nearly 40 per week or 1,920 per year. To create invoices, George uses a ball-point pen to fill out a page in a carbon-copy invoice book. He gives one copy to the customer and keeps the other for his records. George believes that it would be much more efficient to create the invoice with a word processing program, save it on the computer's hard disk, and then print a copy of the invoice for his customer. Although George has used Microsoft Windows, he doesn't know the first thing about using a word processing program.

In this session, you and George learn how to create simple documents, access Word's Help facility, edit documents, use the Undo command, and save your work.

WORD PROCESSING WITH MICROCOMPUTERS

Word processing is the most commonly used application for microcomputers and is often cited as the primary reason for purchasing a computer. Briefly stated, **word processing** is the method by which documents (for example, letters, reports, and other correspondence) are created, edited, formatted, and printed. Although the process of creating a document using a word processing software program is similar to using a typewriter, the methods for editing documents differ greatly. With a typewriter, any changes you make—correcting typos, deleting words or sentences, adding or enhancing text—require you to retype the entire page or pages. Word processing programs, on the other hand, enable you to make changes without retyping any pages, as well as retrieve, edit, and reprint documents quickly and easily.

Some of the more popular word processing software programs include Microsoft Word and WordPerfect. These programs provide not only basic word processing tools but also publishing capabilities previously limited to commercial typesetters and printers. Let's begin exploring the features of word processing.

ENTERING TEXT

You create a document by typing information onto the screen. As you type, text appears at the **insertion point** or cursor. In Windows, the insertion point is displayed as a flashing vertical bar[1] and is positioned using the arrow keys or by clicking the mouse. Text is entered into a document in one of two modes: Insert mode or Overtype mode. **Insert mode** inserts text at the insertion point and pushes existing text to the right. **Overtype mode** inserts text in place of or over top of existing text. In most word processing programs, you press the INSERT key to toggle between these modes.

Novices and experts alike make typing errors when creating a document. You correct these errors using the BACKSPACE and DELETE keys. The BACKSPACE key removes text to the left of the insertion point on each key press, while the DELETE key removes text to the right of the insertion point. Although these keys are useful for deleting text one character[2] at a time, more efficient methods exist for deleting sentences and paragraphs.

One significant advantage that word processing programs have, compared with typewriters, is a feature called **word wrap**. Word wrap describes the process by which the insertion point is automatically moved to the beginning of the next line when the end of the current line is reached. In other words, you may type continuously without regard to pressing the carriage return or ENTER key to advance to the next line. The ENTER key is used only to end paragraphs and insert blank lines in a document.

EDITING TEXT

Word processing programs have numerous editing features to assist you in making corrections and modifications to existing documents. Two of the most important features involve methods for inserting, deleting, and rearranging text. First, the Insert mode enables you to insert text anywhere in a document. This process works well for inserting a sentence or phrase in the middle of an existing paragraph. Second, the copy and move functions allow you to change the order of paragraphs or sections in a document and limit the need to retype similar information. Most word processing programs also possess sophisticated search and replace capabilities for changing information throughout an entire document. These editing features are often underutilized, and an awareness of them is the first step to becoming a "power user" of word processing software.

[1]Be careful not to mistake the insertion point for the vertical I-beam mouse pointer.

[2]*Character* is a computer term meaning letter, number, punctuation mark, or symbol.

FORMATTING

Formatting refers to changing the appearance or position of text in a document. There are four different levels of formatting:

- *Character formatting* selects typefaces, font sizes, and styles for text. The most common way to emphasize text is to apply boldface, italic, or underline character formatting styles.
- *Paragraph formatting* specifies text alignment, line spacing, indentations, tab settings, and borders. A paragraph can be a single line of text or an entire page. Each paragraph may be formatted independently from the rest of the document.
- *Section formatting* lets you specify page numbers, headers, and footers for different sections or chapters of a document.
- *Document formatting* specifies the overall page layout. Formatting topics at this level include choosing the paper size (letter or legal), page orientation (portrait[3] or landscape[4]), and margins.

PROOFING TOOLS

Most word processing programs offer spell-checking capabilities. When you request a spelling check of a document, the word processing program loads a standard spelling dictionary into the computer's memory. Each word in the document is then compared to the words stored in the dictionary. If no match is found, the **spelling checker** (Figure 1.1) typically marks the word and suggests correctly spelled words. At this point, you can type a new word, accept a word from the list, or keep your original word. Many programs also offer the ability to create custom dictionaries for storing proper names, terminology, and abbreviations.

Another writing tool commonly found in word processing programs is the electronic **thesaurus**. A thesaurus (Figure 1.2) provides a list of synonyms (and antonyms) for a given word or phrase. As with the spelling checker, you can either type a new word, accept a word from the presented list of synonyms, or keep your original word

Microsoft Word was one of the first word processing software programs to incorporate a full-featured **grammar checker** (Figure 1.3) to analyze punctuation, sentence structure, and word usage. You can often choose the intensity of analysis based on rules from different writing styles, such as business or personal. These tools commonly display summary statistics on readability and assign your document an audience grade level.

[3]*Portrait* orientation refers to a page that is taller than it is wide.

[4]*Landscape* orientation refers to a page that is wider than it is tall.

FIGURE 1.1 WORD'S SPELL CHECKER

Spelling: English (US)
Not in Dictionary:
superfulous
Change To:
superfluous
Suggestions:
superfluous
Ignore
Ignore All
Change
Change All
Add
Suggest
Add Words To:
CUSTOM.DIC
AutoCorrect
Options...
Undo Last
Cancel
Help

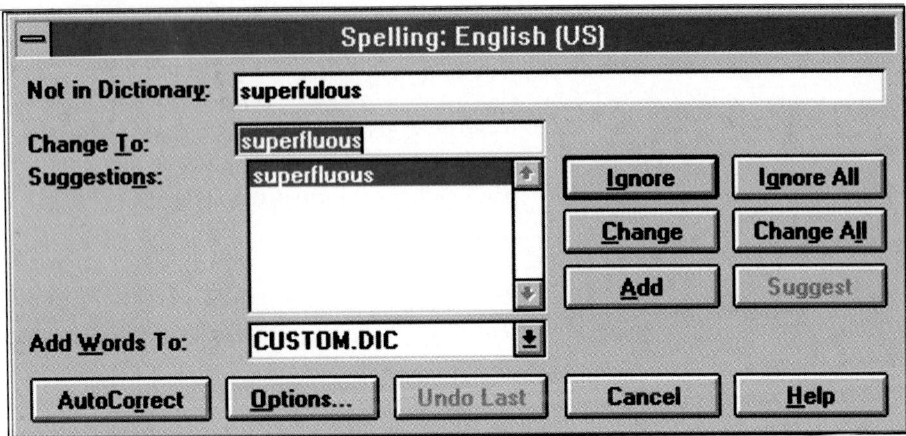

FIGURE 1.2 WORD'S THESAURUS

Thesaurus: English (US)
Looked Up:
superfluous
Replace with Synonym:
excessive
Meanings:
excessive (adj.)
Antonyms
excessive
extravagant
exorbitant
superabundant
extra
excess
inordinate
needless
profuse
Replace
Look Up
Cancel
Previous
Help

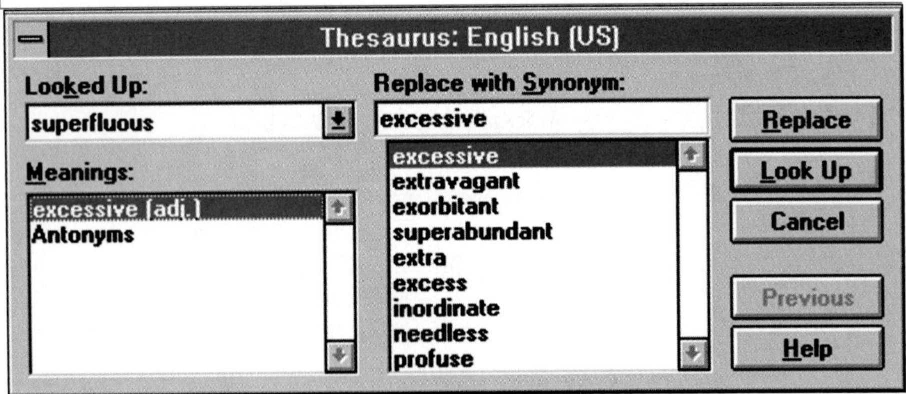

FIGURE 1.3 WORD'S GRAMMAR CHECKER

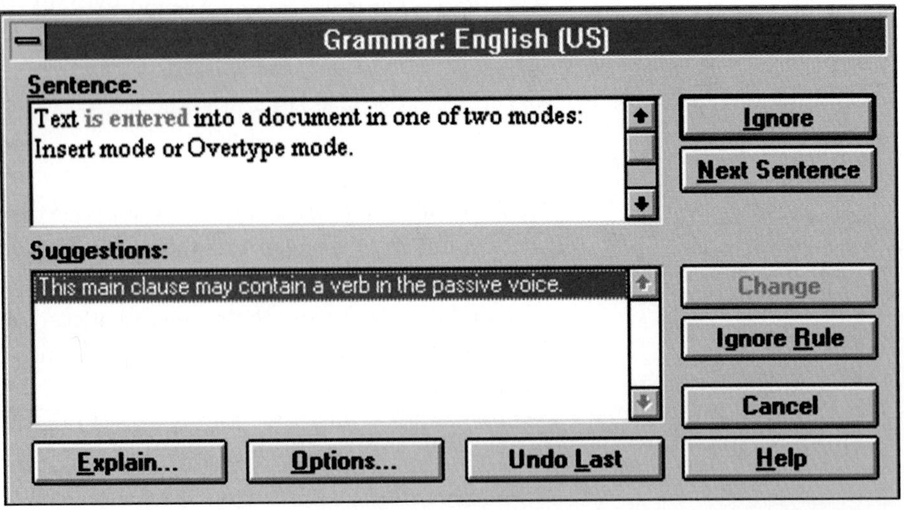

Grammar: English (US)
Sentence:
Text is entered into a document in one of two modes: Insert mode or Overtype mode.
Ignore
Next Sentence
Suggestions:
This main clause may contain a verb in the passive voice.
Change
Ignore Rule
Cancel
Explain...
Options...
Undo Last
Help

PRINTING

After creating, editing, formatting, and proofing a document, you'll usually want to send it to the printer. Before performing this step, you should make sure your computer is connected to a printer. Your options for printing a document often include printing multiple copies and limiting the print selection to specific pages. Most word processing programs also allow you to preview a document on-screen before printing. Besides saving trees, this feature allows you to see the effects of formatting changes without having to print the document.

MERGING

One of the most powerful features of word processing software is the ability to merge names and addresses into standard documents for printing. This process, called **mail merge**, allows you to create a single document and then print personalized copies for numerous recipients. Mail merge activities are not limited, however, to producing form letters. Merging can be used to print a batch of invoices, promotional letters, or legal contracts.

THE WINDOWS ADVANTAGE

Microsoft Word is the best-selling word processing software program for the Windows environment. With tens of millions of copies sold in the last few years, Windows is fast becoming the environment of choice for personal computer users worldwide. This section explains some of the benefits of working in the Windows environment.

Microsoft Windows is a software program that works with DOS to provide a **graphical user interface** (GUI) for programs. A graphical interface makes using computers easier and more intuitive for most people. With Windows, you use a pointing device called a **mouse** to select from **icons** (pictures that represent programs or functions).

Some of the advantages of working in the Windows environment include these factors:

- *Windows programs are easy to learn and easy to use.*
  Windows provides a standardized interface for all programs, whether they are word processing, spreadsheet, or database applications. As a result, you can use the knowledge acquired from one Windows product in working with other Windows products.

- *The ability to run more than one application at a time.*
  Windows is a **multitasking** environment whereby more than one application or program may be running at the same time. For example, multitasking

allows you to simultaneously receive an electronic mail message, calculate a spreadsheet, and print a report.

- *The ability to exchange information among applications.*
  Windows provides a program called Clipboard that lets you copy and move information within an application or among applications. For example, it's easy to copy a budget from an Excel spreadsheet to the Clipboard and then paste that budget into a Word document.

- *The ability to display on the screen what you will get from the printer.*
  This feature is called **WYSIWYG** ("What You See Is What You Get"); it allows different fonts, borders, and graphics to be displayed on the screen at all times.

FEATURES OF MICROSOFT WORD 6.0

At the time of this writing, the latest release of Microsoft Word for Windows is version 6.0. To ensure its competitiveness in the marketplace, Microsoft introduced several significant features in Word 6.0. This section highlights some of these enhancements.

- Word 6.0 lets you access context-sensitive commands on a shortcut menu by pointing at text or an object, such as a toolbar or a picture, with the mouse pointer and clicking the right mouse button.

- Word 6.0 provides eight toolbars for single-step mouse access to menu commands. You can display, hide, move, and customize toolbars as required. In addition, you can assign macros to toolbar buttons and add new commands to the pull-down menus.

- The new wizards and templates simplify the process of creating tables, performing mail merges, and writing standard documents, such as letters, agendas, résumés, and brochures.

- Multilevel Undo lets you reverse mistakes made several steps previously. Word also provides a Redo command to undo an Undo. Are you confused? Don't worry, you'll learn these features in this session!

- A new "thumbnail" print preview lets you show and edit several pages on-screen at the same time. You can quickly position graphics and rearrange text between pages using this display mode.

- Several "Auto" features make it easier for you to perform your work. For example, AutoCorrect corrects your typing errors and capitalization mistakes, AutoText replaces your abbreviations with full text entries or graphics, AutoFormat enhances your document with professionally created formatting styles, and AutoCaption adds captions to your graphics.

Now, let's begin our journey through Microsoft Word 6.0.

WORKING WITH WORD

Microsoft Word 6.0 is a complex yet easy-to-learn program. As you proceed through this guide, you will find that there are often three methods for performing the same command or procedure in Word:

- Menu — Select a command or procedure from the Menu bar.
- Mouse — Point to and click a toolbar button or use the Ruler.
- Keyboard — Press a keyboard shortcut (usually CTRL +*a letter*).

Although this guide concentrates on the quickest and easiest methods, we recommend that you try the others and decide which you prefer. *Don't memorize all of the methods and information in this guide! Be selective.*

HOW THE MOUSE IS USED

You may use Word with only a keyboard, but much of the program's basic design revolves around the availability of a mouse. Regardless of whether your mouse has two or three buttons, you use the left or primary mouse button for selecting text and menu commands and the right or secondary mouse button for displaying shortcut menus.

The most common mouse actions used in Word are:

- Point — Slide the mouse on your desk to position the tip of the mouse pointer over the desired object on the screen.
- Click — Press down and release the left mouse button quickly. Clicking is used to position the insertion point in the document and to choose menu commands.
- Right-Click — Press down and release the right mouse button. Right-clicking the mouse on text or an object displays a context-sensitive shortcut menu.

- Double-Click — Press down and release the mouse button twice in rapid succession. Double-clicking is used in Word to select text. In Windows, double-clicking the Control menu box of a window closes that window.

- Drag — Press down and hold the mouse button as you move the mouse pointer across the screen. When the mouse pointer reaches the desired location, release the mouse button. Dragging is used to select a block of text or to move objects or windows.

You may notice that the mouse pointer changes shape as you move it over different parts of the screen. Each mouse pointer shape has its own purpose and may provide you with important information. There are four primary mouse shapes you should be aware of:

	left arrow	Used to choose menu commands, access the toolbars, and complete dialog boxes.
	right arrow	Used to select text in the document window's Selection bar.
	hourglass	Informs you that Word is occupied with another task and requests that you wait.
I	I-beam	Used to modify and edit text and to position the insertion point.

As you proceed through this guide, other mouse shapes will be explained in the appropriate sections.

HOW THE KEYBOARD IS USED

Aside from being the primary input device for creating a document, the keyboard offers shortcut methods for performing commands and procedures. For example, several menu commands have shortcut key combinations listed to the right of the command in the pull-down menu. Therefore, you can perform a command by simply pressing the shortcut keys rather than accessing the Menu bar. Many of these shortcut key combinations are available throughout Windows applications.

STARTING WORD

This session assumes that you are working on a computer with DOS, Windows, and Microsoft Word 6.0 loaded on the hard disk drive. Before you can use Word, you must turn on the computer and load Microsoft Windows into the computer's memory. Perform the following steps on your computer.

1. Turn on the power switches to the computer and monitor. The C:\> prompt or a menu appears announcing that your computer has successfully loaded the Disk Operating System (DOS). (*Note*: Your computer may automatically load Microsoft Windows when it is first turned on. If this is the case, you can skip to step 3.)

2. To start Microsoft Windows from the C:\> prompt:
   TYPE: `win`
   PRESS: ENTER

   After a few seconds, the Windows logo appears on the screen followed by the **Program Manager** window (Figure 1.4). (*Note*: The icons in your Program Manager window may not be exactly the same as in Figure 1.4; icons represent the programs stored on your hard disk.)

FIGURE 1.4 THE MICROSOFT WINDOWS PROGRAM MANAGER WINDOW

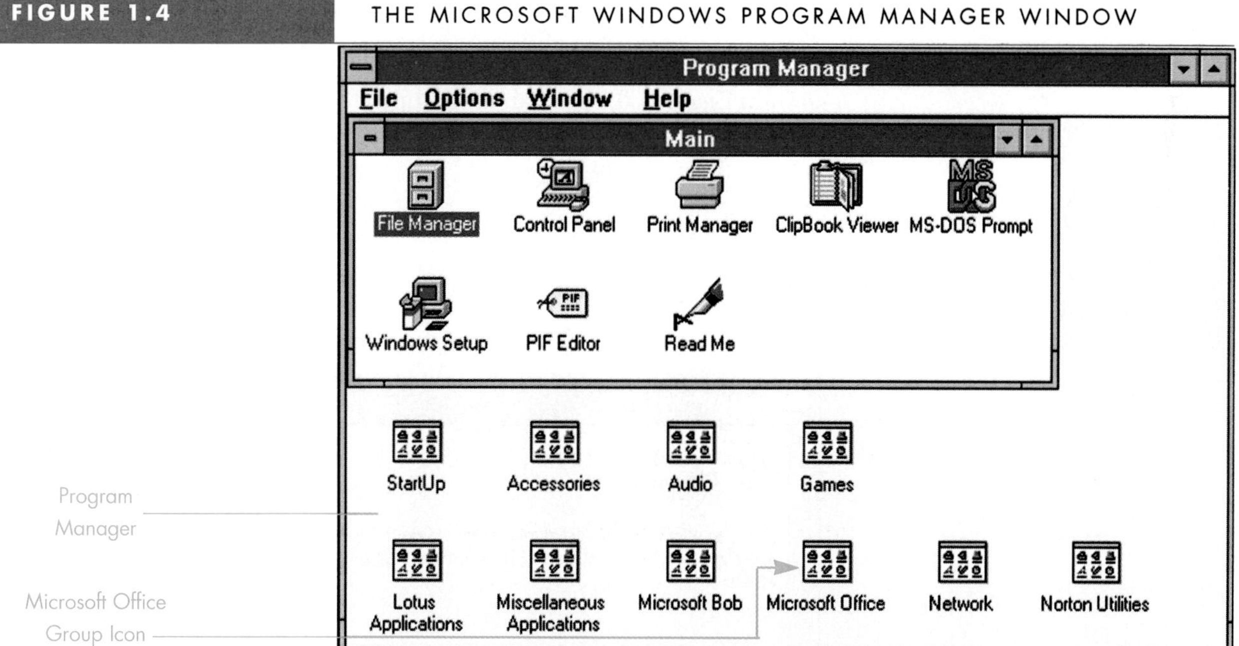

3. The Microsoft Word 6.0 program is often located in a group window called either Microsoft Word for Windows 6.0 or Microsoft Office. To open a group window, you double-click its group icon.

If the Word for Windows 6.0 group icon appears in your Program Manager, double-click it to display its group icon. If you see a Microsoft Office group icon only, double-click it to display a group window similar to the following:

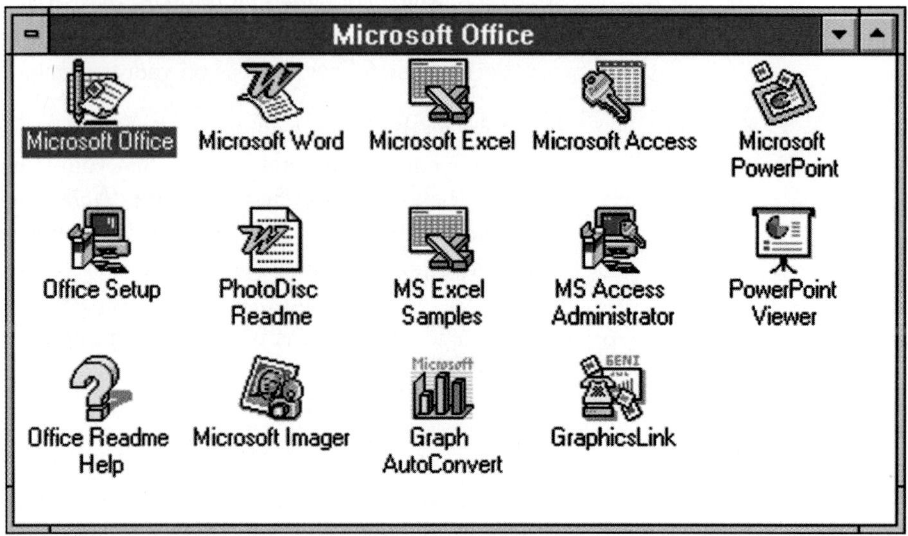

4. Load Microsoft Word from the group window:
   DOUBLE-CLICK: Word program icon ( )

5. Each time you start Word 6.0, a Tip of the Day appears in a dialog box (shown in Figure 1.5). You can easily turn this feature off by deselecting the Show Tips at Startup check box. However, these tips provide a useful reminder of features that you may be underutilizing. Leave the check box selected for now and proceed to the next step:
   PRESS: ENTER or CLICK: OK

FIGURE 1.5 TIP OF THE DAY DIALOG BOX

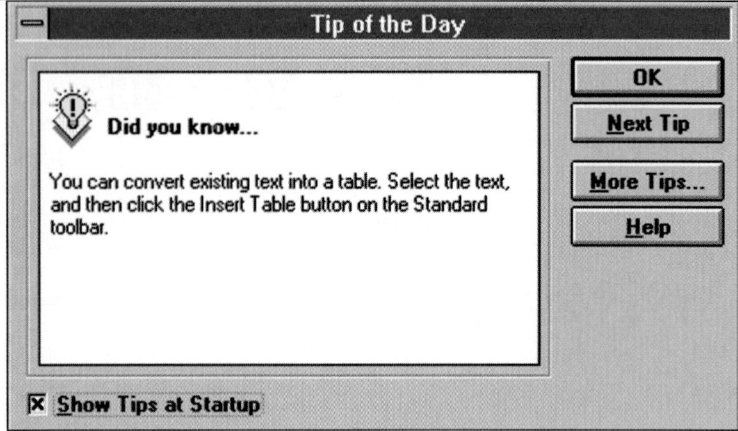

QUICK REFERENCE Loading Microsoft Word 6.0	1. **DOUBLE-CLICK: Word for Windows 6.0 group icon (or Microsoft Office group icon)** 2. **DOUBLE-CLICK: Microsoft Word program icon**

THE GUIDED TOUR

Software programs designed for Microsoft Windows, such as Word, Excel, and PageMaker, have many similarities in screen design and layout. Each program operates in its own application window, while the letters, spreadsheets, and brochures you create are displayed in separate document windows. This section explores the various parts of Word, including the tools for manipulating application and document windows.

APPLICATION WINDOW

The Word screen consists of the **application window** and the **document window**. The application window (Figure 1.6) contains the Title bar, Menu bar, Standard toolbar, Formatting toolbar, Status bar, and document area. Document windows contain the actual documents that you create and store on the disk.

FIGURE 1.6 MICROSOFT WORD'S APPLICATION WINDOW

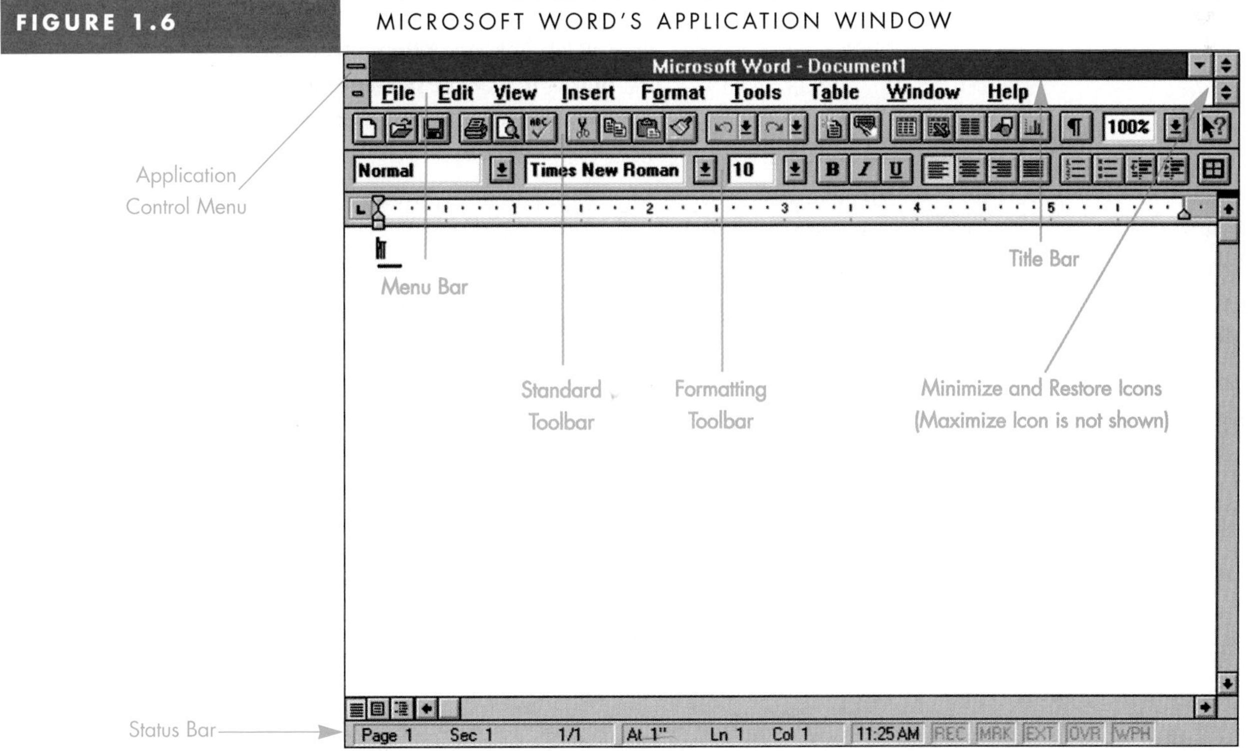

The primary components of the application window are:

Application Control menu[5] (▬)	Used to size and position the application window using the keyboard. To quit Word, you can double-click the Application Control menu.
Minimize (▾) and Maximize (▴) or Restore (⬍) Icons	Located in the top right-hand corner of the application window, these triangular-shaped icons are used to control the display of the application window using the mouse.
Title bar	The Title bar contains the name of the program or document file. Using a mouse, you can move a window by dragging its Title bar.
Menu bar	Contains the Word menu commands.
Standard toolbar	The Standard toolbar displays buttons for opening and saving documents, editing text, and accessing special features using the mouse. (Discussed later in this session.)
Formatting toolbar	The Formatting toolbar displays buttons for accessing character and paragraph formatting commands using the mouse. (Discussed later in this session.)
Status bar	Located at the bottom of the application window, the Status bar displays status or mode information and tracks your current position in a document.

You can size, move, and manipulate the Word application window on the Windows desktop to customize your work environment.

DOCUMENT WINDOW

The document window provides the viewing and editing area for a document. When Word is first loaded, this window is maximized to fill the entire document area. Figure 1.7 shows an example of a document window that is not maximized, as it would appear in the document area of Word's application window.

[5]Sometimes called the *Control box*.

FIGURE 1.7 A "WINDOWED" DOCUMENT WINDOW

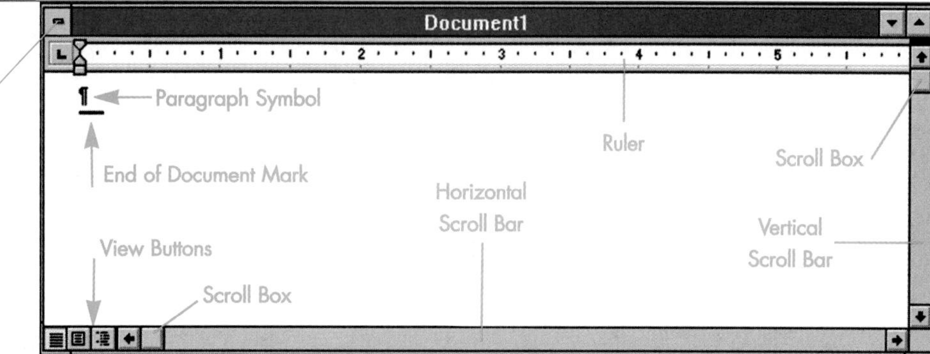

The parts of a document window are:

Document Control menu[6] (▭)	Used to size and position the window using the keyboard. To close a document, you can double-click the Document Control menu.
Ruler	Located beneath the Formatting toolbar in a maximized window, each document window has its own Ruler that provides information about tab settings, paragraph indentations, and margins.
Scroll bars	Placed at the right and bottom borders of the document window, scroll bars facilitate moving around a worksheet using the mouse. By dragging the scroll box along the scroll bar, you can skim quickly through a document.
View buttons	Located at the bottom left-hand corner of the document window, the View buttons let you easily switch between Normal View, Page Layout View, and Outline View. Whereas the Normal view is used for the majority of your work, the Page Layout and Outline views provide additional features for finalizing and managing documents.
End of Document mark and Paragraph symbol	The End of Document mark informs you that you cannot move the insertion point beyond this point in the document. Although not always displayed, the Paragraph symbol (¶) shows where you have pressed the ENTER key to start a new line.

[6]Sometimes called the *Control box.*

You should recognize some familiar components in the document window that appear in all windows. For example, the Minimize and Maximize icons appear in the top right-hand corner of the document window. To restore a maximized document to a window, you click the Restore icon ( ). To maximize the document window, you click the Maximize icon ( ). Before proceeding, make sure that your document window is maximized, resembling Figure 1.6.

MENU BAR

Word commands are grouped together on the Menu bar, as shown below.

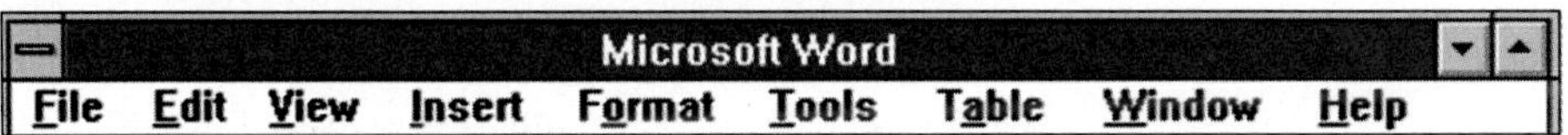

Commands in this guide are written in the following form: Edit, Copy, where Edit is the Menu bar option and Copy is the command to be selected from the pull-down menu. To execute a command using the mouse, click once on the Menu bar option and then click once on the pull-down menu command. Using the keyboard, you hold down the ALT key and tap the underlined letter of the desired option on the Menu bar. When the pull-down menu is displayed, press the underlined letter of the command you want to execute. Commands that are not available for selection appear dimmed. Commands that are followed by an ellipsis (...) require further information to be collected in a dialog box.

To practice accessing the Menu bar, perform the following steps on your computer.

1. To choose the Help command, position the tip of the mouse pointer on the word Help in the Menu bar and click the left mouse button once. A pull-down menu appears below the Help option.

2. To display the pull-down menu for the File option:
   CHOOSE: File
   This instruction tells you to click the mouse pointer on File in the Menu bar. (*Note*: All menu commands that you execute in this guide begin with the word "CHOOSE.")

3. To leave the Menu bar without making a selection:
   CHOOSE: File
   (*Note*: Clicking the menu option twice removes the pull-down menu. You can also click the Title bar to remove a menu.)

SHORTCUT MENUS

Word 6.0 introduces context-sensitive shortcut menus for quick access to menu commands. Rather than searching for commands in the Menu bar, you position the mouse pointer on text or an object, such as a table or a graphic, and click the right mouse button. A pop-up menu appears with the most commonly selected commands for the text or object.

√Standard
√Formatting
Borders
Database
Drawing
Forms
Microsoft
Toolbars...
Customize...

To practice accessing a shortcut menu, perform the following steps:

1. To display a shortcut or pop-up menu, position the mouse pointer over any button on the Standard toolbar and click the right mouse button. The shortcut menu at the right should appear.

2. To remove the shortcut menu from the screen, move the mouse pointer away from the menu and click the right mouse button a second time. The shortcut menu disappears.

QUICK REFERENCE
Using Shortcut Menus

1. **Position the mouse pointer over an item, such as a toolbar button.**
2. **CLICK: the right mouse button to display a shortcut or pop-up menu**
3. **CHOOSE: *a command from the menu,* or**
   CLICK: the right mouse button away from the menu to remove it

TOOLBARS

Assuming that you haven't yet customized your Word screen, you will see the Standard and Formatting toolbars appear below the Menu bar. Word provides eight toolbars and hundreds of buttons[7] and drop-down lists for quick and easy mouse access to its more popular commands and features. Don't worry about memorizing the button names appearing in the following graphics—the majority of these buttons are explained elsewhere. You can also point at any toolbar button and pause until a yellow ToolTip appears with the button name.

The Standard toolbar provides access to file management and editing commands in addition to special features like AutoFormat and AutoText:

[7] Sometimes called *icons.*

The Formatting toolbar lets you access character and paragraph formatting commands:

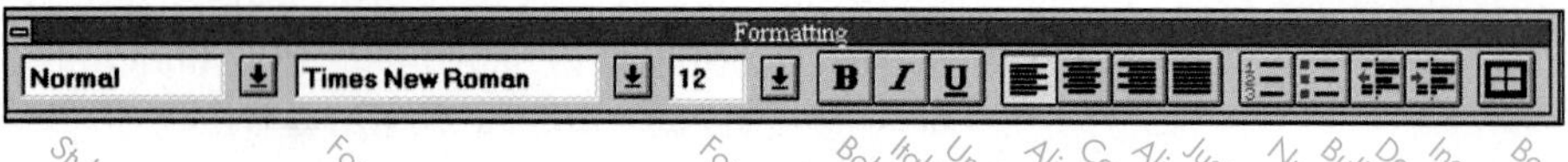

To select additional toolbars, you point to an existing toolbar and click the right mouse button. From the shortcut menu that appears, you can display and hide toolbars by clicking their names in the pop-up menu. If a toolbar is currently being displayed, a check mark appears beside its name.

To practice displaying and hiding toolbars, perform the following steps.

1. Position the mouse pointer over any button on the Standard toolbar.

2. CLICK: right mouse button to display the shortcut menu

3. To display the Drawing toolbar:
   CHOOSE: Drawing
   The new toolbar appears, usually positioned at the bottom of the application window.

4. To remove the Drawing toolbar:
   RIGHT-CLICK: Drawing toolbar
   This instruction tells you to position the mouse pointer over the Drawing toolbar and click the right mouse button.

5. CHOOSE: Drawing
   The Drawing toolbar disappears from the application window.

RULER

The Ruler (shown below) displays the tab, paragraph, and margin settings for the current line. Rather than accessing menu commands to adjust paragraph and document formatting options, you can move the appropriate symbols on the Ruler using the mouse.

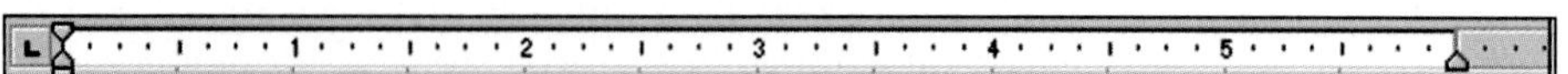

STATUS BAR

The Status bar (shown on the next page) provides editing and status information for a document, including the current page number, section number, and total number of pages. The insertion point's current depth from the top of the page is displayed in inches, along with the line and column numbers.

The Status bar also provides some helpful information. For example, pressing the INSERT key results in the word "OVR," which stands for Overtype mode, to appear. You can also toggle between Overtype and Insert modes by double-clicking the "OVR" indicator on the Status bar. When the menu is accessed, the Status bar displays a description of the currently highlighted command.

DIALOG BOX

Word uses dialog boxes (Figure 1.8) to collect information necessary to execute a command. An ellipsis (...) following a command on a pull-down or pop-up menu informs you that Word will present a dialog box when the command is selected. Dialog boxes are also used to display messages or ask for confirmation of commands.

FIGURE 1.8 ONE EXAMPLE OF A DIALOG BOX

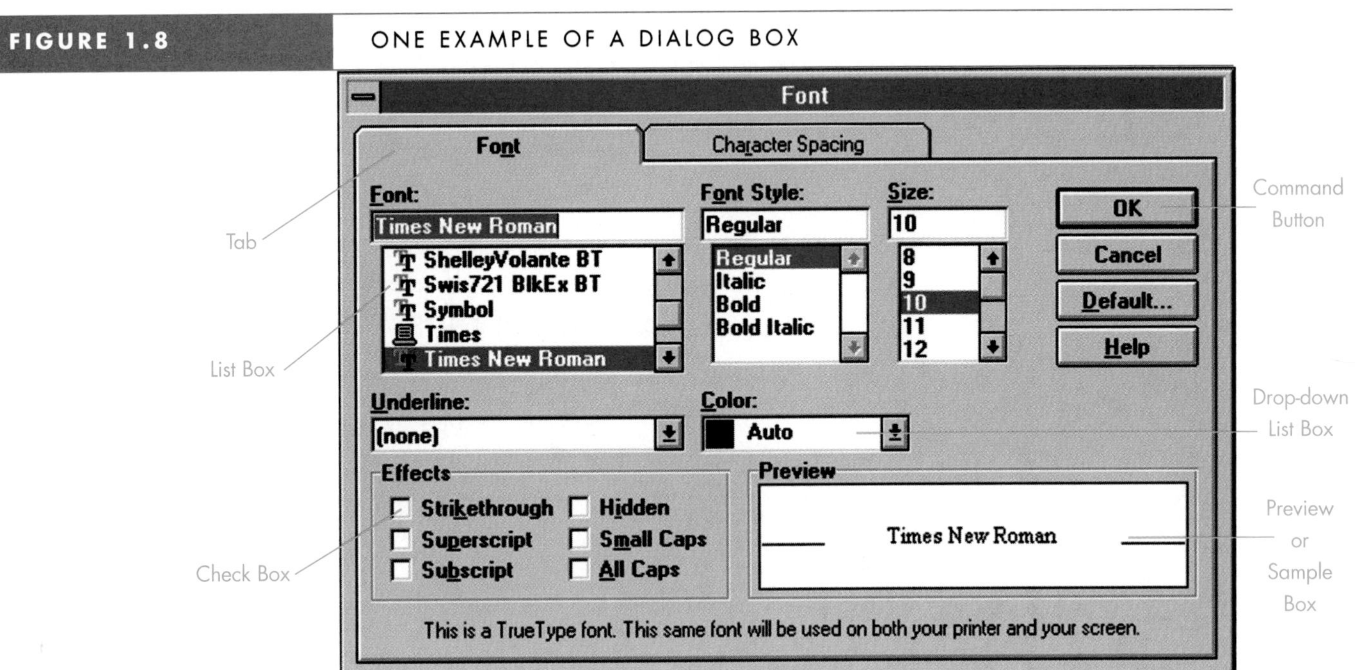

A dialog box uses several methods for collecting information, as shown in Figure 1.8 above and described in Table 1.1 below.

TABLE 1.1

Parts of a Dialog Box

Component	*Description*
Tabs	A new feature in Word 6.0: dialog boxes with tabs allow you to access other pages of options by simply clicking on a named tab at the top of the window.
List box	A scrollable list of choices. Use the scroll bars or arrow keys to browse the list.
Text box	A box for collecting typed information. Before typing your entry, you must click in the text box to select it.
Drop-Down list box	A list of available choices in which only one item is displayed at a time. Using a mouse, click on the adjacent arrow to display the full list of choices. To select an item, use the scroll bars to move through the list and then click the desired item.
Check box	An option that can be toggled on or off. Click the mouse pointer in the box to toggle the × mark on and off. The option is turned on when an × appears.
Option button	One option that can be selected from a group of related options. Click the mouse pointer on the desired option button to select it. There are no option buttons in Figure 1.8.
Command button	A button that executes an action when selected. Most dialog boxes provide the Help button to offer quick access to a help screen explaining the items in the dialog box. You accept the selections in a dialog box by pressing ENTER or clicking the OK command button. You cancel your selections in a dialog box by pressing ESC or clicking the Cancel button.

GETTING HELP

Similar to most software programs, Word provides context-sensitive Help when you press the F1 key. *Context-sensitive* refers to Word's ability to retrieve Help information reflecting your current position in the program. For example, you can highlight a menu option and press F1 to display a Help window containing a description of the command. Perhaps an easier method for accessing Help for menu commands is to click the Help button (?) on the Standard toolbar and then select the desired command using the question mark mouse pointer. Rather than executing the command, Word displays its Help window.

To access the table of contents for Word's Help facility, choose the Help, Contents command from the menu. The resulting Help window is shown at the right. You can browse the contents by clicking on words and phrases that are green and have a solid underline. These are called **jump terms** because they allow you to jump quickly to topics of interest. Words or phrases that are green and have a dotted underline provide definition boxes when they are clicked. To remove the definition, you simply click the box a second time.

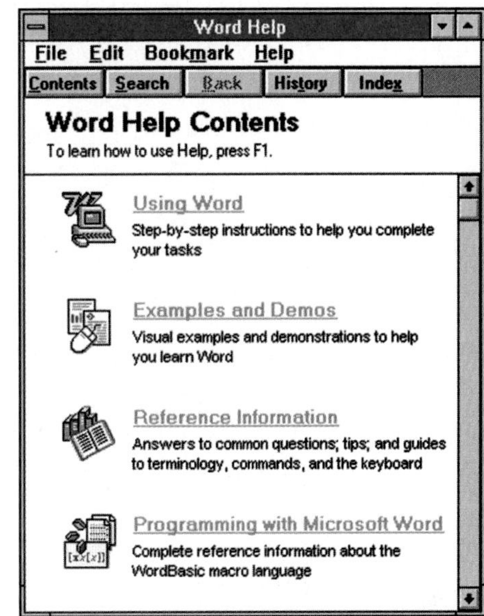

If you have access to a computer for practice, you may want to peruse the Word 6.0 Quick Preview. To start this tour of Word's features, you choose Help, Quick Preview from the menu. To return to Word, you click the Return to Word command button on the main screen (shown below in Figure 1.9).

FIGURE 1.9 WORD'S QUICK PREVIEW

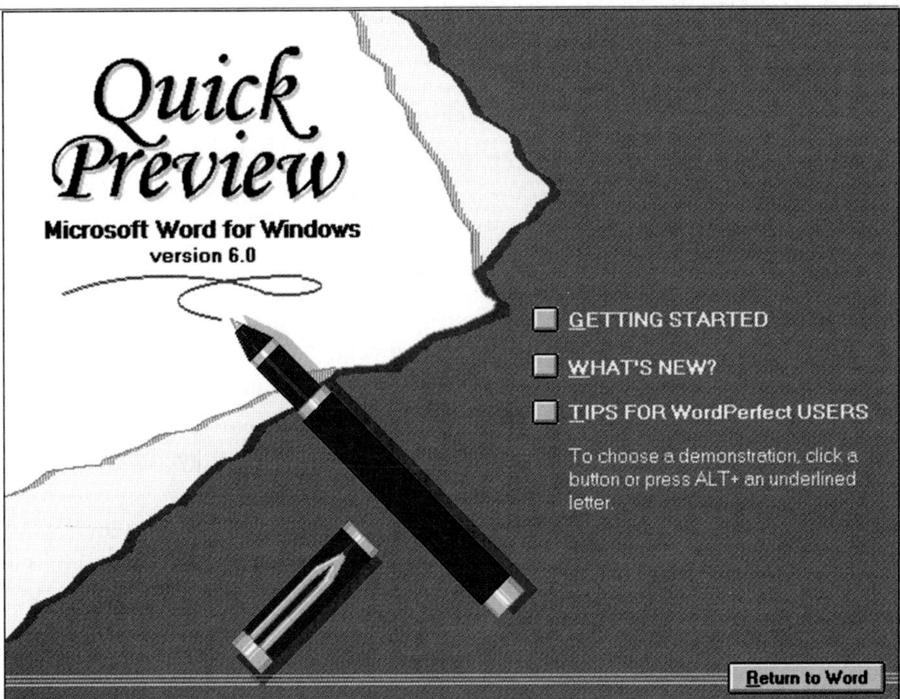

The best way to learn about Word's Help facility is to practice using it. Perform the following steps.

1. In the next several steps, you'll access Help for the File, New command, the File, Print command, and one of the toolbar buttons. Let's start with the File, New command. Position the tip of the mouse pointer over the Help button ( ) on the Standard toolbar.

2. To activate the question mark mouse pointer:
   CLICK: Help button ( ) once

3. CHOOSE: File, New
   Rather than executing the command, Word retrieves a Help window.

4. Read the contents of the Help window. Once finished, you close the window by executing the following command from its Menu bar:
   CHOOSE: File, Exit from the Help window's Menu bar
   (*Note*: You can also close a Help window by double-clicking its Control menu.)

5. To access Help for the Save button ( ) on the Standard toolbar:
   CLICK: Help button ( ) to get the question mark mouse pointer

6. CLICK: Save button ( )
   A Help window appears describing the Save command.

7. To close the Help window:
   DOUBLE-CLICK: Control menu ( ) for the Help window

   (*CAUTION*: Ensure that you are clicking the Help window's Control menu and not Word's Control menu.)

8. To search for Help on a specific topic or command (for example, printing), do the following:
   DOUBLE-CLICK: Help button ( )
   The Help window appears followed by the Search dialog box. Make sure that the dialog box is displayed before continuing to the next step.

9. TYPE: `print`
   The list box automatically scrolls to the first occurrence of "print."

10. With the "Print command" option highlighted, do the following:
    SELECT: Show Topics command button
    The word SELECT means to click the command button with the mouse or to highlight the option and press ENTER.

11. Two Help options appear for the Print command. With the "Print command" option highlighted in the bottom window, do the following:
    SELECT: Go To command button

12. Read the contents of the resulting Help window and then close it using either method described above.

QUICK REFERENCE
Using Help

- **PRESS: F1, or**
- **CLICK: Help button (), or**
- **CHOOSE: Help, Contents**

CREATING A DOCUMENT

Creating a document in Word is easy. You type information onto the screen, save the document to the disk, and, if desired, send it to the printer. Before you begin typing, make sure that you have a blinking insertion point in the upper left-hand corner of the document window. This marks the location where text is inserted. Below the insertion point, you should see a horizontal black bar called the **End of Document Marker**. As you enter information, this marker automatically moves downward.

In the next section, you will create the paragraph appearing in Figure 1.10.

FIGURE 1.10 PRACTICE PARAGRAPH

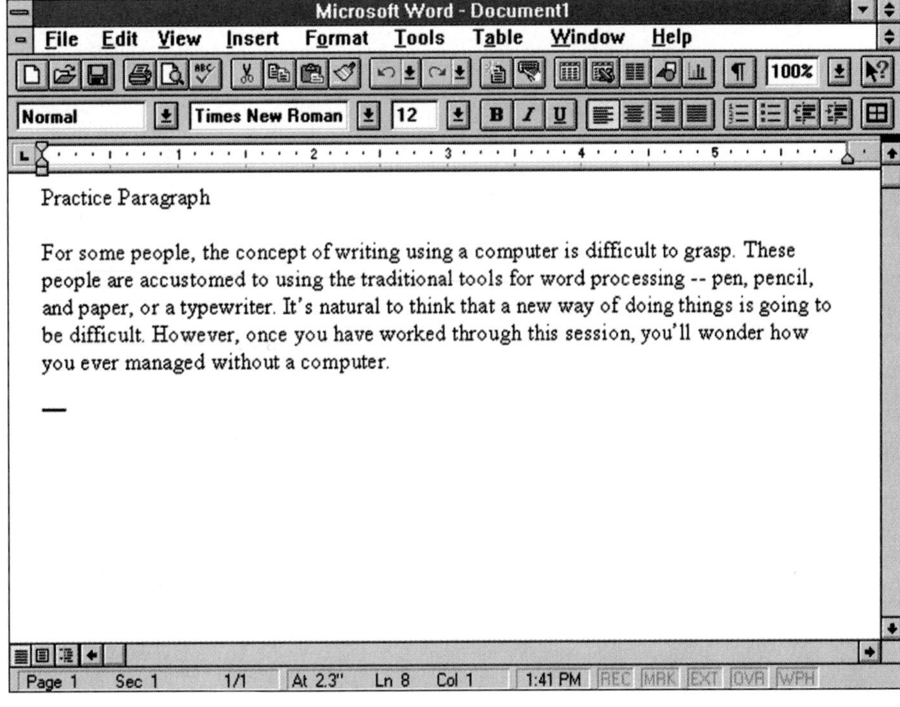
Microsoft Word - Document1
File Edit View Insert Format Tools Table Window Help
100%
Normal
Times New Roman
12
Practice Paragraph
For some people, the concept of writing using a computer is difficult to grasp. These people are accustomed to using the traditional tools for word processing -- pen, pencil, and paper, or a typewriter. It's natural to think that a new way of doing things is going to be difficult. However, once you have worked through this session, you'll wonder how you ever managed without a computer.
Page 1 Sec 1 1/1 At 2.3" Ln 8 Col 1 1:41 PM REC MRK EXT OVR WPH

INSERTING TEXT

To illustrate the fundamentals of inserting text, this section leads you through an exercise for editing the words "Practice Paragraph." You will also learn about Word's new AutoCorrect feature which automatically corrects simple typographical errors in spelling and capitalization. For example, you can type "teh" and Word replaces the text with "the" as soon as you press the Space Bar. Let's proceed—perform the following steps.

1. TYPE: `Paragraph`
   The insertion point appears one character to the right of the word "Paragraph."

2. To move the insertion point back to the beginning of the line:
   PRESS: HOME
   The insertion point should now appear to the left of thc "P" in "Paragraph."

3. Make sure that the letters OVR in the Status bar appear dimmed. This tells you that Word's current mode is Insert mode and not Overtype mode. If the letters OVR are not dim, double-click the letters in the Status bar before continuing. Type the following, exactly as it appears:
   TYPE: `PRactice`
   PRESS: Space Bar
   Notice that Word's AutoCorrect feature automatically corrected your capitalization error at the beginning of the word. Also, the Insert mode let you insert text and spaces at the current position by simply typing the characters and pressing the Space Bar. The existing information was pushed to the right.

4. To illustrate the difference between Insert mode and Overtype mode, position the insertion point to the left of the letter "P" in the word "Practice."

5. PRESS: INSERT
   The letters OVR, the abbreviation for Overtype mode, appear highlighted (not dimmed) in the Status bar.

6. TYPE: `My`
   The word "My" overwrites the first two characters of "Practice."

7. To toggle the Insert mode on using the mouse:
   DOUBLE-CLICK: OVR in the Status bar
   The letters OVR should now appear dimmed.

8. Let's complete the phrase:
   PRESS: Space Bar to insert a space
   TYPE: `Pr`
   The line should now read "My Practice Paragraph."

9. The ENTER key inserts blank lines into a document and signifies the end of a paragraph. To illustrate, position the insertion point to the left of the letter "P" in the word "Paragraph."

10. PRESS: ENTER four times
The word "Paragraph" moves down with the insertion point and blank lines are inserted into the document. In the next section, you learn how to delete blank lines from a document.

QUICK REFERENCE
Inserting Text

- **Insert text into a document by typing.**
- **Insert spaces between words by pressing the Space Bar.**
- **Insert blank lines in a document by pressing the ENTER key.**
- **To toggle between Insert and Overtype modes:**
PRESS: INSERT or DOUBLE-CLICK: OVR in the Status bar

DELETING TEXT

The BACKSPACE and DELETE keys are the most common keystrokes for removing information from a document one character at a time. To practice each keystroke, perform the following steps.

1. To quickly move to the top of the document:
PRESS: CTRL + HOME
This instruction tells you to press and hold down the CTRL key and tap HOME once. You then release both keys. The insertion point jumps to the first column of the first line in the document. (*Note*: If your keyboard does not have separate arrow keys, you must ensure that the Num Lock status is off before performing this keystroke combination.)

2. To move to the end of the line, click the I-beam mouse pointer to the right of the word "Practice."

3. In order to get the word "Paragraph" back to its original location, you must delete the blank lines.
PRESS: DELETE four times

4. To illustrate the use of the BACKSPACE key, position the insertion point to the left of the word "Practice" using the mouse or keyboard.

5. PRESS: BACKSPACE three times
   The word "My" and the space are deleted. The text now reads "Practice Paragraph" once again.

6. To move the insertion point down two lines without moving the text:
   PRESS: END to move to the end of the line
   PRESS: ENTER twice
   The insertion point is now in the correct position for you to begin typing the practice paragraph.

QUICK REFERENCE
Deleting Text

- **PRESS: DELETE to delete text to the right of the insertion point**
- **PRESS: BACKSPACE to delete text to the left of the insertion point**

WORD WRAP

The word wrap feature of Word allows you to continuously type without having to press the ENTER key at the end of each line. If you have worked on a typewriter, resist the temptation to hit a carriage return (ENTER) when the right margin approaches. Word will take you to the next line automatically. In this section, you will complete the practice paragraph.

1. TYPE: `For some people the concept of writing using a computer is difficult to grasp. These people are accustomed to using the traditional tools for word processing -- pen, pencil, and paper, or a typewriter. It's natural to think that a new way of doing things is going to be difficult. However, once you have worked through this session, you'll wonder how you ever managed without a computer.`

2. PRESS: ENTER
   Your screen should now appear similar to Figure 1.10.

QUICK REFERENCE
Word Wrap

When typing a paragraph, do not press the ENTER key at the end of each line. The ENTER key is used only to end a paragraph or to insert a blank line in a document.

IN ADDITION HYPHENATING WORDS

Words sometimes wrap to the next line in such a way that your paragraphs have a very ragged right margin. You can hyphenate words yourself or direct Word to hyphenate long words where needed.

To access the hyphenation feature, choose Tools, Hyphenation from the Menu bar. For more information, click the Help button in the dialog box.

USING THE UNDO COMMAND

The **Undo command** allows you to cancel the last several commands you performed in a document. There are three methods for executing the Undo command. You can choose Edit, Undo from the menu, press the keyboard shortcut of CTRL +z, or click the Undo button ( ) on the Standard toolbar.

Let's practice using the Undo button ( ):

1. Make sure that you are in Insert mode (the letters OVR should appear dimmed in the Status bar) and then insert another blank line in the document:
   PRESS: ENTER

2. TYPE: `This is a test of the Undo command.`

3. To undo the typing you just performed:
   CLICK: Undo button ( ) on the Standard toolbar

   (*CAUTION*: You place the tip of the mouse pointer over the curved arrow on the left side of the button, as opposed to the downward pointing arrow, before clicking the left mouse button.)

4. TYPE: `This is a test of the shortcut key method.`

5. To undo the typing again:
   CLICK: Undo button ( )

6. To view all the actions that you can undo:
   CLICK: down arrow adjacent to the Undo button ( )

7. To remove the drop-down list without selecting an item:
   CLICK: down arrow adjacent to the Undo button ( ) again

QUICK REFERENCE
Undo a Command

- **CLICK: Undo button ( ) on the Standard toolbar, or**
- **CHOOSE: Edit, Undo, or**
- **PRESS: CTRL +z**

SAVING AND CLOSING A DOCUMENT

When you are creating a document, it exists only in the computer's RAM (random access memory), which is highly volatile[8]. To permanently store your work, you must save the document to the hard disk or to a floppy diskette. Saving your work to a disk is similar to placing it into a filing cabinet. For important documents (ones that you cannot risk losing), you should save your work every 15 minutes, or whenever you're interrupted, to protect against an unexpected power outage or other catastrophe.

To save a document to a disk, you click the Save button ( ) on the Standard toolbar or you select the File, Save command from the menu. If you haven't saved the document before, a dialog box appears and you must type in a file name of up to eight characters with no spaces. When you are finished typing, press ENTER or click the OK command button. Word automatically attaches the letters .DOC, which stand for document, to the end of each file name. As the document is being written to the disk, a series of boxes appears in the Status bar indicating its progress.

Perform the following steps to save the current document.

1. Make sure that the Advantage Diskette is placed into drive A: or drive B:.

2. CLICK: Save button ( ) on the Standard toolbar
   Word displays a dialog box similar to the one shown in Figure 1.11; the file names and directories will differ from your dialog box.

3. To specify a file name for the document:
   TYPE: `practice`

4. To specify that the document be saved onto the Advantage Diskette:
   CLICK: down arrow adjacent to the Drives drop-down list box
   SELECT: a: (or b:, depending on where the Advantage Diskette is located)
   (*Note*: In addition to the drive, you can select a specific folder location for your file in the Directories list box. The Advantage Diskette has no folders, unlike the example in the dialog box displayed above.)

[8]RAM is wiped clean when you turn off your computer or experience a power failure.

FIGURE 1.11 SAVE AS DIALOG BOX

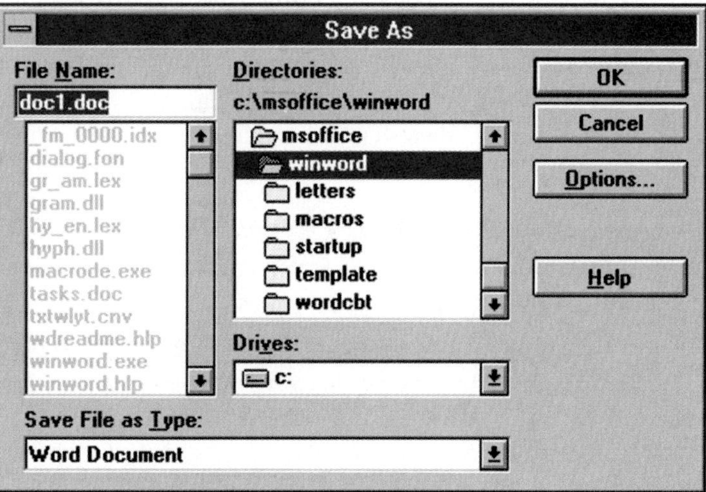

5. To proceed with saving the document:
   PRESS: ENTER or CLICK: OK
   If Word's Summary Info feature is turned on, a dialog box similar to the one shown in Figure 1.12 may appear. The information that you enter into this dialog box is useful for locating files using Word's advanced search capabilities.

FIGURE 1.12 SUMMARY INFO DIALOG BOX

Summary Info
File Name: PRACTICE.DOC
Directory: A:
Title: Practice Paragraph
Subject:
Author: Sarah E. Hutchinson
Keywords:
Comments:
OK
Cancel
Statistics...
Help

6. To accept the contents of the Summary Info dialog box:
   PRESS: ENTER or CLICK: OK
   You may hear a noise from the computer's diskette drive as the file is being saved to the Advantage Diskette.

There are times when you'll want to save an existing document under a different file name. For example, you may want to keep different versions of the same document on your disk. Or, you may want to use one document as a template for future documents that are similar in style and format. Rather than retyping an entirely new document, you can retrieve an old document file, edit the information, and then save it under a different name using the File, Save As command. If you want to replace the old file instead, you use File, Save or click the Save button ( ).

QUICK REFERENCE
Saving a File

- **CLICK: Save button ( ) on the Standard toolbar, or**
- **CHOOSE: File, Save, or**
- **CHOOSE: File, Save As to save a file under a different name**

IN ADDITION AUTOMATICALLY SAVING DOCUMENTS

For more peace of mind, you can tell Word to save your documents automatically at predefined time intervals. To access this feature, choose Tools, Options from the Menu bar and select the Save tab in the dialog box. Select the Automatic Save Every check box and enter a time interval in minutes. For more information, click the Help button.

IN ADDITION SAVING A DOCUMENT AS A PROTECTED FILE

If you're sharing your computer with other people, but don't want anyone else to be able to look at or modify your files, consider assigning a Protection Password to your individual files. Before opening a protected file, you must type in the correct password.

To assign a password to a document, choose File, Save As and then click the Options button. The Save tab should already be selected. The file sharing options are displayed at the bottom of this dialog box. For more information, click the Help button.

When you are finished working with a document, you should close the file to free up valuable RAM. To close a document window, choose File, Close from the menu or double-click its Control menu. Let's close the PRACTICE document file.

1. CHOOSE: File, Close

2. If there are other documents appearing in the document area, repeat step 1 to clear them from memory.

QUICK REFERENCE Closing a File	• **CHOOSE: File, Close, or** • **DOUBLE-CLICK: Control menu for the document window**

BEGINNING A NEW DOCUMENT

When Word is first loaded, a blank document is automatically displayed on the screen. If you have already typed information into this document and would like to continue working with Word in a new document, you must request a new document by choosing the File, New command or by clicking the New button ( ) on the Standard toolbar.

Perform the following steps to display a new blank document.

1. Ensure that there are no open documents in the document area.

2. CLICK: New button ( ) on the Standard toolbar
   A new document appears.

QUICK REFERENCE Creating a New Document	• **CLICK: New button ( ) on the Standard toolbar, or** • **CHOOSE: File, New**

OPENING AN EXISTING DOCUMENT

Now that your document is stored in this electronic filing cabinet called a disk, how do you retrieve the document for editing? Your first step is to display the Open dialog box by choosing the File, Open command or by clicking the Open button ( ) on the Standard toolbar. When this dialog box appears, you make selections in much the same way that you used the Save As dialog box earlier in this session. After selecting the appropriate drive and folder locations, you load a document by double-clicking its file name in the File Name list box or by highlighting it and pressing ENTER.

Perform the following steps to retrieve the PRACTICE document from the Advantage Diskette.

1. Make sure that the Advantage Diskette is placed into drive A: or drive B:.

2. To practice using the Open dialog box:
   CLICK: Open button (📂) on the Standard toolbar

3. To view the files on the Advantage Diskette that is in either drive A: or drive B:, do the following:
   CLICK: down arrow adjacent to the Drives drop-down list box
   SELECT: a: (or b:)

4. DOUBLE-CLICK: PRACTICE.DOC in the File Name list box
   PRESS: ENTER or CLICK: OK

QUICK REFERENCE
Opening a Document

1. **CHOOSE: File, Open, or**
   CLICK: Open button (📂) on the Standard toolbar
2. **SELECT: *desired drive, directory, and file name from the list boxes***
3. **PRESS: ENTER or CLICK: OK**

IN ADDITION OPENING A FILE FROM THE FILE PULL-DOWN MENU

Near the bottom of the File pull-down menu, you'll notice that Word lists the four most recent documents that you have opened. Rather than using the Open dialog box to retrieve a document, you can simply choose its name from this menu. Obviously, this feature is only useful if the desired document is one of the last four files you have opened. However, you can also specify on the General tab in the Options dialog box the number of files that you want to have appear in this list.

LEAVING WORD

When you are finished using Word, save your work and exit the program before turning off the computer. If you have made modifications to the document and have not saved the changes, Word asks whether the document should be saved or abandoned before exiting the program.

Perform the following steps to finish working with Word.

1. To exit Word:
   CHOOSE: File, Exit
   Assuming that no changes were made to the document, the application is closed and you are returned to the Program Manager.

2. To exit Windows:
   CHOOSE: File, Exit
   Rather than using the menu commands, you can double-click the Control menus for both Word and the Program Manager.

QUICK REFERENCE
Exiting Word

- **CHOOSE: File, Exit, or**
- **DOUBLE-CLICK: Word's Control menu ( )**

SUMMARY

This session introduced you to word processing software, specifically Microsoft Word 6.0. We began the session exploring the advantages of word processing using microcomputers. After loading Microsoft Windows and Word, you were led on a guided tour of the program's major components. We also used the Help facility to retrieve information on menu commands and toolbar buttons.

In the latter half of the session, you created a practice document using the Insert and Overtype modes. You also learned how to remove characters using DELETE and BACKSPACE and enter blank lines using ENTER. The session finished with discussions on saving, closing, and opening document files. Many of the commands and procedures appearing in this session are provided in the command summary in Table 1.2.

TABLE 1.2

Command Summary

Task Description	*Menu Command*	*Toolbar Button*	*Keyboard Shortcut*
Create a new document file	File, New		CTRL+n
Open an existing document file	File, Open		CTRL+o
Close a document file	File, Close		
Save a document to the disk	File, Save		CTRL+s
Save a document to the disk, specifying the file name	File, Save As		
Leave Word	File, Exit		

continued

TABLE 1.2
concluded

Task Description	*Menu Command*	*Toolbar Button*	*Keyboard Shortcut*
Reverse the last command(s) executed	Edit, Undo		CTRL +Z
Access the Word Help facility	Help, Contents		F1

application window
In Microsoft Windows, each running application program appears in its own application window. These windows can be sized and moved anywhere on the Windows desktop.

document window
In Microsoft Windows, each open document appears in its own document window. These windows can be sized and moved anywhere within the document area.

End of Document Marker
The black, horizontal bar that appears at the end of a Word document. You cannot move the insertion point beyond this marker.

grammar checker
In word processing programs, a program that checks the grammar and word usage in a document.

graphical user interface
Software feature that allows the user to select menu options and icons; makes software easier to use and typically employs a mouse.

icons
Pictures that represent different application programs and processing procedures you can execute. The Macintosh, IBM OS/2, and Microsoft Windows operating environments use icons extensively.

Insert mode
A mode of entering text. Insert mode allows the user to insert text at the current position without typing over existing text.

insertion point
The vertical flashing bar in Word that indicates your current position in the document. The insertion point shows where the next typed characters will appear.

jump terms

In the Windows Help facility, a phrase that appears green with a solid underline that lets you jump from topic to topic by clicking it with the mouse.

mail merge

A procedure that typically involves combining data that is stored in a data file with a form letter created in a word processing software program.

Microsoft Windows

Graphical user interface software.

mouse

Hand-held input device connected to a microcomputer by a cable; when you slide the mouse across the desktop, the mouse pointer moves on the screen. A button on the mouse allows users to make menu selections and to issue commands.

multitasking

Activity in which more than one task or program is executed at a time.

Overtype mode

A mode of entering text. With Overtype mode, the newly typed text overwrites the existing text.

Program Manager

The primary window or shell for Microsoft Windows. Applications are organized in and launched from the Program Manager window.

spelling checker

In word processing programs, a program that checks the spelling of words in a document.

thesaurus

In word processing programs, a program that provides a list of synonyms and antonyms for a selected word.

Undo command

In a software application, a command that reverses the last command executed.

word processing

Preparation of a document using a microcomputer.

word wrap

When the insertion point reaches the right-hand margin of a line, it automatically wraps to the left margin of the next line; the user does not have to press ENTER at the end of each line.

WYSIWYG

Acronym for What You See Is What You Get. A Windows feature that allows you to see the final version of a document on the screen before it is printed out.

EXERCISES

SHORT ANSWER

1. What are the advantages of using a word processing program over a typewriter?
2. List the advantages of working in the Microsoft Windows environment.
3. What are the four levels of formatting in a document?
4. What are some examples of mail merge activities?
5. Why is it significant to know that the default mode in Word is the Insert mode?
6. Why is it important to close a document before retrieving another file?
7. What happens if you press ENTER when the insertion point is in the middle of a paragraph?
8. How do you delete a single character to the left of the insertion point?
9. What is meant by the term *word wrap*?
10. What is the difference between the File, Save and File, Save As commands?

HANDS-ON

(*Note*: In the following exercises, save your documents onto and retrieve files from the Advantage Diskette.)

1. Create the document pictured in Figure 1.13.

FIGURE 1.13 MOVING DOCUMENT

```
WE'RE MOVING TO SPAIN on January 15, 1996!

Our new address and phone are:

     Calle Blanca de Rivera, 19
     28010 Madrid, Spain
     Local Phone: 311-0001

ADIOS!
```

a. Save the document as MOVING onto the Advantage Diskette.

b. Close the MOVING document.

c. Retrieve the MOVING document from the Advantage Diskette and insert the following after the first sentence: `Please come visit us!`

d. Save and close the MOVING document once again.

2. Pretend you're having a garage sale. Open GARAGE from the Advantage Diskette and edit it to include the date March 16, 1996, the time 10 A.M. to 12 P.M., and your name and address. When finished, save it back to the Advantage Diskette as GARAGE using the Save button (💾).

3. Create the document appearing in Figure 1.14. Make sure you include your name and job title (real or imaginary) in the closing of the letter. Save this document onto the Advantage Diskette as WORDLTR.

FIGURE 1.14 WORDLTR DOCUMENT

```
September 24, 1995

Mr. Al Martino
210 Spruce Way
Stanford, CA  94305

Dear Mr. Martino:

Thank you for your letter regarding the upcoming
event. I am in complete agreement with you that
the number of persons attending must be limited
to 200. Your idea of having this event catered
sounds fantastic!

Moving to a different subject, I noticed that
the letter you wrote me was typed using a
typewriter. (You certainly make use of
correction fluid!) With the number of letters
you write, you really should consider purchasing
a microcomputer and word processing software
program.

If you are interested, come over to my office
and I'll show you some word processing
fundamentals. We could even use my computer to
design and print the invitations for the event.

Best regards,

your name
```

a. Insert the following text between the second and third paragraphs:

```
Specifically, word processing software makes
it easier to change a document by allowing
you to:

1. Insert text
2. Delete text
3. Move text
4. Copy text
```

b. In the first line of the last paragraph, delete the words "If you are interested," and start the sentence with "You should."

c. In the second paragraph, replace the phrase "correction fluid" with "white out" using Overtype mode and the DELETE key.

d. Save the document back to the Advantage Diskette as WORDLTR, replacing the original version.

e. Close the WORDLTR document.

f. Open a new document.

4. Create the document appearing in Figure 1.15. Make sure you include your name in the closing of the letter. Save this document onto the Advantage Diskette as ABCLTR.

a. In the second paragraph, perform the following editing changes:

Text Before Editing	Text After Editing
`DOS 3.3`	`Microsoft DOS 6.2`
`WordPerfect 5.1`	`Microsoft Word 6.0`
`at that time`	`the next morning`

b. Remove the entire third paragraph, starting with "Training on."

c. Enter the phone number (800) 581-8799 below the last line.

d. Save the document as ABCLTR using the Save button (💾).

e. Close the document.

f. Retrieve the ABCLTR document from the Advantage Diskette.

g. Edit the phone number to read (800) 588-1799.

h. Save and close the document once again.

FIGURE 1.15 ABCLTR DOCUMENT

```
June 28, 1995

Mr. S. Luis Obispo
Manager, Sales
ABC Realty Inc.
1388 Primrose Lane
Albany, GA  31705

Dear Luis:

Per our conversation yesterday, please accept this
letter as confirmation for your order of computer
equipment, deliverable next week.

As discussed, five computers will be installed: one
at reception, two for sales, one for accounting, and
the last one for yourself. We will also be
installing DOS 3.3 and WordPerfect 5.1 at that time.

Training on these software programs will begin the
week after installation, per the schedule arranged in
our conversation. By the way, I've included the cost
for training in the total cost of the equipment.

If I can be of further assistance or if you have
any questions, please do not hesitate to contact me.

Yours sincerely,
Tech Talk Technology

your name
Accounts Representative
```

CASE PROBLEMS

THE EXPERT HANDYMAN, INC.

(*Note*: In the following case problems, assume the role of the primary characters and perform the same steps that they identify. You may want to re-read the session opening.)

1. George is determined to use Microsoft Word to create invoices. He has outlined the information by hand (as shown below) that he wants to include on every invoice.

   The Expert HandyMan, Inc.
   1990 Jillson Street
   Irvine, California 92718

Invoice Number:
Date:
Customer Name:
Address:
City, State, Zip:

[Insert a sentence describing the job performed and result.]

[Number of hours] hours at $30 per hour = [Insert total amount due]

We appreciate your business.

Sincerely,

George Perrera
President, The Expert HandyMan, Inc.

Referring to the handwritten notes, create a generic invoice document that George can edit each time he needs to generate a new invoice. When finished, save the document as INVOICE onto the Advantage Diskette.

2. Yesterday, George completed a job for Kenneth Richards at 436 Wetlands Way, Irvine, California, 92718. Kenneth's dryer wasn't working properly, and George had to clean the fan unit and replace the main airflow tube. George must now generate an invoice for the two hours of work for Mr. Richards. Retrieve the blank invoice stored on the Advantage Diskette, edit the invoice to reflect Mr. Richards' information, add the Invoice Number GP-946, and then save the document as INV-KR.

3. George feels so confident with his new word processing skills that he decides to tackle a proposal using Word. In a conversation with a friend, George heard that Isabel Perez at the Holiday Retreat Hotel is looking for someone to spend five days performing odd jobs around the hotel. The types of problems that need attending to include doors that won't close properly, locks that stick, faucets that leak, and tables that wobble.

   George wants the business at the Holiday Retreat Hotel. He decides to prepare a written proposal stating his hourly wage and describing some of his accomplishments, including the job he just completed for Kenneth Richards. The Holiday Retreat Hotel is located at 2987 W. Howard Street, Irvine, California, 92718. Prepare a proposal document for George and save it as HOLIDAY onto the Advantage Diskette.

4. George has decided to put an advertisement in the local paper for The Expert Handyman, complete with his address, phone number, and his new slogan: "We can fix anything that needs fixing!" He wants the ad to run for the next month in the Business Classifieds section of the weekend edition. Two hours

after calling the local paper about the procedure for submitting an ad, George receives a message on his answering machine. The message is from Rachel Yenkel, the advertising manager, and provides the following information.

Hi, Mr. Perrera. Please send me the text for your advertisement. Insert the words "BEGIN TEXT" one line above the text of your advertisement and "END TEXT" one line below. Send the ad text in a letter to my attention at 4910 S. Commerce Street, Irvine, California, 92718. Also, you will have to let me know what section you want the ad to appear in and how many days you want the ad to run. Bye.

When you've finished creating the advertisement, save the document onto the Advantage Diskette as AD-TEXT.

Microsoft Word 6.0

Formatting Commands

SESSION OUTLINE

INTRODUCTION

Word processing programs include default values or assumptions that determine how a document appears when printed. For most business documents, these default settings work well. However, on occasion you may need to use formatting commands to tailor documents to meet your specific needs or to enhance a document for presentation purposes. This session teaches you how to use Word's tools for professionally formatting your work.

CASE STUDY ADVANCED SOFTWARE DESIGN, INC.

Advanced Software Design, Inc. (ASD) is a software development company that specializes in writing Windows-based software applications. When requested, ASD submits proposals to companies and individuals who express a need for custom-written applications. For example, Harry Zidell of Business Assistance Services, an employment agency, recently contracted with ASD to build a skill-testing program for candidates. A few days after talking to Alethia Montera at ASD about his needs, Harry received a proposal in the mail. The proposal looked fair, and the project is now underway.

While speaking to a client on the phone or in person, Alethia takes handwritten notes outlining the client's needs. After the conversation or meeting, she estimates the number of hours required to complete the project and calculates the cost of the job. She then sends her notes to Mary, who types them up using Microsoft Word and returns them to Alethia for final review. Mary likes working for Alethia and hopes that one day she can work side-by-side with her in assessing clients' needs. To show her initiative and desire for advancement, Mary decides to improve the look of ASD's proposals using Word's formatting commands. But where to begin? Mary has never formatted a document before, just inserted text.

In this session, you and Mary learn more about Word's default settings and how they affect your documents, how to select text, how to format characters, and how to format a paragraph. Finally, you learn the various options for printing your documents.

WORD'S DEFAULT SETTINGS

Why bother formatting a document? First of all, while the words in a document contain the message, a formatted document can better communicate that message. And not only does formatting let you add your own personality to your work, it also improves a document's readability. With proper formatting, you can direct readers' attention to important concepts, improve overall comprehension of the material, and better the chance of recall. And last, it looks really nice!

You begin this session by learning how to change Word's formatting assumptions, or default settings. These settings affect how your documents appear on the screen and how they look when printed. The majority of the session teaches you Word's most commonly used character and paragraph formatting commands. With these commands in your software arsenal, you can produce professional-looking résumés, letters, and reports with minimal effort.

When you first load Word or click the New button (▢) on the Standard tool bar, a new document appears based upon Word's Normal template. This template provides a set of basic formatting assumptions about your new document, including the size of paper, margin widths, and desired font. Although you can modify these initial assumptions directly in the template, most people prefer to start with the original template and then customize the settings later. The **default settings** for a new document based on the Normal template are listed in Table 2.1.

TABLE 2.1

Settings for the Normal Template

Option	*Setting*
Paper Size	8.5-inches wide by 11-inches tall
Top and Bottom Margins	1 inch
Left and Right Margins	1.25 inches
Page Numbering	None
Line Spacing	Single space
Font (Typeface)	Times New Roman
Font Size	10 point
Tabs	Every 0.5 inches
Justification	Left-justified with a ragged right margin

Before you start using Word's character and paragraph formatting commands, you need to learn how to modify the default page layout options for your documents. Let's learn by doing rather than by reading. Perform the following steps on your computer.

1. Ensure that a new document appears in the Word application window and that the Advantage Diskette is inserted in the diskette drive. If you have a document on your screen, close it using the File, Close command and then click the New button (▢) on the Standard toolbar.

2. To view the default page layout settings for this new document:
   CHOOSE: File, Page Setup
   The dialog box shown in Figure 2.1 appears. Notice that there are four tabs along the top of this dialog box: Margins, Paper Size, Paper Source, and Layout.

FIGURE 2.1 PAGE SETUP DIALOG BOX: MARGINS TAB

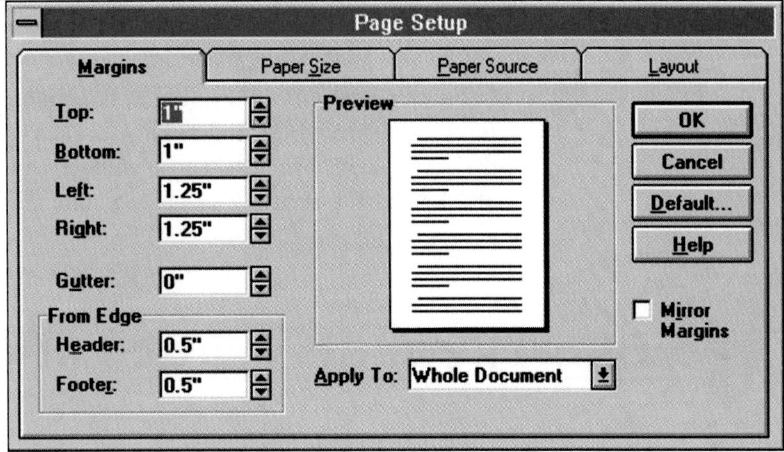

3. To increase and decrease the values for the margin settings, you click the up and down triangular-shaped increment buttons positioned to the right of each text box. Let's increase the top margin to 1.5 inches:
   CLICK: up increment button until 1.5 appears in the Top text box
   Notice that the Preview area immediately shows the increase in the top margin.

4. To ensure that you are using letter-size paper:
   CLICK: Paper Size tab
   The dialog box displayed in Figure 2.2 appears. As you can see in this figure, the default paper size is Letter with a portrait orientation.

FIGURE 2.2 PAGE SETUP DIALOG BOX: PAPER SIZE TAB

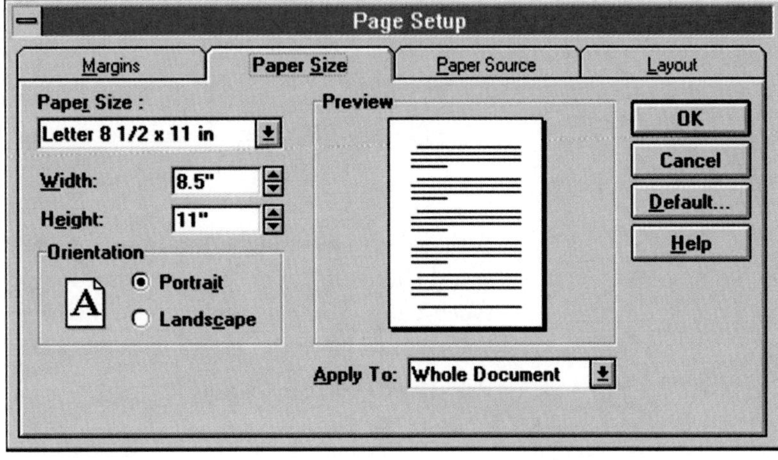

5. To return to the document:
   PRESS: ENTER or CLICK: OK
   The document is now conforming to the 1.5-inch top margin.

For now, we're finished looking at the options for page setup. In the next few sections, you learn how to move efficiently through a document and to block text using the mouse and keyboard. These skills are important for selecting text and issuing character and paragraph formatting commands.

MOVING THROUGH A DOCUMENT

Before inserting or editing text in a document, you must position the insertion point using the mouse or keyboard. Like many procedures in Word, the mouse provides the easiest method for traversing a document. To position the insertion point, you scroll the document window until the desired text appears and then click the I-beam mouse pointer in the text. Scrolling the document window does not automatically move the insertion point! If you forget to click the mouse and start typing or press an arrow key, Word takes you back to the original location of the insertion point before you started scrolling.

Common methods for scrolling the document window are provided below:

To scroll the window ...	*Do this...*
• One line at a time	Click the up (↑) and down (↓) arrows on the vertical scroll bar.
• One screen at a time	Click the vertical scroll bar itself, above and below the scroll box (□).
• Pages at a time	Drag the scroll box (□) along the vertical scroll bar.
• In Page Layout view (discussed later)	In addition to the above methods, you can click on these scroll bar symbols to move to the previous page (▲) or to the next page (▼).

Although not as straightforward as the mouse procedures, there are several keyboard shortcuts for moving the insertion point through a document. If you are a touch-typist, you may prefer these methods to reaching for the mouse every time you need to move the insertion point. Table 2.2 provides a summary of the more popular keystrokes.

TABLE 2.2

Using the Keyboard to Move the Insertion Point

Key	*Description*
↑ or ↓	Moves up or down one line
CTRL + ↑	Moves to the previous paragraph
CTRL + ↓	Moves to the next paragraph
← or →	Moves to the previous or next character
CTRL + ←	Moves to the beginning of the previous word
CTRL + →	Moves to the beginning of the next word
PgUp or PgDn	Moves up or down one screen
HOME or END	Moves to the beginning or end of the current line
CTRL + HOME	Moves to the beginning of the document
CTRL + END	Moves to the end of the document
F5 (GoTo)	Moves to a specific line, section, or page number
SHIFT + F5 (GoBack)	Moves to the last three areas edited in a document

Perform the following steps to practice moving through a document.

1. Make sure that the Advantage Diskette is inserted into drive A:.

2. To practice moving the insertion point, we'll open an existing document that is located on the Advantage Diskette:
   CLICK: Open button ( )
   SELECT: a: (or b:) from the Drives drop-down list box

3. To retrieve the ETHICS document:
   DOUBLE-CLICK: ETHICS.DOC in the File Name list box
   Your screen should now appear similar to Figure 2.3.

FIGURE 2.3 THE ETHICS DOCUMENT

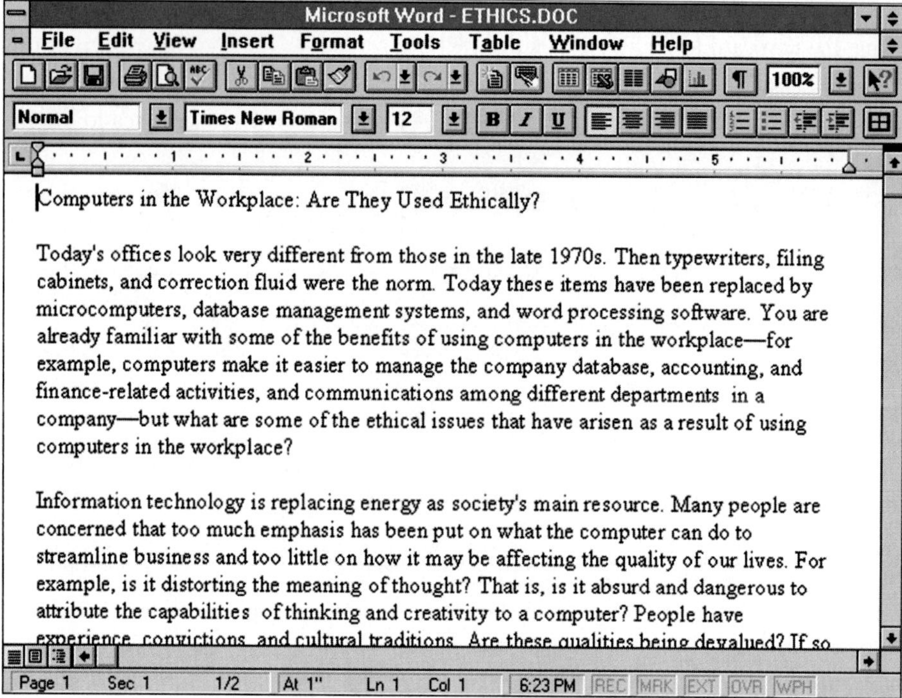

4. To move down through the document one screen at a time:
   CLICK: below the scroll box on the vertical scroll bar repeatedly

5. To move to the top of the document:
   DRAG: the scroll box to the top of the vertical scroll bar

6. To move to the bottom of the document using the keyboard:
   PRESS: CTRL + END

7. To move back to the top of the document using the keyboard:
   PRESS: CTRL + HOME

8. To move to the end of the current line:
   PRESS: END

9. To move to the beginning of the current line:
   PRESS: HOME

10. To move to the top of the second page in the document:
    DOUBLE-CLICK: on the page area at the left side of the Status bar
    The Go To dialog box appears in Figure 2.4.

FIGURE 2.4 THE GO TO DIALOG BOX

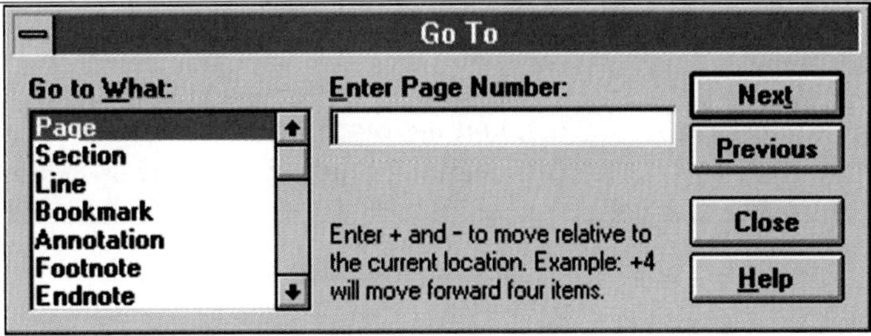

11. Enter the page number where you want to go:
    TYPE: 2
    PRESS: ENTER or CLICK: Next
    The insertion point automatically moves to the first line of page 2.

12. To call up the Go To dialog box again:
    DOUBLE-CLICK: on the page area at the left side of the Status bar
    TYPE: `P1L8`
    PRESS: ENTER or CLICK: Next
    The "P" tells Word that the following number is a page number, and the "L" tells Word that the next number is a line number. The letters can be typed in either uppercase or lowercase characters. In this step, the insertion point is moved to line 8 on page 1.

13. To move to the top of the document:
    PRESS: CTRL + HOME

QUICK REFERENCE

Using the Go To Dialog Box

To access the Go To dialog box:

- **DOUBLE-CLICK: on the page area at the left side of the Status bar, or**
- **PRESS: F5 (GoTo), or**
- **PRESS: CTRL +g, or**
- **CHOOSE: Edit, Go To**

IN ADDITION MARKING LOCATIONS WITH BOOKMARKS

You can also name locations, called *bookmarks*, in your document and then display the Go To dialog box to move to them easily.

To create a bookmark, position the cursor at the location you want to name and then choose Edit, Bookmark from the Menu bar. Type in a name for the bookmark (up to 40 characters) and then click the Add button.

To move to a bookmark, display the Go To dialog box, select Bookmark from the list, and then type in the Bookmark name. For more information, choose Edit, Bookmark and then click the Help button.

SELECTING TEXT

Once text has been typed into a document, formatting changes are made by first selecting the text and then issuing the appropriate command. Selected text always appears highlighted in reverse video. A selection may include letters, words, lines, paragraphs, or even the entire document. When you finish formatting a selection, press an arrow key or click anywhere in the document to remove the highlighting from the text.

BLOCKING TEXT

Word provides an invisible column in the extreme left margin of the document window called the **Selection bar.** When the mouse is moved into this area, the pointer changes from an I-beam to a right-pointing diagonal arrow. This area provides shortcuts for selecting text using the mouse, as summarized in Table 2.3 along with other selection methods.

To practice selecting text, perform the following steps.

1. To select the word "Computers" in the title, first position the I-beam mouse pointer on the word.

2. DOUBLE-CLICK: Computers
   The word and its trailing space should be highlighted in reverse video.

3. To select the letters "Work" of the word "Workplace," you must first position the I-beam pointer to the left of the "W" in "Workplace."

TABLE 2.3

Selecting Text Using the Mouse

To select this...	*Do this...*
Single Letter	Position the I-beam pointer to the left of the letter you want to select. Press down and hold the left mouse button as you drag the mouse pointer to the right.
Single Word	Position the I-beam pointer on the word and double-click the left mouse button.
Single Sentence	Hold down CTRL and click once with the I-beam pointer positioned on any word in the sentence.
Block of Text	Move the insertion point to the beginning of the block of text and then position the I-beam pointer at the end of the block. Hold down SHIFT and click once.
Single Line	Move the mouse pointer into the Selection bar, beside the line to be selected. Wait until the pointer changes to a right-pointing arrow and then click once.
Single Paragraph	Move the mouse pointer into the Selection bar, beside the paragraph to be selected. Wait until the pointer changes to a right-pointing arrow and then double-click. You can also triple-click with the I-beam mouse pointer positioned inside a paragraph.
Entire Document	Move the mouse pointer into the Selection bar. Wait until the pointer changes to a right-pointing arrow and then hold down CTRL and click once.

4. PRESS: left mouse button and hold it down
   DRAG: I-beam to the right until Work is highlighted

5. To select the first sentence in the first paragraph below the title, first position the I-beam pointer on the word "offices." (*Note*: The mouse pointer can be placed over any word in the sentence.)

6. PRESS: CTRL and hold it down
   CLICK: left mouse button once
   The first sentence, including the period and spaces, are highlighted.

7. To select only the third line in the first paragraph, position the mouse pointer to the left of the line in the Selection bar. The mouse pointer should change from an I-beam to a right-pointing diagonal arrow.

8. CLICK: the Selection bar beside the third line

9. To select the entire first paragraph:
   DOUBLE-CLICK: the Selection bar beside the first paragraph
   (*Note:* You can also position the I-beam pointer on any word in the paragraph and triple-click the left mouse button to select the entire paragraph.)

10. To select the entire document:
    PRESS: CTRL and hold it down
    CLICK: *once anywhere in the Selection bar*
    (*Note:* You can also position the mouse pointer in the Selection bar and triple-click the left mouse button to select the entire document.)

11. To remove the highlighting from the text:
    CLICK: *once anywhere in the text area*

12. To return to the top of the document:
    PRESS: CTRL + HOME

To select text using the keyboard, you can use any combination of the keyboard shortcuts for moving the insertion point around the document while holding down the SHIFT key. Most people find that the mouse methods provide all the flexibility required for selecting blocks of text.

DELETING BLOCKS OF TEXT

Before this section, you deleted text one character at a time using the BACKSPACE and DELETE keys. However, selecting text allows you to easily perform editing procedures on larger blocks of text. Perform the following steps to practice deleting and replacing text in a document.

1. To select the phrase in the title that reads "Are They Used Ethically?" first position the I-beam pointer to the left of the word "Are."
   CLICK: the left mouse button once to position the insertion point

2. Position the I-beam pointer to the right of the question mark. To select the text between the insertion point and the I-beam pointer:
   PRESS: SHIFT and hold it down
   CLICK: the left mouse button once

   The entire phrase is selected.

3. To remove this phrase from the title:
   PRESS: DELETE

4. Move the I-beam pointer on the word "Computers" in the title:
   DOUBLE-CLICK: Computers
   The word is selected.

5. TYPE: `Technology`
   PRESS: Space Bar
   Rather than using the Overtype mode, you can select the text to be replaced and type in the new information. The typing automatically replaces the text selection.

6. To Undo this last editing change:
   CLICK: Undo button ( ) in the Standard toolbar
   The word "Computers" reappears.

7. To demonstrate a basic formatting command, let's change the capitalization of the selected word "Computers":
   CHOOSE: Format, Change Case
   SELECT: UPPERCASE
   PRESS: ENTER or CLICK: OK
   The word changes from "Computers" to "COMPUTERS."

8. Close the document without saving the changes:
   CHOOSE: File, Close
   SELECT: No button

Now that you know how to move through documents and select text, formatting your documents will be much easier. The next section begins with an introduction to the character formatting commands.

CHARACTER FORMATTING COMMANDS

In word processing software, enhancing text is referred to as character formatting. Specifically, character formatting involves selecting typefaces, font sizes, and attributes for text. Some of the attributes available in Word include bold, italic, underline, strikethrough, small capitals, all capitals, superscript, and subscript. Although these enhancement features are effective in drawing attention to text, they can also detract from the message of a document. Some publishing professionals advocate four typefaces or fonts as the maximum for any one document. Still, there is no better gauge than common sense and good taste!

Word's character formatting commands are accessed through the Format, Font command (Figure 2.5), the Formatting toolbar, or by using shortcut keyboard combinations. Since many of the features are accessible from the Formatting toolbar and shortcut keys, you may never need to access the menu except to see a preview of a desired font in the dialog box. Table 2.4 summarizes the mouse and keyboard methods for choosing character formatting commands after you have selected the desired text.

FIGURE 2.5 FONT DIALOG BOX

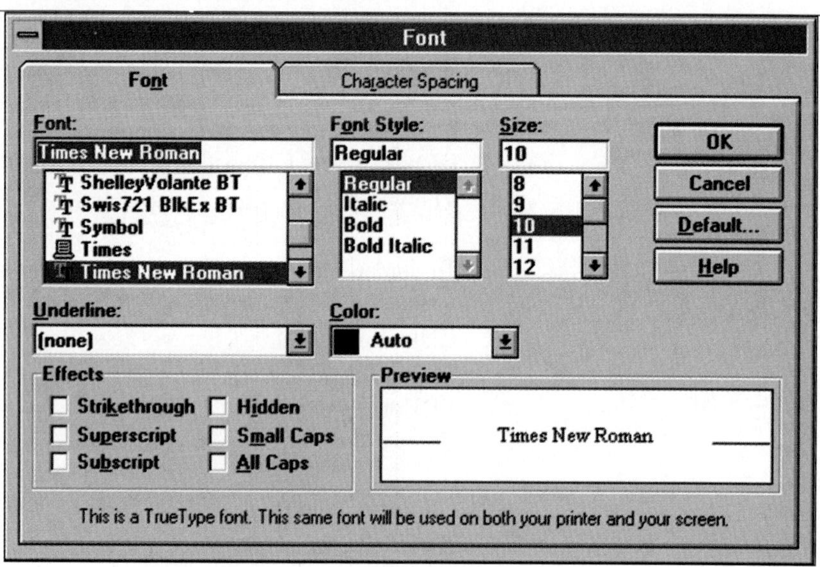

TABLE 2.4

Character Formatting Summary

Toolbar Button	*Keyboard Shortcut*	*Description*
B	CTRL+b	Makes the selected text **bold**
I	CTRL+i	*Italicizes* the selected text
U	CTRL+u	Applies a single underline
	CTRL+SHIFT+d	Applies a double underline
	CTRL+SHIFT+w	Applies underlining to words only

TABLE 2.4 *concluded*

Character Formatting Summary

Toolbar Button	*Keyboard Shortcut*	*Description*
Times Roman	CTRL + SHIFT +f	Specifies a font or typeface
10	CTRL + SHIFT +p	Specifies a point size for the font
	CTRL + SHIFT +a	CAPITALIZES the selection
	CTRL + SHIFT +k	Applies SMALL CAPS
	SHIFT + F3	Changes the case of the selection
	CTRL + =	Applies a $_{\text{sub}}$script style
	CTRL + SHIFT + =	Applies a ^{super}script style
	CTRL +Space Bar	Removes all character formatting

BOLDFACE, ITALIC, AND UNDERLINES

Word allows you to apply character formatting commands as you type or after you have selected text. Perform the following steps to apply boldface, italic, and underlines to the ETHICS document.

1. Retrieve the ETHICS document from the Advantage Diskette. (*Note:* The last four documents that you opened are listed at the bottom of the File pull-down menu. Choose ETHICS.DOC from this list.)

2. To insert a new line between the title and the first paragraph:
   PRESS: END
   PRESS: ENTER

3. To add an italicized subtitle for this document:
   CLICK: Italic button (*I*) on the Formatting toolbar
   TYPE: `The Information Age and the Age of Humanity`

4. To stop typing in italic:
   CLICK: Italic button (*I*)

5. To select this subtitle, position the mouse pointer in the Selection bar to the left of the line and click the left mouse button once.

6. Make the subtitle bold and underlined using the buttons on the Formatting toolbar:
   CLICK: Bold button (**B**)
   CLICK: Underline button (U)

7. To remove the highlighting:
   CLICK: *anywhere in the text area*

8. Perform the following formatting changes in the first paragraph using either the Formatting toolbar buttons or the keyboard shortcuts:

Text to be formatted	*Formatting to apply*
microcomputers	italic and bold
database management system	italic
word processing software	italic
ethical issues	word underline only

QUICK REFERENCE
Boldface, Italic, and Underlines

- **To make text bold, click the Bold button (B) or press CTRL +b**
- **To italicize text, click the Italic button (*I*) or press CTRL +i**
- **To underline text, click the Underline button (U) or press CTRL +u**

TYPEFACES, FONTS, AND POINT SIZES

Some of the more interesting character formatting tasks include selecting typefaces to use in a document. A **typeface** is a style of print, whereas a **font** is defined as all the symbols and characters of a particular typeface for a given point size. Many DOS word processing programs do not utilize a variety of fonts, unless they are available through an individual software vendor or resident in the printer's memory. Microsoft Windows, on the other hand, provides easy access to several different typefaces.

The font and point size can be changed before typing new text or after selecting text. Although you can access the Format, Font dialog box to set the font and point size, it is easier to use the drop-down lists on the Formatting toolbar. Perform the following steps to change some of the fonts and point sizes in the ETHICS document.

1. SELECT: the main title on the first line

2. To display a list of the available fonts:
   CLICK: down arrow adjacent to the Font drop-down list (Times Roman ⊻)

3. Scroll through the font choices by clicking the up and down arrows on the drop-down list's scroll bar or by dragging the scroll box.

4. SELECT: Arial
   You select a font from the drop-down list by clicking on it.

5. To display the range of available font sizes:
   CLICK: down arrow adjacent to the Font Size drop-down list (10 ▾)

6. SELECT: 16-point font size
   CLICK: Bold button (**B**)
   PRESS: HOME to remove the highlighting
   Your document should now appear similar to Figure 2.6.

FIGURE 2.6 THE ETHICS DOCUMENT AFTER CHARACTER FORMATTING

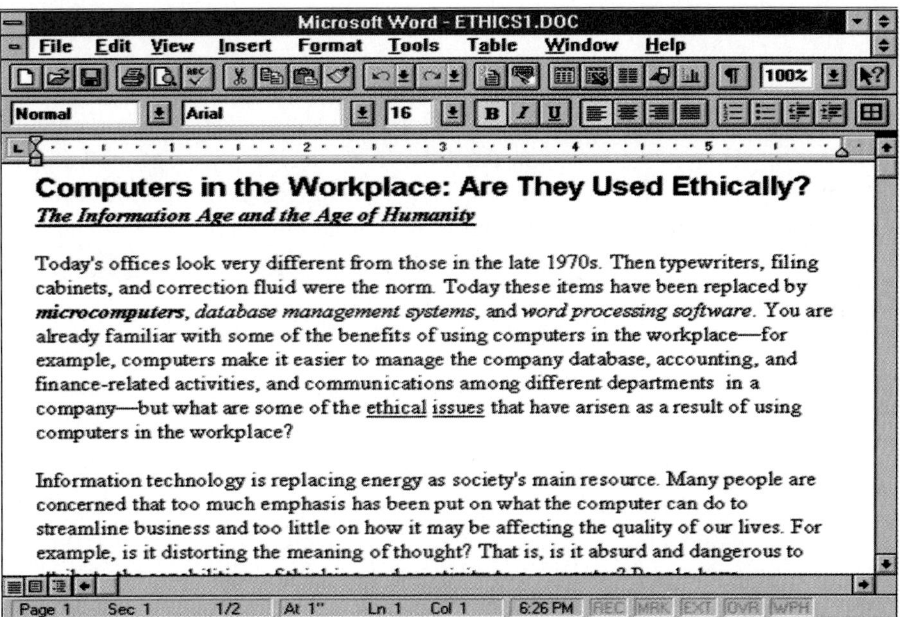

7. To save the document to the Advantage Diskette as ETHICS1:
   CHOOSE: File, Save As
   TYPE: `ethics1`
   SELECT: a: drive (or b: drive)
   PRESS: ENTER or CLICK: OK to accept the Save As dialog box
   PRESS: ENTER or CLICK: OK to accept the Summary Info box

QUICK REFERENCE
Typefaces, Fonts, and Point Sizes

- **To select a typeface, click the Fonts drop-down list (Times Roman) in the Formatting toolbar and then click on the desired font.**
- **To change the font size, click the Font Size drop-down list (10) in the Formatting toolbar and then click on the desired point size.**

USING THE FORMAT PAINTER

Word's new Format Painter feature lets you copy character and paragraph formatting from one area in your document to another area. To copy character formatting, you select the text with the desired formatting and click the Format Painter button ( ) on the Standard toolbar. When you move the mouse pointer into the document area it becomes an I-beam attached to a paintbrush. To apply the formatting, you drag the mouse pointer over the text that you want formatted. When you release the mouse button, the formatting characteristics are copied from the original selection to your new selection.

To copy formatting to multiple areas in a document, you double-click the Format Painter button ( ) after selecting the originally formatted text. Similar to before, you paint the first selection by dragging the mouse pointer over the desired text. However, this time the mouse pointer doesn't disappear when you finish applying the first coat. You continue applying formatting to additional text selections and then click the Format Painter button ( ) when you are finished.

Let's practice—perform the following steps.

1. Retrieve a document called PAINT from the Advantage Diskette.

2. SELECT: Current Status

3. To format the heading:
   CLICK: Bold button (B)
   CLICK: Italic button (I)
   SELECT: Arial font from the Font drop-down list (Times Roman)
   SELECT: 14-point size from the Font Size drop-down list (10)

4. To copy the formatting characteristics that you just selected:
   DOUBLE-CLICK: Current

5. CLICK: Format Painter button ( )

6. Move the mouse pointer into the document area. Notice that it becomes an I-beam attached to a paintbrush.

7. To copy the formatting to the second heading:
   DRAG: mouse pointer over the words Future Potential
   When you release the mouse button, the second heading is formatted with the same characteristics as the first heading.

8. To format the third word in the first paragraph:
   DOUBLE-CLICK: IBM

9. CLICK: Bold button (B)
   CLICK: Italic button (I)

10. To copy this formatting to several areas in the paragraph:
    DOUBLE-CLICK: Format Painter button ()

11. Using the I-beam paintbrush mouse pointer, select all occurrences of "Microsoft" and "Windows NT" in the first paragraph. (*Tip*: You can double-click words as you would with the regular I-beam mouse pointer to apply the formatting.)

12. To finish using the I-beam paintbrush mouse pointer:
    CLICK: Format Painter button ()

13. Save the document as PAINTED to the Advantage Diskette.

14. Close the document.

QUICK REFERENCE
Using the Format Painter Button ()

1. **SELECT: the text with the desired formatting characteristics**
2. **CLICK: Format Painter button ()**
3. **SELECT: the text that you want formatted**

IN ADDITION

FORMATTING CHARACTERS WITH STYLES

A *character style* is a set of formats that can contain any specification found in the Font dialog box (Figure 2.5), such as font type, type style, and point size. When you apply a style to a selection of text, all the formatting instructions in the style are executed at once. When you edit a style, any text that conforms to the style is updated at once.

If you work with documents that contain lots of formatting, styles will (1) save you time, (2) promote consistent formatting throughout your documents, and (3) make it easier for you to edit a document's format.

To find out more about styles, choose Format, Style from the Menu bar, and then click the Help button.

PARAGRAPH FORMATTING COMMANDS

Paragraph formatting involves changing indentation, alignment, line spacing, and tab settings for a paragraph. As with character formatting, many paragraph formatting commands are accessible using the mouse or keyboard shortcut combinations. Using a mouse, you can change alignments and indent paragraphs by clicking buttons on the Formatting toolbar or create hanging indents and set tab stops by dragging symbols on the Ruler. For entering specific measurements and accessing the full gamut of paragraph formatting options, choose the Format, Paragraph command to yield the dialog box shown in Figure 2.7.

FIGURE 2.7 PARAGRAPH DIALOG BOX

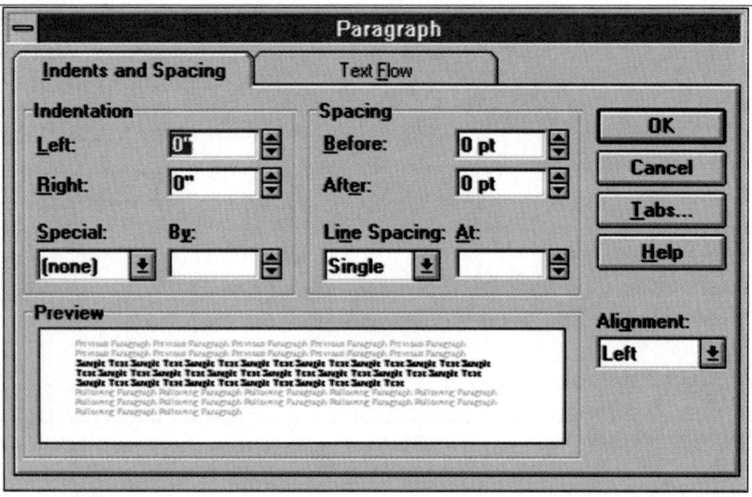

Word stores formatting information in the **Paragraph Symbol** (¶). To apply paragraph formatting commands to a paragraph, position the insertion point anywhere in the paragraph—you do not need to select any text—and then issue the desired command. To remove paragraph formatting, you simply delete the paragraph mark. The current paragraph automatically assumes the paragraph formatting characteristics of the subsequent paragraph.

When you first load Word, the paragraph marks are hidden from view. To display the paragraph marks and all other hidden symbols, click the Show/Hide button (¶) on the Formatting toolbar. Along with the paragraph marks, Word reveals spaces (as dots), tabs (as right-pointing arrows →), and other formatting codes and symbols. It's very important to note that these are *nonprinting symbols*—they will not show up on the printed page.

One new feature available in Word 6.0 is the ability to display a help bubble showing you the formatting characteristics of your text. To display the bubble, click the Help button (?) and then click the question mark mouse pointer on the desired text area. A bubble will appear with character and paragraph formatting information. To remove the Help bubble, you click the Help button (?) a second time.

Perform the following steps to display the hidden symbols and formatting information for the ETHICS1 document.

1. Ensure that the ETHICS1 document appears on your screen.

2. To show all of the hidden symbols in the document:
   CLICK: Show/Hide button (¶)
   Paragraph marks (¶) are displayed in the document wherever the ENTER key was pressed. This view is useful for checking codes and spaces, but you may find it too distracting to use all the time.

3. To show the formatting characteristics for the title:
   CLICK: Help button (?)

4. Position the question mark mouse pointer over any letter in the title:
   CLICK: left mouse button once
   Your screen should appear similar to Figure 2.8.

FIGURE 2.8

HELP BUBBLE FOR SHOWING FORMATTING CHARACTERISTICS

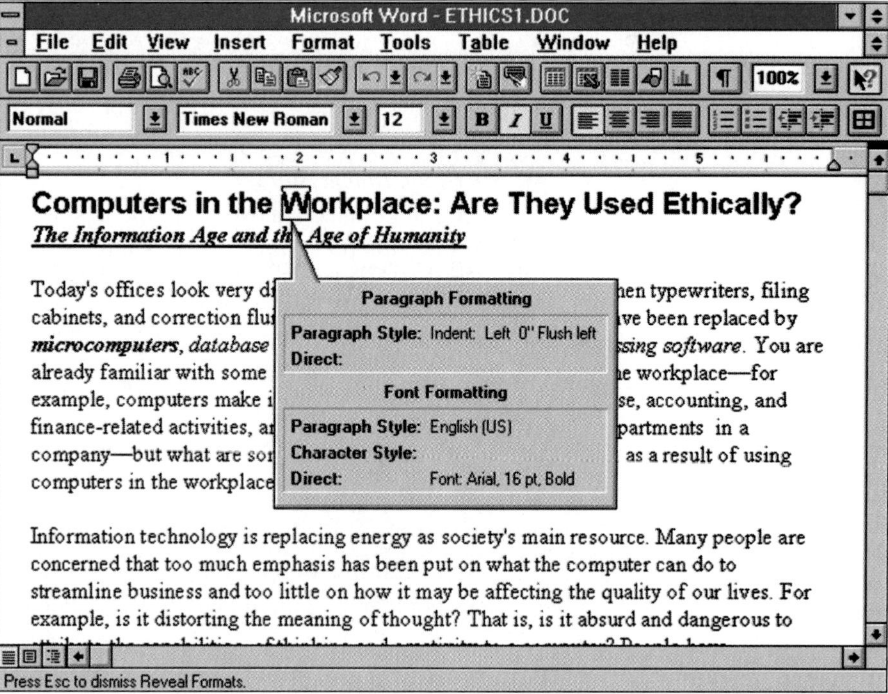

5. To remove the Help bubble:
   CLICK: Help button (![?])

6. Before proceeding, let's hide the symbols:
   CLICK: Show/Hide button (¶)

INDENTING PARAGRAPHS

Indenting a paragraph means to move a body of text in from the normal text borders. When you indent a paragraph, you temporarily change the text's positioning relative to the left and right margins. You can indent a paragraph on the left side only, right side only, or on both sides (known as a nested paragraph).

If you use the Increase Indent () and Decrease Indent () buttons on the Formatting toolbar, indentation is determined by the tab settings in the Ruler. If the tab positions have not been modified, Word assumes you want to use the default 0.5 inch settings. Each time you indent a paragraph, the text moves to the next tab stop. Therefore, to create larger indentations you can set larger gaps between tabs or select the indent command multiple times. You can also customize your indents by dragging the indent markers on the Ruler (shown below).

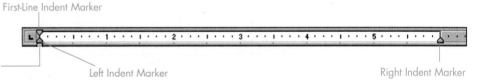

First-Line Indent Marker

Moves First-Line and Left Indent Markers in Tandem

Left Indent Marker

Right Indent Marker

- *First-Line Indent Marker*
  This indent marker moves only the first line of a paragraph in from the left margin. This paragraph format is often used in letters to avoid having to press the TAB key at the start of each new paragraph.

- *Left Indent Marker*
  The left indent marker moves the body of the entire paragraph in from the left margin.

- *Right Indent Marker*
  The right indent marker moves the body of the entire paragraph in from the right margin. Left and right indents are often used together to set quotations apart from normal body text in a document.

By default, Word positions the first-line and left indent markers on the left margin, and the right indent marker on the right margin. You will now practice changing the paragraph indents using the mouse.

Perform the following steps.

1. Ensure that the ETHICS1 document appears on your screen.

2. Move the insertion point to the second paragraph, starting with the words "Information technology." Position the insertion point to the left of the letter "I" in the word "Information."

3. To add a left indent to this paragraph:
   CLICK: Increase Indent button ()
   The paragraph moves 0.5 inches to the next tab stop. Notice the new location of the indent markers on the Ruler.

4. To view the new settings as they appear in the Paragraph dialog box, position the mouse pointer on the paragraph and click the right mouse button to bring up the shortcut menu.

5. CHOOSE: Paragraph
   The Paragraph dialog box appears. Notice the new value in the Left Indentation text box and the sample paragraph in the Preview area.

6. To return to the document:
   PRESS: ESC or CLICK: Cancel

7. To indent the paragraph 1 inch from the right margin:
   DRAG: right indent marker to the left by 1 inch (to 5 inches on the Ruler)

8. To remove the left indent:
   CLICK: Decrease Indent button ()
   Notice that this button has no effect on the right indent marker.

9. To remove the right indent:
   DRAG: right indent marker back to the right margin (at 6 inches on the Ruler)

10. Move to the last paragraph in the ETHICS1 document. Position the insertion point at the start of the second line in the paragraph, beginning with "Keep in mind."

11. To split this paragraph into two parts:
    PRESS: ENTER twice

12. To indent the newly created paragraph by 1 inch:
    CLICK: Increase Indent button ( ) twice

    The text should appear similar to the following:

    These are only a few of the many computer-related issues that are being discussed today.

    > Keep in mind, however, that although these problems certainly deserve everyone's attention, they should not obscure the opportunities that will be opened up to if you know how to use computers in your chosen occupation.

    ---

13. Move the insertion point to the end of the sentence in the previous paragraph, immediately after the word "today."

14. A paragraph's formatting characteristics are stored in its paragraph mark. When that mark is deleted, the paragraph assumes the formatting characteristics of the next paragraph mark. To demonstrate:
    PRESS: DELETE two or three times until the paragraphs join together
    (*Note:* The first sentence should assume the indented characteristics of the second paragraph.)

15. A handy keystroke to remember is CTRL + `q`; it removes all paragraph formatting characteristics from a paragraph. To demonstrate:
    PRESS: CTRL + `q`
    The paragraph indentations return to their normal settings against the left and right margins.

16. Move to the end of the document and insert a new blank line.

17. In this next step, you insert a hanging indent where the first line of the paragraph lines up with the left margin and the remainder of the paragraph is indented. To begin:
    DRAG: left indent marker to 1 inch on the Ruler

    (*CAUTION:* Make sure that the tip of your mouse pointer points to the triangle and not to the bottom rectangle when dragging. If performed correctly, the first-line indent marker should remain at the margin.)

18. TYPE: `Summary`
    PRESS: TAB

19. TYPE: `Information systems technology provides a clear opportunity for the disabled to perform in the workplace.`
    Your document should now appear similar to Figure 2.9.

20. Save and then close the ETHICS1 document.

FIGURE 2.9 INDENTING PARAGRAPHS IN THE ETHICS1 DOCUMENT

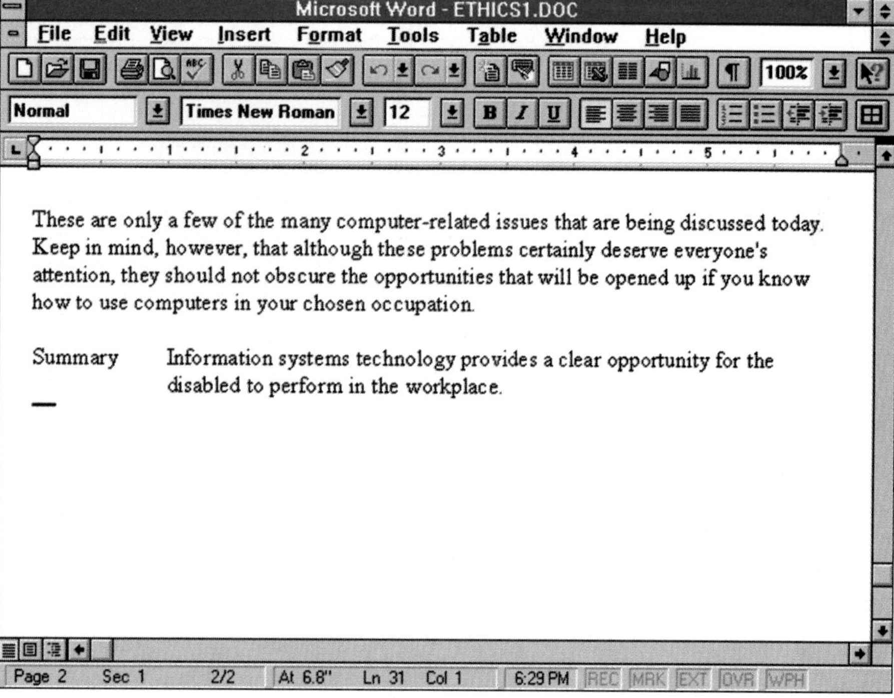

QUICK REFERENCE
Indenting Paragraphs

- **To indent a paragraph from the left margin:**
  CLICK: Increase Indent button ( )
- **To remove a left indent for a paragraph**
  CLICK: Decrease Indent button ( )
- **To customize the first-line, left, and right indents:**
  DRAG: the indent markers on the Ruler

CREATING BULLETED AND NUMBERED LISTS

Word offers a utility for automatically creating lists with leading **bullets** or numbers. Although round circles are the standard shape for bullets, you can select shapes from a variety of symbols. Numbered lists can use numerals, letters, or numbers. If you want to modify the bullet symbols or numbering scheme, choose the

Format, Bullets and Numbering command to display the dialog box appearing in Figure 2.10. This screen graphic also shows the resulting dialog box when you click the Modify button.

FIGURE 2.10 BULLETS AND NUMBERING DIALOG BOX

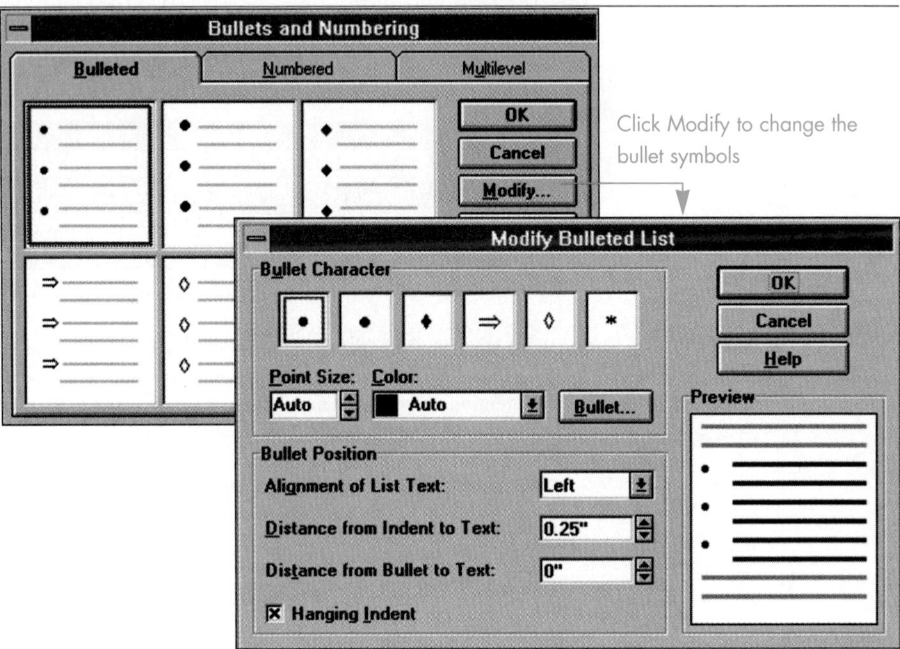

Perform the following steps to create bulleted and numbered lists.

1. If you do not have an empty document on the screen, open a new document using the New button ( ).

2. TYPE: `To Do List`
   PRESS: ENTER twice

3. To create a bulleted list:
   CLICK: Bullets button ( )

4. Enter the following text, pressing ENTER at the end of each line:

   ```
   Pick up dry cleaning
   Meet Jesse at the gym
   Go grocery shopping
   Mail letter to Mom
   ```

5. You will notice that Word automatically starts each new line with a bullet when you press ENTER. To turn off the bullets, ensure that your insertion point is on the line below "Mail letter to Mom" and then:
   CLICK: Bullets button ( )

6. PRESS: ENTER

7. In this next example, you create a numbered list after you've already entered information into your document. To begin:
   TYPE: `Travel Itinerary`
   PRESS: ENTER twice

8. Enter the following lines of text, as before:

```
Aug 12: Flight 455 to Sydney.
Aug 28: Flight 87 to Auckland.
Aug 29: Flight A101 to Christchurch.
Sep 11: Flight 110 to Vancouver.
```

9. Using the mouse pointer in the Selection bar, select the text that you just entered in step 8.

10. CLICK: Numbering button ( )
    The selected text is automatically numbered.

11. To use letters rather than numbers for the list, position the mouse pointer over the highlighted text and click the right mouse button. From the shortcut menu that appears:
    CHOOSE: Bullets and Numbering

12. Ensure that the Numbered tab is displayed in the dialog box.

13. CLICK: the option that shows a), b), c), and d)

14. PRESS: ENTER or CLICK: OK
    CLICK: *anywhere in the document to remove the highlighting*
    Your document should now appear similar to Figure 2.11.

15. To add an item to your travel itinerary between Christchurch and Vancouver, position the I-beam pointer at the end of the Christchurch line or item c) and press ENTER.

16. TYPE: `Sep 10: Flight 904 to Seattle`
    Notice that Word automatically renumbers, or in this case re-letters, the list for you when you insert entries.

17. Save the document as LISTS onto the Advantage Diskette.

18. Close the document.

QUICK REFERENCE
Bulleted and Numbered Lists

- **To create a bulleted list, click the Bullets button ( )**
- **To create a numbered list, click the Numbering button ( )**
- **To modify the bullet symbols or numbering scheme:**
  CHOOSE: Format, Bullets and Numbering

FIGURE 2.11 NUMBERED AND BULLETED LISTS

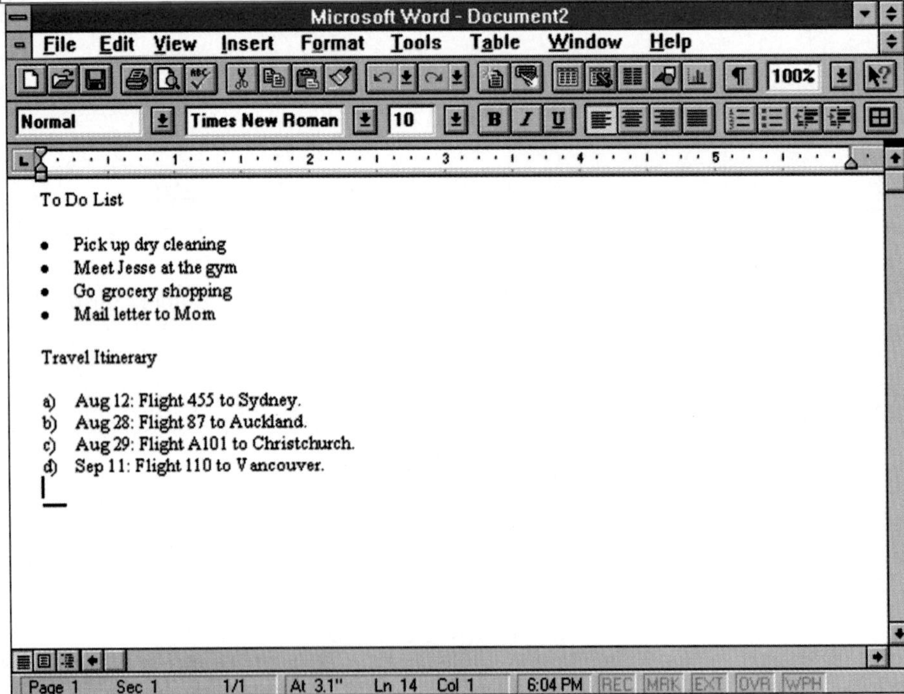

CHANGING PARAGRAPH ALIGNMENT

Justification refers to how text aligns with the margins of a document. You can apply justification to a paragraph either before or after text is typed. Word provides four different types of justification or alignment:

- *Left justification* aligns text at the left margin but leaves jagged right edges as a typewriter does.
- *Center justification* centers the line or paragraph between the margins.
- *Right justification* positions text flush against the right margin.

- *Full justification* provides even text columns at the left and right margins by automatically spacing words on the line.

You specify the justification for a paragraph using the Format, Paragraph command, Formatting toolbar buttons, or keyboard shortcut combinations (summarized in Table 2.5). Remember, paragraph formatting requires the insertion point to be placed in the paragraph to be formatted, but you need not select any text.

TABLE 2.5

Alignment and Justification

Toolbar Button	*Keyboard Shortcut*	*Description*
	CTRL +l	Left-justifies the selected paragraph
	CTRL +e	Centers the selected paragraph
	CTRL +r	Right-justifies the selected paragraph
	CTRL +j	Fully justifies the selected paragraph

Perform the following steps to practice justification.

1. Retrieve the ETHICS document from the Advantage Diskette.
2. To change the justification for the title, first position the insertion point at the beginning of the title.
3. CLICK: Center button ( )
   The line is immediately centered between the two margins.
4. CLICK: Align Right button ( )
   The line is positioned flush against the right margin.
5. To move the line back to its original position:
   CLICK: Align Left button ( )
6. Practice changing the first paragraph's justification using the buttons on the Formatting toolbar.

QUICK REFERENCE
Changing Justification

- **To left-align a paragraph, click the Align Left button ( )**
- **To center a paragraph, click the Center button ( )**
- **To right-align a paragraph, click the Align Right button ( )**
- **To justify a paragraph, click the Justify button ( )**

IN ADDITION

ALIGNING TEXT VERTICALLY

On a page, text is usually aligned with the top margin. That is, the first line of text that you type prints on the first line after the top margin. In some cases, such as when including a cover page or a table of data in your document, you may want the text to be centered or justified between the top and bottom margins.

To align text vertically, choose File, Page Setup from the Menu bar. Select the Layout tab. In the Vertical Alignment list, select Center to center the text on the page or Justify to spread the paragraphs evenly between the top and bottom margins. For more information, click the Help button in the Layout tab.

CHANGING LINE SPACING

Another common paragraph formatting procedure lets you change the line spacing in a document. The standard options for line spacing are single- and double-spaced, but your choices aren't limited to these. You can specify various line spacing options using the Format, Paragraph dialog box. However, the shortcut keys in Table 2.6 provide the quickest methods for selecting line spacing in a paragraph.

TABLE 2.6

Changing Line Spacing

Keyboard Shortcut	*Description*
CTRL+1	Single-spaces the selected paragraph
CTRL+2	Double-spaces the selected paragraph
CTRL+5	Applies 1.5-line-spacing to the selected paragraph

Perform the following steps to change line spacing.

1. Move the insertion point into the first paragraph of the ETHICS document.

2. To double-space this paragraph:
   PRESS: CTRL+2
   Notice that only the first paragraph is double-spaced.

3. To apply 1.5-line-spacing:
   PRESS: CTRL+5

4. To return the paragraph to single spacing:
   PRESS: CTRL+1

5. To double-space the document, you need to first select the entire document. Move the mouse pointer into the Selection bar and triple-click the left mouse button. The entire document should be highlighted in reverse video before proceeding.

6. PRESS: CTRL+2
   The ETHICS document should be double-spaced.

7. CLICK: *anywhere in the document to remove the highlighting*

8. Close the document and do not save the changes.

QUICK REFERENCE
Line Spacing Shortcuts

- **To single-space a paragraph, select the text, press CTRL +1**
- **To space a paragraph by 1.5 lines, press CTRL +5**
- **To double-space a paragraph, press CTRL +2**
- **To select a specific line spacing option:**

  CHOOSE: Format, Paragraph

  CLICK: down arrow next to the Line Spacing box

  SELECT: *any spacing option*

  PRESS: ENTER or CLICK: OK

CHANGING TAB SETTINGS

Tabs enable you to neatly enter text and numbers into columns. If your past experience includes using a typewriter, you are likely familiar with using the Space Bar to line up columns of text on a page. This works fine when you are using a monospaced font in which all letters are an equal width. However, most word processing fonts are not monospaced and, therefore, you cannot line up columns by simply pressing the Space Bar a fixed number of times. To accomplish the same objective in Word, you place tabs on the Ruler and use the TAB key to move the insertion point between tab stops. The four basic types of tabs are described in Table 2.7.

TABLE 2.7

Types of Tabs

Tab Name	*Ruler Symbol*	*Description*
Left-Aligned		Starting at the tab, text extends to the right as you type
Center-Aligned		Starting at the tab, text is centered on the tab stop
Right-Aligned		Starting at the tab, text extends to the left as you type
Decimal-Aligned		At the tab, the integer portion of a number extends to the left and the decimal fraction extends to the right

Before you start adding your own tabs to the Ruler, you should be aware that Word supplies left-aligned tabs every 0.5 inches by default. If you require greater flexibility, you begin by selecting a tab type using the Tab Alignment button () located at the far left of the Ruler. On each mouse click, Word switches to the next tab symbol. Once the desired tab type appears, you position the tip of the mouse pointer on the Ruler and click once to place the tab. If you need to fine-tune a tab's position on the Ruler, you simply drag it back and forth. To remove a tab, you drag it downwards and off the Ruler. Be forewarned that all the default tabs to the left of the new tab are automatically cleared.

You can also set tabs using the Format, Tabs command (its dialog box appears in Figure 2.12.) An added benefit to using the Tabs dialog box to set tabs is that you can also set leaders. A tab **leader** is a dotted, dashed, or solid line that fills the space between text and tab stops. Leaders are commonly used in tables of contents to visually join the section headings with the page numbers. Some examples of leaders are provided below:

Dot leader . . . . .A Right-Aligned tab

Dashed leader -Another Right-Aligned tab

Solid leader ______________________And yet a third Right-Aligned tab

In the following steps, you create a document that uses customized tabs.

1. If you do not have an empty document on the screen, open a new document using the New button ().

FIGURE 2.12 TABS DIALOG BOX

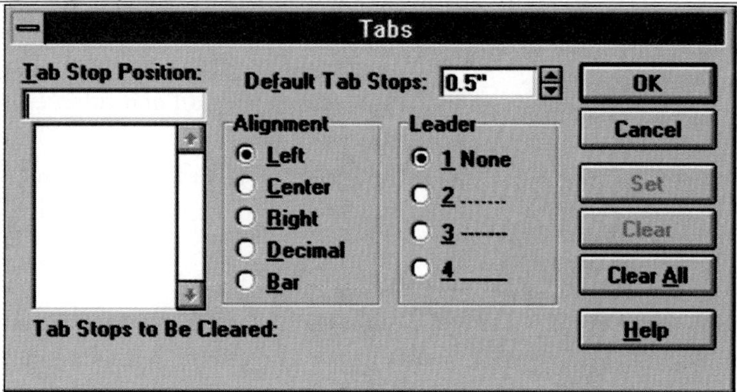

2. To center the title and specify double spacing:
   CLICK: Center button
   PRESS: CTRL+2

3. TYPE: `Marketing Memo`
   PRESS: ENTER

4. To change the paragraph alignment to fully justified:
   CLICK: Justify button

5. TYPE: `It is my pleasure to announce to Sporting Life's marketing and sales staff that sales have increased steadily for the past six months. As you well know, Sporting Life is known for carrying quality sporting items at reasonable prices. But without you, Sporting Life would be "just another sports store." Keep up the good work!`

6. To add a blank line and change to single spacing:
   PRESS: ENTER
   PRESS: CTRL+1

7. In the remainder of the document, you will create an income and expense report for January through June. The first step is to label the columns that will contain the figures. The first column heading will center at 3 inches and the second column at 4.5 inches on the Ruler.

   Perform the following steps to set the two tab stops:
   CLICK: Tab Alignment button at the far left of the Ruler until the center-aligned tab symbol appears

8. Position the tip of the mouse pointer on the 3-inch mark and click the left mouse button once. If done properly, you will see a center-aligned tab mark appear on the Ruler. If the tab stop is not placed correctly, drag the tab mark into position using the mouse. To delete the tab and start over, drag the tab downward and release the mouse button.

9. To position the second tab stop, position the mouse pointer on the 4.5-inch mark and click the left mouse button once.

10. PRESS: TAB
    The insertion point moves to the first tab stop. Notice that Word deletes the default tab stops to the left of the customized tabs.

11. TYPE: `REVENUE`
    PRESS: TAB

12. TYPE: `EXPENSES`
    PRESS: ENTER twice
    The headings are centered on their respective tab marks.

13. The next step is to set the decimal tabs for aligning the numbers correctly. Before proceeding, remove the two center-aligned tab stops by dragging them down and off the Ruler.

14. To specify a tab position for the row headings:
    SELECT: Left-aligned tab using the Tab Alignment button
    CLICK: 1 inch on the Ruler

15. To specify a tab position for the REVENUE figures:
    SELECT: Decimal-aligned tab using the Tab Alignment button
    CLICK: 3.25 inches on the Ruler
    (*Tip*: To display a measurement helper, try holding down the ALT key as you drag the tab symbol on the Ruler.)

16. To specify a tab position for the EXPENSES figures:
    CLICK: 4.75 inches on the Ruler

17. For fun, let's turn on the Show/Hide symbols feature:
    CLICK: Show/Hide button (¶)

18. Now, let's enter January's REVENUE and EXPENSES:
    PRESS: TAB
    TYPE: `January`
    PRESS: TAB
    TYPE: `18,900.75`
    PRESS: TAB
    TYPE: `13,534.67`
    PRESS: ENTER
    Notice that each press of the TAB key results in the tab symbol (→).

19. Enter the following information to finish the Marketing Memo:

	REVENUE	EXPENSES
February	22,050.00	15,356.48
March	17,354.45	11,225.32
April	18,239.00	15,006.95
May	26,884.69	19,322.55
June	28,677.41	21,632.10

20. Save the document as MEMO95 onto the Advantage Diskette. Your document should now appear similar to Figure 2.13.

FIGURE 2.13 SPORTING LIFE MARKETING MEMO

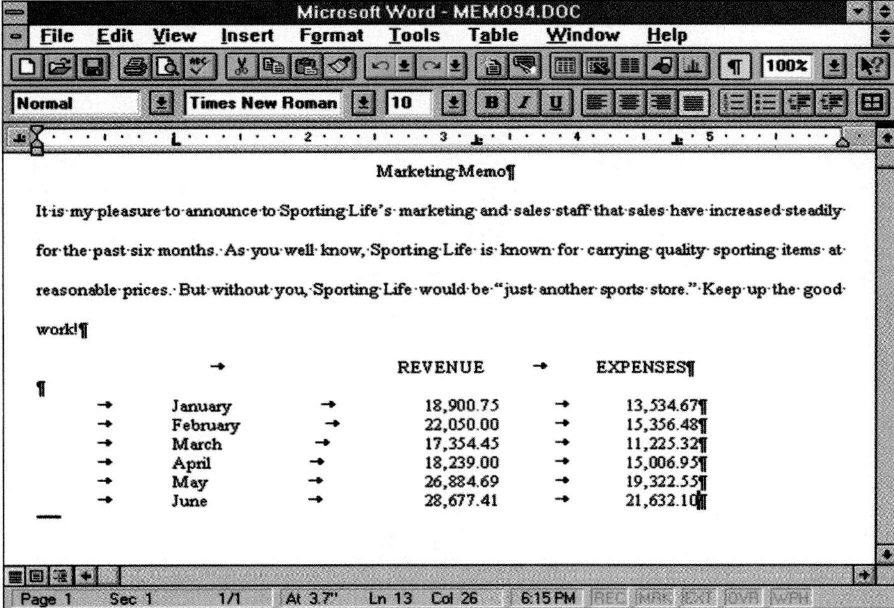

QUICK REFERENCE
Setting Tabs

1. **SELECT: a tab type ([L], [⊥], [⅃], or [⊥.]) using the Tab Alignment button on the Ruler**
2. **CLICK: desired location on the Ruler to set the tab stop**

FORCING A PAGE BREAK

Word automatically repaginates a document as you insert and delete text. In Word's Normal view, a dotted line appears wherever Word inserts a floating page break, sometimes splitting an important paragraph or a table of figures. Rather than leaving the text on separate pages, you can instruct Word to start a new page at the insertion point by inserting a hard page break. The quickest way to force a hard page break is to press CTRL+ENTER. You can also choose the Insert, Break command from the Menu bar.

In the following exercise, you force a page break so that the table created in the MEMO95 document appears on a separate page.

1. Position the insertion point at the beginning of the line containing the headings REVENUE and EXPENSES. Make sure that the insertion point is in the first column, next to the left margin.

2. PRESS: CTRL+ENTER
   A solid line with the words "Page Break" appears above the headings. The Status bar should contain "Pg 2" and "2/2."

3. To delete the hard page break, position the insertion point directly on the page break line and press DELETE.

QUICK REFERENCE
Inserting a Forced Page Break

1. **Position the insertion point at the beginning of the line that you want moved to the top of a new page.**
2. **PRESS: CTRL+ENTER**

IN ADDITION

FORMATTING PARAGRAPHS WITH STYLES

A *paragraph style* is a set of formats that can contain character formatting (such as font type, type style, and point size) and paragraph formatting such as line spacing and tab settings commands. When you apply a style to a selection of text, all the formatting instructions in the style are executed at once. When you edit a style, any text that is based on the style is updated at once.

If you work with documents that contain lots of formatting, styles will (1) save you time, (2) promote consistent formatting throughout your document, and (3) make it easier for you to edit a document's format.

To find out more about styles, choose Format, Style from the Menu bar, and then click the Help button.

PRINTING A DOCUMENT

Now that you've learned how to create and format documents, this section explains how to send them to the printer. This section provides only a brief glimpse at the tools available.

The quickest method for sending the active document to the printer is to click the Print button ( ) on the Standard toolbar. When you click this button, no dialog boxes appear asking you to confirm your choice, so ensure that the printer is online and has sufficient paper. You may want to save a few trees by previewing the document on screen first using the Print Preview button ( ). You can always click the Print button ( ) from the Print Preview screen if you want to send the document to the printer.

Perform the following steps to print a document.

1. To display a preview of how the MEMO95 document will appear when printed:
   CLICK: Print Preview button ( )
   Your screen should appear similar to Figure 2.14.

2. Assuming that you are pleased with the Print Preview results:
   CLICK: Print button ( )
   The MEMO95 document will print to your default printer.

3. Close the MEMO95 document and exit Word.

FIGURE 2.14 PRINT PREVIEW

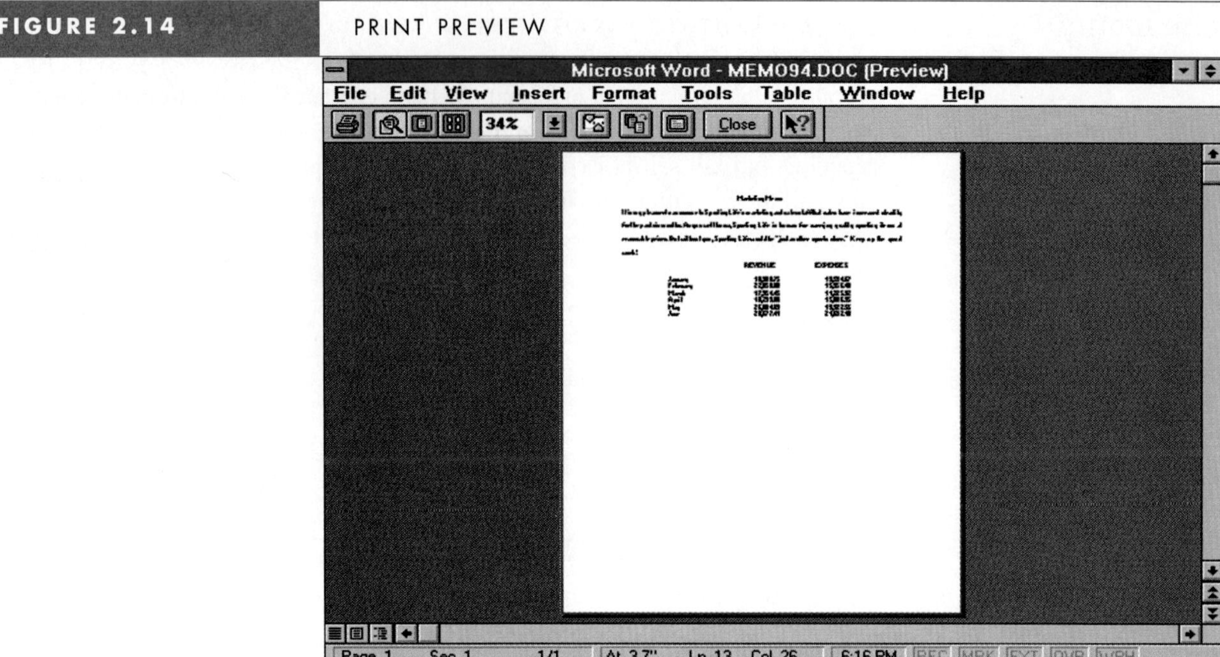

QUICK REFERENCE Quick Printing	1. **CLICK: Print Preview button ( ) to see a preview of your document** 2. **CLICK: Print button ( ) to send your document to the printer**

SUMMARY

This session introduced several methods for moving around a document and selecting text. As with most Windows programs, Word is based upon a Select and then Do approach to formatting and editing. Therefore, the proper selection of text is extremely important for executing commands and working effectively with Word.

This session concentrated on character and paragraph formatting commands. Besides applying boldface, italic, and underline character styles to text, character formatting involves changing the typeface, font, and point size. Paragraph formatting commands enable you to customize paragraphs in your text without affecting the entire document. This section explored indenting paragraphs, creating bulleted and numbered lists, aligning text, setting tabs, and forcing page breaks. The session ended with an opportunity to print a document.

Table 2.8 provides a summary of the commands introduced in this session.

TABLE 2.8

Command Summary

Task Description	*Menu Command*	*Toolbar Button*	*Keyboard Shortcut*
Move to a specific location in your document	Edit, Go To		CTRL+g, or F5
Make text bold Italicize text Underline text	Format, Font	B I U	CTRL+b CTRL+i CTRL+u
Select a typeface Change the font size	Format, Font	Times Roman 10	
Increase Indent Decrease Indent	Format, Paragraph		
Create a bulleted list Create a numbered list	Format, Bullets and Numbering		
Specify bullet symbols or numbering schemes	Format, Bullets and Numbering		
Provide options for setting up your page layout	File, Page Setup		
Left-align a paragraph Center-align a paragraph Right-align a paragraph Justify a paragraph	Format, Paragraph		
Single-space a paragraph Space a paragraph by 1.5 lines Double-space a paragraph	Format, Paragraph		CTRL+1 CTRL+5 CTRL+2
Specifies tab positions and leaders	Format, Tabs		
Copy formatting options			

continues

TABLE 2.8 concluded

Command Summary	*Task Description*	*Menu Command*	*Toolbar Button*	*Keyboard Shortcut*
	Force a page break	Insert, Break		CTRL + ENTER
	Preview a document for printing	File, Print Preview		
	Print a document	File, Print		CTRL +p

KEY TERMS

bullets
The symbols used to set apart points in a document. Bullets are typically round dots and appear in paragraphs with a hanging indent.

default settings
Assumptions made by Word, if no other specific selections are made.

font
All of the symbols and characters of a particular typeface for a given point size.

leader
The symbols, lines, dots, or dashes that fill the gap between text and tab stops.

Paragraph Symbol
The symbol (¶) at the end of a paragraph that stores all of Word's paragraph formatting information.

Selection bar
The leftmost column of the document window. The Selection bar provides shortcut methods for selecting text in a document using the mouse.

typeface
A style of print.

EXERCISES

SHORT ANSWER

1. How do you select an entire document using the mouse?
2. What are the keyboard shortcut keys for applying bold, italics, and underlines to text?
3. What is the difference between a typeface and a font?
4. What are the different paragraph alignment options?
5. Describe the four types of tabs you can include in a document.
6. Describe some methods for moving the cursor around a document.
7. Provide an example of when you would use a dot leader.
8. How would you set line spacing to 1.5 lines?
9. How do you force a hard page break?
10. What is the difference between a hard page break and a floating page break? How can you tell the difference between the two in a Word document?

HANDS-ON

(*Note*: In the following exercises, save your documents onto and retrieve files from the Advantage Diskette.)

1. Create the memo appearing in Figure 2.15. Make sure to include the current date in the DATE: area and your name in the FROM: area of the memo.

FIGURE 2.15 KATHMEMO DOCUMENT

MEMORANDUM

DATE: [*current date*]

TO: Kathy Jordan
Administrative Support Manager

FROM: [*your name*]
V.P., Marketing

SUBJECT: Appearance of Documents

It has come to my attention that our two clients are finding our proposals difficult to read. When queried further, they both mentioned (as personal preference dictates) that the sentences seemed to have gaps between the words. (Similar to this paragraph.)

After speaking with several people in our Word Processing department, I understand that we have been using full justification for paragraphs. As these two clients are our lifeblood, please prepare a letter to the staff stating that the use of full justification in documents is no longer acceptable. All documents are to be typed using left justification only.

Please send me a draft of the letter by Monday.

Thanks, Kathy – Enjoy your weekend!

a. Make sure that your memo has the following formatting features:

- Center the title "MEMORANDUM."
- Use tabs to right-align the memo headings for DATE:, TO:, FROM:, and SUBJECT:.
- Fully justify the first paragraph.
- Left-align (or left-justify) the second and third paragraphs.
- Right-align (or right-justify) the last line.

b. Make the title and the memo headings (DATE:, TO:, FROM:, and SUBJECT:) bold.

c. Italicize the word "justification" throughout the memo.

d. Underline "Monday" in the third paragraph.

e. Save the document as KATHMEMO onto the Advantage Diskette.

f. Print the document.

2. This exercise uses tabs to align a table of numbers.

a. Open a new document.

b. Specify decimal tab settings on the Ruler at 2 inches, 3.5 inches, and 5 inches.

c. Enter the following information into the document.

	January	February	March
East	50,000	65,000	75,000
West	125,000	105,000	100,500
Central	55,000	50,000	75,000

d. PRESS: **ENTER** three times.

e. TYPE: `These are the forecasted commissions for the first part of 1995. Please add a discussion of these figures to the Sales Planning agenda next week.`

f. Save the document as FORECAST onto the Advantage Diskette.

g. Print the document.

3. The objective of this exercise is to practice using tabs, leaders, and character formatting commands.

a. Open a new document.

b. Create the document appearing in Figure 2.16.

FIGURE 2.16 AGENDA DOCUMENT

SALES PLANNING AGENDA

DATE: October 4th, 1995 TIME: 9 A.M. to 4 P.M.

Who Is Our Customer?
Demographic Analysis................9:00-9:45 A.M.
Psychographic Analysis ....9:50-10:30 A.M.
Lifestyles and AIO Study ....10:45-12 P.M.

What Are We Selling?
Research and Development............1:00-2:00 P.M.
Product Packaging ....2:05-2:45 P.M.
Pricing Structures..................3:00-3:30 P.M.

Incentives and Commissions ....3:35-4:00 P.M.

Please be prepared to give a ten-minute impromptu presentation on the status of your department. Specifically, mention the following issues:

- Employee Productivity
- Employee Satisfaction
- Resource Management
- Future Requirements

Your faithful V.P. of Marketing,

[*your name*]

c. Make the first two lines of the agenda, including the title, date, and time, bold.

d. Increase the font size for the title to 18 points.

e. Select an Arial font for the main agenda items.

f. Make the three main agenda items bold and 14 points in size.

g. Underline the word "faithful" in the closing of the document.

h. Save the document as AGENDA onto the Advantage Diskette.

i. Print the agenda.

4. The objective of this exercise is to practice including a page break in a document, changing the font of an entire document, indenting, and changing line spacing.

   a. Create the document pictured in Figure 2.17 (make sure to perform the steps described in brackets):

FIGURE 2.17 POINTING DOCUMENT

```
THE POPULAR POINTING DEVICES
USED WITH MICROCOMPUTERS

DATE: [insert the current date]

BY: [your name]

[insert a page break here]

The following is a summary of the types of pointing
devices that are commonly used with microcomputers:

The mouse: A small, hand-held device connected to
  the computer by a cable and rolled around the
  desktop to move the cursor around the screen.

The trackball: Essentially an upside down mouse.The
  ball is rolled around in a socket to move the
  cursor. Trackballs are used where space is
  limited.

The light pen: A pen-shaped input device that uses a
  photoelectric (light-sensitive) cell to signal
  screen position to the computer. The pen, which is
  connected to the computer by a cable, is placed on
  the display screen at the desired location.

The touch screen: A special display screen that is
  sensitive to touch. The user touches the screen at
  desired locations, marked by labeled boxes, to
  "point out" choices to the computer.

The digitizer: A tablet covered by a grid of wires
  that are connected to the computer by a cable.
  Drawings placed on the tablet can be traced with a
  special pen or mouse-like device to translate the
  image into computer-usable code.

Pen-based computing: Uses special software and
  hardware to interpret handwriting done directly on
  the screen.
```

b. Before you continue, save the document onto the Advantage Diskette as POINTING.

c. Double-space the entire document.

d. Change the font of the entire document to Arial.

e. Increase the point size of the title on the first page to 16 point.

f. Center all the text positioned on the first page.

g. Boldface the name of each pointing device on page 2.

h. Save the document again onto the Advantage Diskette as POINTING.

CASE PROBLEMS

ADVANCED SOFTWARE DESIGN, INC.

(*Note*: In the following case problems, assume the role of the primary characters and perform the same steps that they identify. You may want to re-read the session opening.)

1. For the past year, Mary's proposals have all looked similar to the one appearing in Figure 2.18. She wants to create a new document that contains the same information but with formatting enhancements. For example, she would like to make the company's name and address look more like a letterhead on printed stationery, perhaps centered and with a different font at the top of the page. She would also like to add emphasis to the different titles on the proposal (Date, Client Name, Project Description, and so on).

   Create the document appearing in Figure 2.18 and then perform the steps that Mary has identified. Print it and then save the document as ASDPROP onto the Advantage Diskette.

2. Having just completed a telephone conversation with Mountain Wear, Inc., Alethia hands Mary her proposal notes for typing. The project description reads as follows:

   Mountain Wear, Inc., a manufacturer of rugged footwear, needs a better program for keeping track of its inventory. It has one warehouse, with several truckloads of shoes coming and going each day. The company would like to generate hourly reports and gather demographic data on the people who buy Mountain Wear shoes. I estimate this job will take 122 programming hours.

   Mary retrieves the ASDPROP document from the Advantage Diskette and edits it to include the information from Alethia's notes. When finished, she prints it and then saves the proposal as MWIPROP onto the Advantage Diskette.

FIGURE 2.18 A STANDARD ASD PROPOSAL DOCUMENT

```
ADVANCED SOFTWARE DESIGN, INC.
221 FOREST DRIVE
Lakewood, NJ 08701
Tel: 333-333-3333
Fax: 333-333-3331

DATE: [enter current date]

CLIENT NAME: [enter client name]

PROJECT DESCRIPTION: [enter project description]

HOUR ESTIMATE: [enter hours]

COST ESTIMATE: [multiply the hours by $50]

Signature ________________________________
          Alethia Montera, Vice President
```

3. Now that Alethia has seen what Mary can do with Microsoft Word, she asks Mary to format the company's client list for the upcoming board meeting. She gives Mary the list on the Advantage Diskette with the following instructions:

   Mary, you will find the document file, called CLIENTS, on the Advantage Diskette. Please format the contents to make it look more professional. Thanks, Alethia.

   Upon retrieving the CLIENTS document, Mary decides to print it so she can get a complete picture of the document before she applies any formatting commands. With the printed document in hand, Mary sees clearly that she needs to center and apply a larger point size to the title. Also, she decides to indent and number the names, format all text using the Times New Roman font, and add emphasis to the company names by making them italic. After incorporating her changes, she saves the file onto the Advantage Diskette as GOOD-CL.

   Mary now decides to preview GOOD-CL on the screen to see if she likes the overall look of the document. Although pleased with the list, she decides to insert some extra blank lines at the top of the document and a few just below the main heading to balance the page. Mary saves the document again, prints it, and puts a copy in the message box outside Alethia's office.

4. Upon returning to her cubicle, Mary finds a note tacked to her computer monitor from Alethia.

   Mary, I need someone to create a splashy advertising piece for an upcoming customer mailing, and I think you're the one to do it! Use one side of an 8x10 piece of paper. I want you to make the following points: (1) Advanced Software Design can satisfy any programming requirement because of its staff of highly talented programmers. (2) ASD always supplies accurate cost estimates. (3) Your satisfaction is guaranteed—should you be dissatisfied with a product, we'll either modify it at our own cost or give you a full refund. (4) ASD provides a 24-hour support hotline should questions arise once an application is delivered. And lastly, after the name, address, and phone number of our company (positioned at the top of the page), try to draw the reader's attention to the following sentence: The Small Business Association, in conjunction with the Hapstead Publishing Group, did an assessment of software development companies and gave Advanced Software Design the "Best Pick" award for 1996. By the way, I need this by tomorrow. Let me know if you have any questions. Thanks, Alethia.

   Although she's flattered, it's already late in the day and Mary is concerned about completing the advertising piece on time. She realizes that without Microsoft Word she wouldn't have stood a chance at finishing this ad. When you finish the project, print the document and then save it as ASDAD onto the Advantage Diskette.

Microsoft Word 6.0

Editing and Proofing Tools

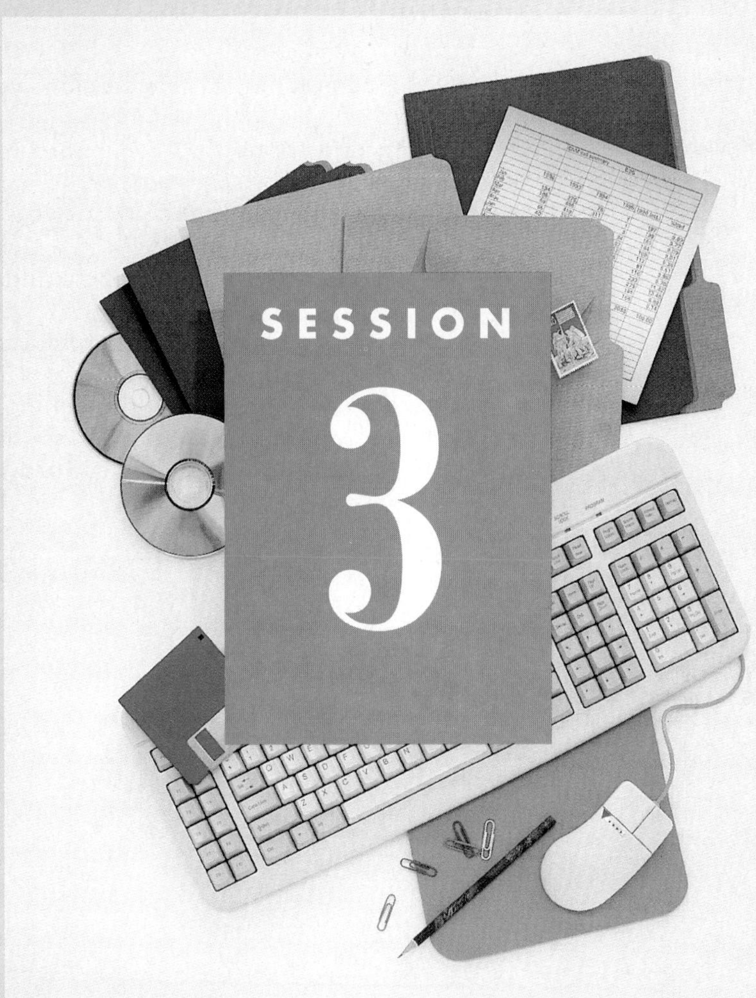

SESSION OUTLINE

Working with Multiple Documents
Copying and Moving Information
Finding and Replacing Text
Using AutoText
Using the Spell Checker
Using the Thesaurus
Using the Grammar Checker
Summary
Key Terms
Exercises

INTRODUCTION

By the completion of this session, you will know the editing and formatting commands required to develop error-free documents. Also, you'll learn how to use Word's proofing tools including the Spell Checker, Grammar Checker, and Thesaurus. Whether you require assistance with spelling, sentence structure, or just finding the right word, these tools are invaluable.

CASE STUDY

THE RIVER REPORT

The *River Report* is a weekly publication that provides news reports, announcements, and general interest stories for the Sacramento River region. Linda James, a graduate of Stanford's journalism program, just accepted the position of editor for the small-town newspaper. In her new position, Linda is responsible for identifying leads, editing articles written by her reporters, and, most importantly, getting the paper out every Friday.

Her new office is well-appointed with a large oak desk and a new Pentium™ computer system. On the computer screen, her predecessor, Hank Leary, left the following message:

Linda, welcome! Just so you know, the reporters will be submitting their articles on disk for you to edit and print using Microsoft Word. They should have their articles in to you each week by 7:00 P.M. on Wednesday. You have all day Thursday to edit and proof their work. The articles must be sent to Production by 7:00 P.M. on Thursday to meet the deadline. Hope all goes well. Hank.

Linda feels a swelling anxiety overcome her. It's already Wednesday afternoon and, although she has used Microsoft Word before, she has never performed the types of editing tasks that will be required of her to edit and proof these articles. She only has a few short hours to become skilled at editing articles using her fancy computer!

In this session, you and Linda will learn how to copy and move text within a document, search for and replace text, and use Word's proofing tools.

WORKING WITH MULTIPLE DOCUMENTS

Word 6.0 allows you to simultaneously display and work with as many documents as your computer's memory will allow. This feature enables you to open multiple documents and share information among them. You can also use the Window, New Window command to open multiple windows of the same document. For example, you might want to view page 10 of a document while working on page 30. Each document or window view appears in its own document window. These windows can be sized, moved, and arranged anywhere in the document area.

Perform the following steps to display multiple documents.

1. Make sure that you've loaded Word 6.0 and the Advantage Diskette is inserted into drive A:.

2. To close all open documents that may appear in the document area:
   PRESS: SHIFT and hold it down
   CHOOSE: File, Close All
   (*Note*: By holding down the SHIFT key, Word changes the command in the pull-down menu from Close to Close All.)

3. Retrieve the ETHICS document from the Advantage Diskette.

4. Retrieve the HARDWARE document from the Advantage Diskette.

5. When the HARDWARE document is opened, the ETHICS document disappears. Actually, the HARDWARE document is just temporarily covering the ETHICS document. To display the ETHICS document:
   CHOOSE: Window, 1 ETHICS.DOC

6. Notice that the names of the open documents appear at the bottom of the Window pull-down menu. To move between open documents, you simply select the document name. To move back to HARDWARE:
   CHOOSE: Window, 2 HARDWARE.DOC

7. Although this method allows you to work on several documents at the same time, sometimes it's desirable to compare documents side-by-side. To simultaneously display both documents:
   CHOOSE: Window, Arrange All
   Your screen should now appear similar to Figure 3.1.

FIGURE 3.1 USING THE WINDOW, ARRANGE ALL COMMAND TO VIEW TWO DOCUMENTS

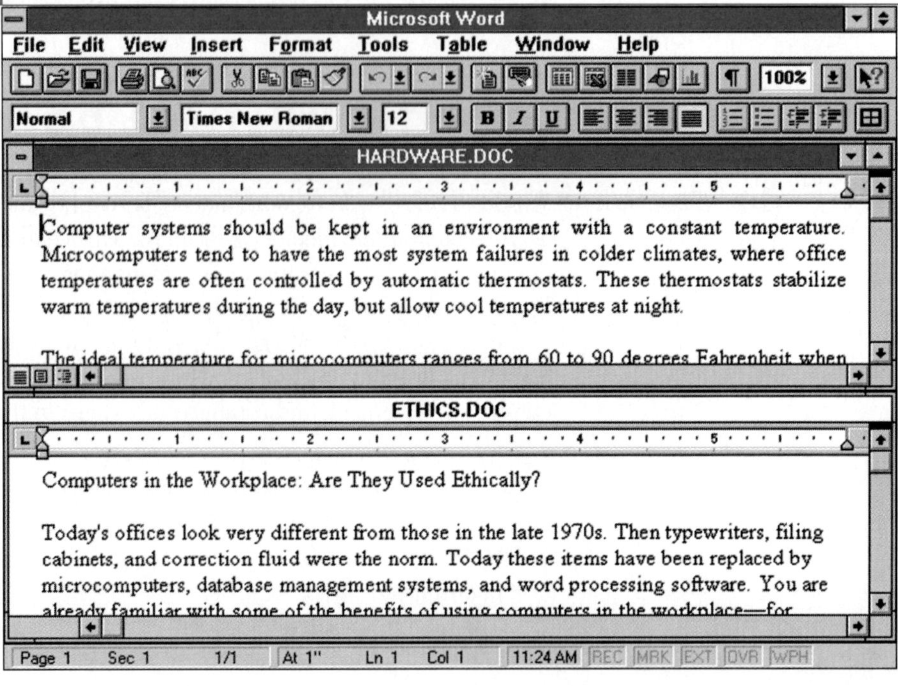

8. The document window with the solid Title bar (HARDWARE.DOC) is the active window. Any editing and formatting commands that you execute will affect the active window only. To move between documents, you click the mouse pointer on a window to make it active:
   CLICK: *anywhere in the ETHICS document window*
   The ETHICS Title bar should change color to reflect that it is active.

9. CLICK: *anywhere in the HARDWARE document window*
   The HARDWARE Title bar changes to reflect that it is now active.

10. Notice that the active window has its own Control menu (▬) in the upper left-hand corner and a Maximize icon (▲) in the upper right-hand corner. To maximize the HARDWARE window:
    CLICK: Maximize icon (▲) on the HARDWARE document window

11. CHOOSE: Window, Arrange All to view both windows again

12. PRESS: SHIFT and hold it down
    CHOOSE: File, Close All
    Both documents are closed and removed from the document area.

QUICK REFERENCE
Viewing Multiple Documents

- **CHOOSE: Window, *document name* to display an open document**
- **CHOOSE: Window, Arrange All to show multiple windows on-screen**
- **CHOOSE: Window, New Window to open a new document window**

COPYING AND MOVING INFORMATION

There are several different methods for copying and moving text in a document. Similar to most Windows applications, Word provides the **Clipboard** for sharing information within a document, among documents, and among applications. For quick "from-here-to-there" operations, Word provides the **drag and drop** method where you use the mouse to drag text around the screen. This section provides examples using both methods for copying and moving information.

USING THE CLIPBOARD

If the drag and drop method is quicker and easier, why use the Clipboard to copy and move information? The Clipboard provides greater flexibility, allows you to copy information to multiple locations in a document, and allows you to copy and move information to and from other applications such as Microsoft Excel. The general process for copying and moving information using the Clipboard is summarized in the following steps:

a. Select the text that you want to copy or move.

b. Cut or copy the selection to the Clipboard.

c. Move the insertion point to where you want to place the information.

d. Paste the information from the Clipboard into the document.

e. Repeat steps c. and d., as desired.

The Clipboard tools for cutting, copying, and pasting text and graphics appear in Table 3.1.

TABLE 3.1

Copying and Moving Information Using the Clipboard

Task Description	*Menu Command*	*Toolbar Button*	*Keyboard Shortcut*
Moves the selected text from the document to the Clipboard	Edit, Cut		CTRL +X
Copies the selected text to the Clipboard	Edit, Copy		CTRL +C
Inserts the contents of the Clipboard at the insertion point	Edit, Paste		CTRL +V

Perform the following steps to practice using the Clipboard.

1. Retrieve the HARDWARE document from the Advantage Diskette.

2. Insert two lines at the top of the document using the ENTER key.

3. To copy the phrase "Computer systems" from the first sentence to the top of the document, first you must select the text:
   SELECT: Computer systems

4. To copy the selection to the Clipboard:
   CLICK: Copy button ( )

5. PRESS: ↑ twice

6. To paste the contents of the Clipboard into the document:
   CLICK: Paste button ( )

7. To center the title:
   CLICK: Center button ( )

8. To change the case of the letters in the title:
   SELECT: Computer systems
   PRESS: SHIFT + F3 once
   The title should now read "COMPUTER SYSTEMS." (*Note*: You can also choose the Format, Change Case command.)

9. Let's move the entire second paragraph to the end of the document:
   DOUBLE-CLICK: *beside the paragraph in the Selection bar*

10. To move the selected paragraph to the Clipboard:
    CLICK: Cut button ( )
    Notice that the paragraph is removed from the document.

11. Move to the bottom of the document and add a blank line:
    PRESS: CTRL + END
    PRESS: ENTER

12. CLICK: Paste button ( )
    The paragraph is inserted at the bottom of the document.

13. Insert another blank line at the end of the document:
    PRESS: ENTER

14. When information is placed on the Clipboard, it can be pasted multiple times. To illustrate, you will insert another copy of the paragraph:
    CLICK: Paste button ( )
    A second copy of the paragraph appears.

QUICK REFERENCE

Copying and Moving Information Using the Clipboard

- **To move information using the Clipboard:**
  CLICK: Cut button ( )
- **To copy information using the Clipboard:**
  CLICK: Copy button ( )
- **To paste information using the Clipboard:**
  CLICK: Paste button ( )

USING DRAG AND DROP

The drag and drop method is the easiest way to copy and move information short distances. The Clipboard is not used during a drag and drop operation; therefore you can only copy or move text from one location to another. In other words, you are not able to perform multiple "pastes" of the selected text. This method is extremely quick for simple copy and move operations.

Perform the following steps to practice using drag and drop.

1. In the HARDWARE document, select the first sentence of the first paragraph by positioning the I-beam mouse pointer over any word in the sentence, holding down the CTRL key, and clicking once.

2. Position the mouse pointer over the selected text. Notice that the pointer shape is a left-pointing diagonal arrow and not an I-beam. To move this sentence using drag and drop:
   CLICK: left mouse button and hold it down

3. The mouse pointer changes shape to include a phantom insertion point at the end of the diagonal arrow. Drag the new mouse pointer into the second paragraph, immediately after the first sentence.

4. Position the mouse pointer and phantom insertion point to the left of the letter "T" in the word "The."

5. Release the left mouse button.
   The sentence is inserted at the mouse pointer, causing the existing text to wrap to the next line.

6. To remove the highlighting from the text:
   CLICK: *anywhere in the unselected area of the document*

7. The drag and drop method can also be used to copy text. Select the word "failures" in the first paragraph:
   DOUBLE-CLICK: failures
   The word should be highlighted.

8. To copy this word into the title area:
   PRESS: CTRL and hold it down

9. Position the mouse pointer over the highlighted word and then drag the selection to the right of the word "SYSTEMS" in the title.

10. Release the left mouse button and then the CTRL key. Notice that Word automatically places a space between the word "SYSTEMS" and the word "failures."

11. To change the copied text to uppercase:
    PRESS: SHIFT + F3 twice
    The title should now read "COMPUTER SYSTEMS FAILURES."

12. Close the document and do not save the changes.

QUICK REFERENCE
Using Drag and Drop

- **To move information, select the text to move and then drag the selected text to the desired location.**
- **To copy information, select the text to copy, press CTRL and hold it down, and then drag the selected text to the desired location.**

FINDING AND REPLACING TEXT

Imagine that you just completed a 200-page proposal supporting the importation of llamas as household pets in North America. As you are printing the final pages, a colleague points out that you spelled *llama* with one *l* throughout the document. The Spell Checker didn't catch the error since both *llama*, the animal, and *lama*, the Tibetan monk, appear in Word's dictionary. Therefore, you must use another of Word's editing features—the Find and Replace utility—to correct your mistake.

The Find and Replace commands under the Edit menu allow you to search for and replace text, special symbols like ™, nonprinting characters like ¶, and formatting characteristics. For example, you might type (c) in your document initially and then use the Replace command to replace it with the true copyright symbol © at a later date. To demonstrate the power of these two commands, perform the following steps.

1. Retrieve the HARDWARE document from the Advantage Diskette.

2. To begin a search for a word or phrase in the document:
   CHOOSE: Edit, Find
   The Find dialog box appears, as shown in Figure 3.2.

FIGURE 3.2 FIND DIALOG BOX

3. With the insertion point in the Find What text box:
   TYPE: `can`

4. In this step, you place an "×" in the Find Whole Words Only check box to stop Word from retrieving all words containing the letters "can" (for example, you don't want to retrieve words like *can*non or s*can*):
   SELECT: "Find Whole Words Only" check box

5. To tell Word to begin the search:
   PRESS: ENTER or CLICK: Find Next

6. Word stops at the first occurrence of "can." To continue the search:
   PRESS: ENTER or CLICK: Find Next

7. To cancel the search at this point:

   PRESS: ESC or CLICK: Cancel

8. Return to the top of the document to begin a new search operation:
   PRESS: CTRL + HOME

9. Let's replace the word "can" with "will" throughout the document:
   CHOOSE: Edit, Replace
   Notice that the word "can" already appears in the Find What text box from the last time we performed the Edit, Find command.

10. To enter the replacement text, you must first click the I-beam mouse pointer in the Replace With text box to position the insertion point.

11. TYPE: `will`
    Your Replace dialog box should appear similar to Figure 3.3.

FIGURE 3.3 REPLACE DIALOG BOX

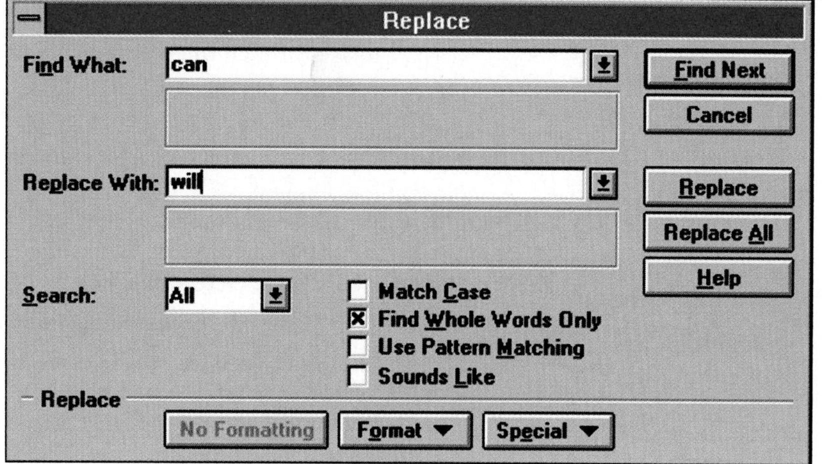

12. To execute the replacement throughout the document:
    SELECT: Replace All command button
    A dialog box appears informing you that four replacements were made in the document.

13. To close the dialog boxes:
    PRESS: ENTER or CLICK: OK
    SELECT: Close command button

14. Now let's make all occurrences of the word "will" bold:
    CHOOSE: Edit, Replace

15. In the Find What text box:
    TYPE: `will`

16. Position the insertion point in the Replace With text box by clicking the I-beam mouse pointer in the text box.

17. Since the word "will" already appears in this text box, you need only specify the bold formatting option. Rather than selecting the Format command button at the bottom of the dialog box, you can use the toolbars and keyboard shortcuts to add your formatting options. For this exercise:
    CLICK: Bold button (B)
    Notice that the formatting characteristics appear below the text box.

18. To perform the replacement:
    SELECT: Replace All command button
    Similar to last time, four replacements are made in the document.

19. To close the dialog boxes:
    PRESS: ENTER or CLICK: OK
    SELECT: Close command button
    If you browse through the document, you will notice that all occurrences of the word "will" have been made bold.

20. Save the document as REPLACED to the Advantage Diskette and then close the document.

QUICK REFERENCE
Finding and Replacing Text

1. **CHOOSE: Edit, Find, or Edit, Replace**
2. **TYPE: text to find and, if necessary, the replacement text**
3. **SELECT: Find Next, Replace, Replace All, or Cancel**

USING AUTOTEXT

Have you ever found yourself repeatedly typing the same text, such as an address or closing salutation? If so, you will appreciate Word's new AutoText feature. With AutoText, you can store frequently used words, phrases, and even graphics, such as a company logo, for easy access. Once defined, you retrieve an **AutoText entry** by typing an abbreviated code and clicking the Insert AutoText button ( ). Rather than reaching for the mouse, you can also press F3 after typing the code. Either way, Word replaces the code with the full text or graphic it represents.

Perform the following steps to create an AutoText entry.

1. Retrieve the PROMOLTR document from the Advantage Diskette.

2. The company name, used quite frequently in this sample letter, is quite long and difficult to type. Therefore, it provides a perfect candidate for an AutoText entry. To define it as an AutoText entry, you begin by selecting the full text in the first sentence:
   SELECT: Sam's Superior Sailboats

   (*CAUTION*: Do not select the formatted company name that appears in the heading area.)

3. To define the selected text as an AutoText entry:
   CHOOSE: Edit, AutoText
   The dialog box shown in Figure 3.4 appears.

FIGURE 3.4 AUTOTEXT DIALOG BOX

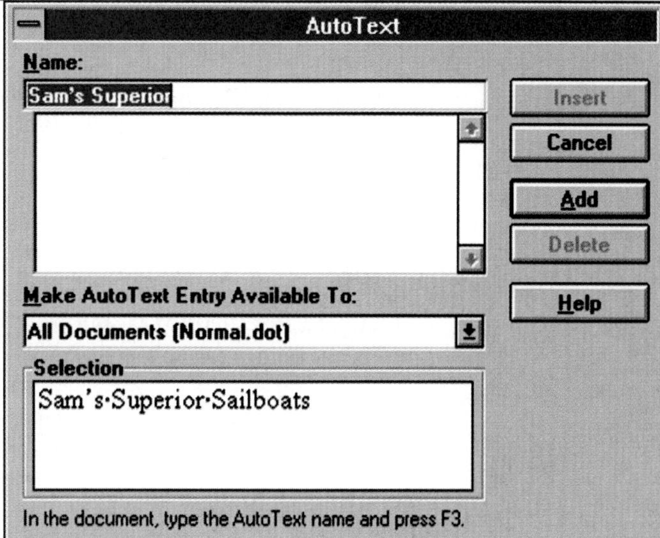

4. Although Word provides an optional name for this entry, you should enter your own abbreviation to use in retrieving the company name.
   TYPE: `sss`
   PRESS: ENTER or CLICK: Add

5. Move to the bottom of the document and try out the AutoText entry:
   PRESS: CTRL + END
   PRESS: Space Bar
   TYPE: `of sss`

6. To replace the abbreviated code with the full text:
   CLICK: Insert AutoText button ( )
   (*Note*: You can also press F3 to insert an AutoText entry.)

Before	*After*
Sincerely	Sincerely
Sam Silverton Founder of sss	Sam Silverton Founder of Sam's Superior Sailboats

7. You are now going to add a graphic to the AutoText library. To select the graphic at the top of the page, position the mouse pointer on the wheel and click the left mouse button once. When properly selected, the graphic appears within a box.

8. To add the graphic as an AutoText entry:
   CHOOSE: Edit, AutoText

9. Enter the following code:
   TYPE: `logo`
   PRESS: ENTER or CLICK: Add

10. Move to the bottom of the document:
    PRESS: CTRL + END
    PRESS: ENTER to add a new line

11. To insert the logo:
    TYPE: `logo`
    CLICK: Insert AutoText button ( )
    The logo appears below the text.

12. Save the document as AUTOTEXT to the Advantage Diskette and then close the document.

QUICK REFERENCE
Creating an AutoText Entry

1. **Select the desired text for an AutoText entry.**
2. **CHOOSE: Edit, AutoText**
3. **Type in the abbreviated code for accessing the entry.**
4. **PRESS: ENTER or CLICK: Add command button**

USING THE SPELL CHECKER

Word provides three major proofing tools: the Spell Checker, Thesaurus, and the Grammar Checker. This section introduces the Spell Checker, which allows you to check a single word, a selection of text, or an entire document for misspellings. You also learn how to add items to the AutoCorrect feature.

Using AutoCorrect AutoCorrect is duly named for its ability to automatically correct your typographical and capitalization errors as you type. You will find this feature extremely handy if you habitually misspell or mistype particular words. For example, people commonly type "thier" instead of "their"—knowing perfectly well how to spell the word but making a simple typing mistake. By adding this word to the AutoCorrect dialog box (see Figure 3.5), Word will correct this error automatically.

Using Spell Checker When you ask Word to perform a spelling check, it begins by comparing each word to entries in Word's main dictionary, which contains well over 100,000 words. If a word cannot be found, the Spell Checker attempts to find a match in a custom dictionary that you may have created. Custom dictionaries usually contain proper names, abbreviations, and technical terms.

FIGURE 3.5 AUTOCORRECT DIALOG BOX

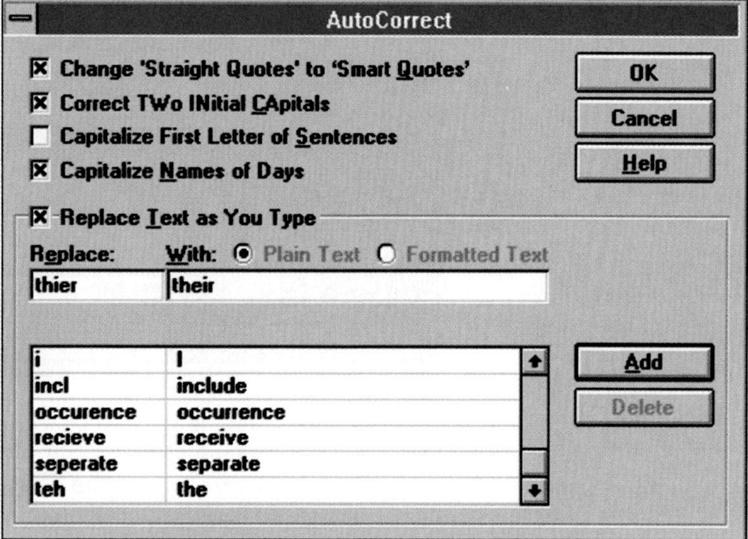

During a spelling check, you can easily add words to the custom dictionary or to the AutoCorrect feature. If the Spell Checker cannot identify a word and believes it to be misspelled, a dialog box appears asking you to correct or ignore the entry. The Spell Checker also flags errors relating to repeated words (for example, "the ball was was red") and mixed case (for example, "the baLL was rEd.")

Perform the following steps to use the Spell Checker.

1. Retrieve the SPELLING document from the Advantage Diskette. This document is a copy of the HARDWARE document with several intentional typographical errors and misspellings.

2. To start a spelling check:
   CLICK: Spelling button ( )
   (*Note*: You can also start a spelling check by choosing the Tools, Spelling command.) When Word finds the first misspelled word, it displays a dialog box (Figure 3.6) and waits for further instructions.

3. You have several options when the Spell Checker cannot find a word in its dictionary:

   - If a word is misspelled and the proper version appears in the Suggestions list box, highlight the word in the list box and select the Change or Change All buttons. You should consider adding the word to the AutoCorrect feature as well.

FIGURE 3.6 SPELLING DIALOG BOX

- If the word is misspelled and none of the suggestions are correct, type the proper version into the Change To text box and then select the Change or Change All buttons. You should consider adding the word to the AutoCorrect feature as well.

- If the word is spelled correctly and not frequently used, select the Ignore or Ignore All buttons to proceed to the next word.

- If the word is spelled correctly and frequently used, select the Add button to add it to the custom dictionary.

- To end the spelling check, press ESC or click the Cancel button.

To correct the misspelled word "enviroment," ensure that the correct spelling of the word appears in the Change To text box and then:
SELECT: Change command button

4. The next word that the Spell Checker finds is "temparature." Let's add this word to the AutoCorrect feature. Make sure the correct spelling of the word appears in the Change To text box and then do the following:
SELECT: AutoCorrect command button

5. Continue the spelling check for the remainder of the document. A message box will appear when it is finished. To clear this dialog box:
PRESS: ENTER or CLICK: OK

6. Save the document back to the Advantage Diskette and then close it.

QUICK REFERENCE
Using the Spell Checker

1. **CLICK: Spelling button ( ) or CHOOSE: Tools, Spelling**
2. **When a misspelled word is found, you can change the entry, ignore the word and the suggested alternatives provided by Word, or add the term to the AutoCorrect feature or custom dictionary.**

USING THE THESAURUS

Have you ever found yourself with the "perfect" word at the tip of your tongue—only to have it stay there? This situation is not limited to authors and professional writers. In fact, most people experience this sensation whenever they sit down to lay their thoughts on paper. Fortunately, Word provides a helping hand with its built-in **Thesaurus**. A thesaurus provides quick access to synonyms (words with similar meanings) and antonyms (words with opposite meanings) for a given word or phrase. You invoke Word's Thesaurus utility by choosing Tools, Thesaurus from the menu or by pressing SHIFT + F7.

Perform the following steps to choose a synonym.

1. Retrieve the ETHICS document from the Advantage Diskette.

2. Using the mouse, select the word "norm" at the end of the second sentence in the first paragraph.

3. CHOOSE: Tools, Thesaurus
   The Thesaurus dialog box appears, as displayed in Figure 3.7.

FIGURE 3.7 THESAURUS DIALOG BOX

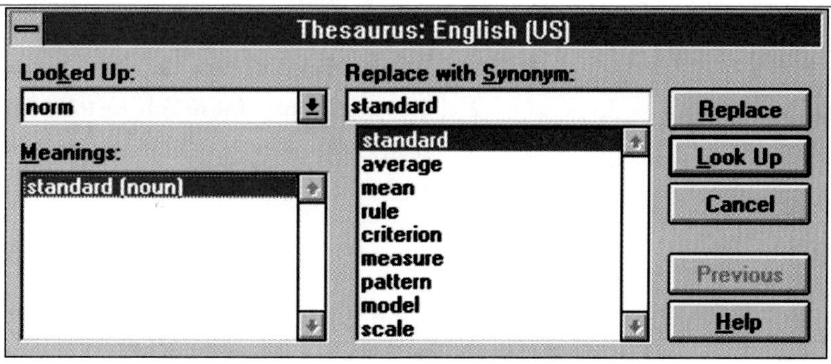

4. Since a word may have several interpretations, you can select the appropriate meaning from the Meanings list box. The Replace with Synonym list box displays the synonyms for the highlighted meaning. You have three options available after selecting a word from the Replace with Synonym list box:

    - Select the Replace command button to replace the word in the document with the highlighted word.
    - Select the Look Up command button to display additional synonyms for the highlighted word.
    - Type a word into the Replace with Synonym text box and then select the Look Up or Replace command buttons.

    To change the word "norm," select the word "standard" in the Replace with Synonym list box and then do the following:
    SELECT: Replace command button

5. Let's find a synonym for the word "era," appearing in the second-to-last sentence of the second paragraph. To begin, select the word "era."

6. CHOOSE: Tools, Thesaurus

7. In the Replace with Synonym list box:
    SELECT: epoch

8. To look up synonyms for "epoch":
    SELECT: Look Up command button

9. To replace the word "era," select the word "period" in the Replace with Synonym list box and then do the following:
    SELECT: Replace command button

QUICK REFERENCE
Using the Thesaurus

1. **Select a word to look up in the Thesaurus.**
2. **CHOOSE: Tools, Thesaurus or PRESS: SHIFT + F7**
3. **Select the desired word in the Replace with Synonym list box.**
4. **SELECT: Replace command button**

USING THE GRAMMAR CHECKER

Word was one of the first word processing programs to include a full-featured grammar checking utility. While the Spell Checker verifies the spelling of words, the Grammar Checker verifies the readability of a document. You can perform a grammar check on a single sentence, paragraph, or the entire document.

Word contains grammatical rules and style considerations for every occasion. By default, Word offers three different levels of grammar checking: strict adherence to all rules, business writing rules only, or casual writing rules only. Fortunately, you can also customize Word to check only for specific rules and styles. Because Word performs a spelling check on words before checking for proper grammar, you need not run both the Spell Checker and the Grammar Checker through a document.

Another feature of the Grammar Checker is the **readability statistics** dialog box (Figure 3.8) displayed at the completion of a grammar check. Besides counting the number of words, this dialog box measures the readability of a document using four different methods. Since each Grade Level method uses formulas based upon the average sentence length and number of multisyllable words, the measures are close to each other but may not always be representative of the document. The grade levels only provide a guideline for measuring the appropriateness of your writing for a particular audience's education level.

FIGURE 3.8 READABILITY STATISTICS DIALOG BOX FOR ETHICS.DOC

Readability Statistics

Counts:	
Words	847
Characters	4,557
Paragraphs	8
Sentences	47
Averages:	
Sentences per Paragraph	5.9
Words per Sentence	18.0
Characters per Word	5.2
Readability:	
Passive Sentences	17%
Flesch Reading Ease	46.7
Flesch-Kincaid Grade Level	10.7
Coleman-Liau Grade Level	15.6
Bormuth Grade Level	10.9

OK Help

To illustrate the use of the Grammar Checker, perform the following steps.

1. Move to the top of the ETHICS document.

2. To start checking the grammar in the ETHICS document:
   CHOOSE: Tools, Grammar
   The Grammar Checker stops at the first mistake or contradiction of its rules and styles. The dialog box, appearing in Figure 3.9, shows the offending sentence and suggests why it was flagged.

FIGURE 3.9 GRAMMAR DIALOG BOX

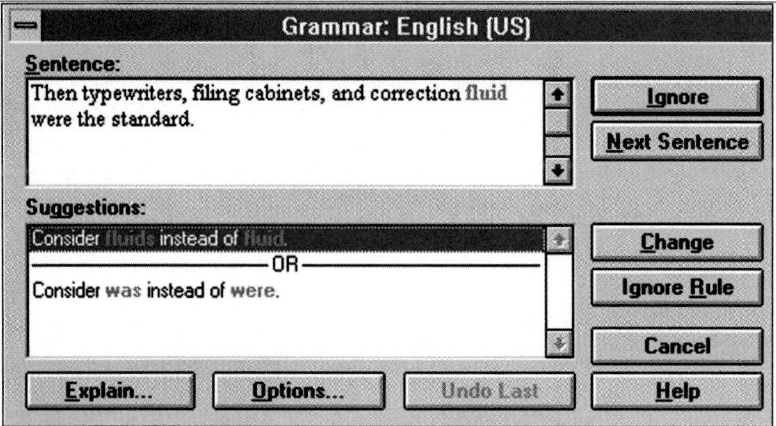

3. For a detailed explanation of the Grammar Checker's suggestion:
   SELECT: Explain command button
   A small window with a vertical scroll bar appears, usually overlaying the Grammar Checker dialog box.

4. Browse the explanation using the scroll bar, and then close the window by double-clicking its Control menu.

5. After the Grammar Checker stops at a sentence and suggests an alternative, you can select a command button to ignore the suggestion, ignore the rule, change the document text as suggested, proceed to the next sentence, or cancel the grammer checking altogether. For now, let's proceed without changing any text:
   SELECT: Next Sentence command button

6. The next suggestion provided by the Grammar Checker is to modify the use of the passive voice. To ignore this rule and proceed:
   SELECT: Next Sentence command button

7. SELECT: Ignore command button for the remainder of the messages
   (*Note*: You may have to select the Ignore command button over thirty times to complete the check and proceed!)

8. When the grammar checking is completed, the Readability Statistics dialog box appears. Review the information and then proceed:
   PRESS: ENTER or CLICK: OK

   The Grammar Checker disappears and you return to the document.

9. The Word Count command is another useful tool that provides some basic document statistics. To display the Word Count dialog box:
   CHOOSE: Tools, Word Count

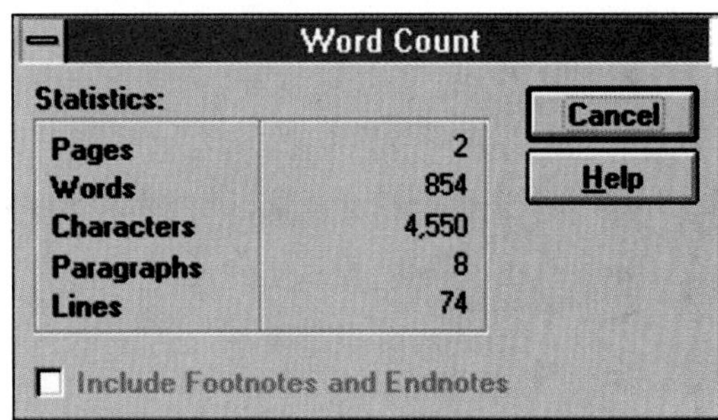

10. To close the Word Count dialog box:
    PRESS: ENTER or CLICK: Close

11. Close the document and do not save the changes.

QUICK REFERENCE
Using the Grammar Checker

1. **CHOOSE: Tools, Grammar**
2. **When an error is located, choose to ignore the suggestion, ignore the rule, change the document text as suggested, proceed to the next sentence, or cancel the grammar checking.**

SUMMARY

This session focused on Word's editing and proofing tools. After a discussion on working with multiple document windows, the session described two methods for copying and moving information: using the Clipboard and using drag and drop. You also used the Find and Replace commands to search for and replace text and formatting in a document. The section on AutoText demonstrated how easy it is to insert frequently used text and graphics into a document by typing abbreviated codes.

The last half of this session concentrated on proofing documents using the Spell Checker, Thesaurus, and Grammar Checker. The ability to add words to a custom dictionary and the AutoCorrect feature highlighted the Spell Checker section. You also used Word's Thesaurus to provide a list of synonyms for words and the Grammar Checker to verify the clarity of a document. Two methods for retrieving document statistics were illustrated using the Grammar Checker's readability statistics and the Word Count command.

Table 3.2 provides a list of the commands covered in this session.

TABLE 3.2

Command Summary

Task Description	*Menu Command*	*Toolbar Button*	*Keyboard Shortcut*
Select a window to make active	Window, *document name*		
Size and display all open document windows	Window, Arrange All		
Create a new window view for the active document	Window, New Window		
Copy the selected text to the Clipboard	Edit, Copy		CTRL+c
Move the selected text to the Clipboard	Edit, Cut		CTRL+x
Insert or paste the Clipboard's contents	Edit, Paste		CTRL+v
Find text in a document	Edit, Find		CTRL+f
Find and replace text in a document	Edit, Replace		CTRL+h
Retrieve an AutoText entry	Edit, AutoText		F3
Perform a spelling check of a document	Tools, Spelling		F7
Display a list of synonyms	Tools, Thesaurus		SHIFT+F7
Perform a grammar check of a document	Tools, Grammar		
Count the number of words in a document	Tools, Word Count		

KEY TERMS

AutoText entry
A frequently used text or graphic that is inserted into a document by typing an abbreviated code and then clicking the Insert AutoText button ( ).

Clipboard
In Windows, the Clipboard is a program that allows you to copy and move information within an application or among applications.

drag and drop
A feature of Windows that allows you to copy and move information by dragging objects or text from one location to another using the mouse.

readability statistics
A statistics page displayed after the Grammar Checker has completed its check; provides a grade level reading equivalency for a document.

Thesaurus
In Microsoft Word, a proofing tool that provides synonyms and antonyms for the selected word or phrase. A synonym is a word that has the same meaning as another word. An antonym has the opposite meaning.

EXERCISES

SHORT ANSWER

1. How many windows can be open in the document area at one time?
2. How do you move between open documents using the mouse?
3. What are the two methods for copying and moving information? How do they differ?
4. Name three types of information that can be searched for using the Find command.
5. How do you create an AutoText entry?
6. How do you insert an AutoText entry?
7. Explain what you would do if the Spell Checker came across a frequently used word that is correctly spelled but Word cannot find it in its main dictionary.

8. How is the Thesaurus tool used?

9. What are the three standard levels of analysis in the Grammar Checker?

10. How are grade levels awarded for the readability statistics?

HANDS-ON

(*Note*: In the following exercises, save your documents onto and retrieve files from the Advantage Diskette.)

1. The objective of this exercise is to practice performing copy and move operations using the Clipboard and drag and drop methods.

   a. Create the document appearing in Figure 3.10.

   b. Save the document as ORDERS onto the Advantage Diskette.

   c. Using the Clipboard, move the text after "P.S." (starting at the word "If") above the line "Yours truly." Leave the "P.S." at the bottom of the letter.

   d. Using the Clipboard, move the first sentence in the first paragraph ("Thank you for your order!") after the "P.S." on the last line.

   e. Using the drag and drop method, change the order of the Items Shipped to the following: CPU, HARD DISK, MONITOR, VIDEO CARD, and OPTIONS.

   f. Using the drag and drop method, copy the company name "Alpha Beta Computer Rentals" from the top of the page to below the title "Accounts Representative" in the closing.

   g. Save the document again, replacing the original version.

   h. Print the document.

   i. Close the document.

FIGURE 3.10 ORDERS LETTER

```
Alpha Beta Computer Rentals
5900 Algonquin Road
Suite 775
Ashton, NC  28804


December 3, 1995


Ms. Lolita Balfour
2910 Freemont Road
Raleigh, NC  27610

Dear Ms. Balfour:

Thank you for your order! I am writing to confirm
that the following items will be delivered to your
premises on December 25th.

Items Shipped

MONITOR:          TLC MultipleSync 4GH Monitor
OPTIONS:          14.4K Baud Internal Fax/Modem
HARD DISK:        MaxStore 512MB Hard Drive
CPU:              Compact 486/66 with 16MB RAM
VIDEO CARD:       ABC Ultrasonic Graphics Card


Yours truly,



your name
Accounts Representative

P.S. If I can be of any assistance, please call me
at 704-250-9987.
```

2. This exercise gives you practice using AutoText entries and the Find and Replace commands.

   a. Open a new document.

   b. Enter the following information at the top of the page, substituting your name and address for the italicized text shown below:

      your name
      your address
      your city, state zip code

c. Define one AutoText entry for all of the text, using your initials as the abbreviated code.

d. PRESS: ENTER twice

e. TYPE: `Management Information Systems Department`

f. Define an AutoText entry called MIS for this term. (*CAUTION*: Do not select the paragraph mark, just the text.)

g. PRESS: ENTER twice

h. TYPE: `OS/2 Version 2.2 Batch Release 2.299`

i. Define an AutoText entry called OS for this term. (*CAUTION*: Do not select the paragraph mark, just the text.)

j. Open a new document.

k. Create the document appearing in Figure 3.11, using the AutoText entries wherever possible.

l. Save the document as MISDEPT onto the Advantage Diskette.

m. Using the Replace command, change the name of the department from "Management Information Systems Department" to "Office Automation Division."

n. Using the Replace command, make every occurrence of "OS/2 Version 2.2 Batch Release 2.299" boldface in the document.

o. Save the document again, replacing the original version.

p. Print the document.

q. Close all the open documents in the document area. Do not save the original document that you used to define the AutoText entries.

FIGURE 3.11 MISDEPT MEMO

```
DATE:          February 14, 1995

TO:            Mr. Tyler French
               Director of Operations
               Management Information Systems Department

FROM:          your name
               your address
               your city, state  zip code

SUBJECT:       OS/2 Version 2.2 Batch Release 2.299

Please be forewarned that the OS/2 Version 2.2 Batch
Release 2.299 operating system will not be available
for the Management Information Systems Department on
March 1, 1995, as previously promised.

Although we understand the requirement for OS/2 Version
2.2 Batch Release 2.299, Research and Development must
fully test the product before allowing any department
access to the code—and that includes the Management
Information Systems Department.

If you require further clarification, please have Alan
Johansen, V.P., Management Information Systems
Department, contact me at the following address:

       your name
       your address
       your city, state  zip code

Thanks for your patience.
```

3. The following exercise uses the proofing tools to correct a poorly written and misspelled document.

   a. Retrieve the BADMEMO document from the Advantage Diskette.

   b. Correct the misspelled words with the help of the Spell Checker.

   c. Correct the poor grammar with the help of the Grammar Checker.

   d. Save the document as GOODMEMO to the Advantage Diskette.

   e. Print the document.

   f. Close the document.

4. The objective of this exercise is to practice using move operations using the Clipboard, Find and Replace commands, the Thesaurus tool, and the Spell Checker.

   a. Open INPUT from the Advantage Diskette.

   b. Using the Clipboard, change the order of the hardware components to match the following: pen-based computing, touch screen, digitizer, mouse, trackball, and light pen.

   c. Using the REPLACE command, change every occurrence of "computer" to "PC." (*Note*: Make sure to select "Find Whole Words Only.")

   d. Use the Thesaurus to find a different word for "Essentially" in the first sentence of the Trackball description.

   e. Correct the misspelled words with the help of the Spell Checker.

   f. Save the document as INPUT onto the Advantage Diskette.

   g. Print the document.

   h. Close the document.

CASE PROBLEMS

THE RIVER REPORT

(*Note*: In the following case problems, assume the role of the primary characters and perform the same steps that they identify. You may want to re-read the session opening.)

1. Linda's first task as editor for the *River Report* is to edit a short article written about a big bass caught in the Sacramento River. Billy Joe Quaker, the staff reporter, left the file on a disk labeled "Advantage Diskette" with the following note:

   Dear Ms. James, I saved the bass article as BASS on the Advantage Diskette. The article was written using Microsoft Word for Windows. If you need me, I'll be at Chatterbox Falls covering the kayaking race. Bye for now, BJQ.

   Upon review of the article, she decides that some of the sentences should be positioned differently and that the spelling must be checked. She also decides to check the article's grammar using Word's Grammar Checker. When finished, she saves the document and then prints it for inclusion in the Sports section.

2. At 5:00 P.M. on Wednesday, reporter Tola McPherson submitted her article about Saturday's baseball game. The article is named BASEBALL and is stored on the Advantage Diskette. Being one of the first articles that Linda has had to review, she doesn't know what to expect when she opens the document. She is pleasantly surprised, however, because the article seems relatively error-free. To be safe, Linda runs the document through Word's Grammar Checker and implements its suggestions where appropriate.

   Sounding embarrassed, Tola calls Linda at 5:45 P.M. to tell her to change the name "Collin Lamas" to "Victor Lamas." Linda swiftly makes the change using Word's Replace command. Now that she has put her stamp of approval on the article, she saves it back to the disk and sets it aside until Thursday evening, when she will give it to Production.

3. As Linda is organizing the articles to give to Production, Tola rushes in with a last-minute change. "Linda, I have some very interesting information about Victor Lamas and I think we need to include it in our BASEBALL article. The information is stored in a file named LAMAS on the Advantage Diskette. I've gotta run to follow up on a lead." With 6:00 P.M. appearing on her desk clock, Linda knows that she doesn't have much time to make the changes! She opens the BASEBALL document into one window and the LAMAS document into another. After reading both documents, she decides to move the first paragraph from the LAMAS document and position it immediately after the second paragraph in the BASEBALL document. She then moves the second paragraph from the LAMAS document and positions it after the last paragraph in the BASEBALL document.

   Satisfied with the revised BASEBALL document, Linda saves and prints her work at 6:30 P.M. She just makes the 7:00 P.M. deadline!

4. As tradition would have it, a complimentary ad is published each year in the *River Report* announcing the upcoming Pear Fair on June 15th. Linda is responsible for creating the advertisement. To begin, she reviews some of the previous document files left by Hank Leary. Fortunately, she finds a file named PEARFAIR stored on the Advantage Diskette. After opening the file, she is even more comfortable with the task at hand. Hank had included bracketed notes throughout the document to help him create the advertisement for this year's fair.

   Linda reviews the document and incorporates all of Hank's suggestions. She then deletes each of his bracketed notes from the document. After saving the document as PEARFAIR onto the Advantage Diskette, she prints it for inclusion in the Special Events section.

5. Linda must write a short article describing the 4th of July parade. She attended the parade and jotted down some notes that are now stored in PARADE on the Advantage Diskette. But the notes are rough and were not placed in a particular order. Therefore, she must edit and move around the text to form a legible paragraph. Also, she has since learned that Bruce Towne drove the fire engine, not Bill Darsie. She can fix that mistake using the Replace utility. As a final step, she corrects the grammar using the Grammar Checker. She saves the document back to the Advantage Diskette as PARADE and prints it for inclusion in the Special Events section.

Microsoft Word 6.0:

Printing and Document Management

SESSION OUTLINE

INTRODUCTION

After the final editing and proofing of a document, there remain only a few optional steps for finalizing its appearance which include specifying page layout, preventing widows and orphans, inserting page numbers, and creating headers and footers. Each of these steps helps to keep your audience on track when reading your document.

Besides discussing how to place the final touches on a document, this session introduces several printing and file management commands. To work efficiently with a word processing software program, it is important that you know how to find, copy, and print a document without having to open each file on your hard disk. This session provides you with the knowledge and experience to perform these functions confidently.

CASE STUDY — GINO'S PIZZA KITCHEN

Gino Lerma is the owner of four pizza restaurants in the Boston metropolitan area. He started with one restaurant 15 years ago. Through hard work and careful planning, Gino was able to open a new restaurant every few years. Gino now considers himself semi-retired, even though he works around the clock and requires a full-time assistant, Larry Ingla. Although he is no longer part of the daily activities, Gino fondly remembers his many years working from 11:00 a.m. until midnight, six days per week, in the restaurants.

Each month, Gino's managers use Microsoft Word to create a summary report of their restaurant's activities. Each manager then sends his or her report over the Internet to Larry Ingla. Larry uses the Windows Clipboard to create a single document from the four reports and then prints the consolidated document for Gino to review. After receiving feedback from his bank manager on the consolidated reports, Gino asks Larry to format the reports with headers, footers, and page numbers. He also wants Larry to improve the general page layout of the reports and has given him specific suggestions for improvement. Larry immediately said "no problem" to Gino's request, but in truth, he doesn't know where to begin.

In this session, you and Larry will learn how to take control of the way your document appears on the screen and when printed, use document formatting commands, and manage the files you create using several file-management commands.

CUSTOMIZING YOUR WORK AREA

Microsoft Word has many advantages over character-based word processing programs like WordPerfect 5.1. Not only can you see the effects of character and paragraph formatting commands immediately on-screen, you can also edit text using features such as drag and drop. One of the disadvantages of working in this WYSIWYG environment is that it may take longer to page through a document on-screen. For example, Word must continuously update the screen with all of the special fonts and character styles that you have selected, unlike a character-based program which simply displays basic characters. Since most people haven't learned how to type faster than the computer can think, this last point may be a little academic.

As a compromise, Word provides three primary views for working with documents: Normal, Outline, and Page Layout. While each view has its own advantages, it is their combination that gives you the best overall working environment. For faster data entry, you can also select a Draft Font for the Normal and Outline views. Since the Draft Font presents text without WYSIWYG formatting, the screen is updated and redrawn as fast as most character-based word processing programs. This section describes and demonstrates the Normal and Page Layout views.

SELECTING A VIEW

You select a view for your document using the View command on the Menu bar or by clicking the desired View button on the horizontal scroll bar. On the pull-down menu, a bullet appears next to the active or currently selected view. Table 4.1 summarizes the primary view options.

TABLE 4.1

View Options

Task Description	*Menu Command*	*View Button*
Change to Normal view	View, Normal	
Change to Page Layout view	View, Page Layout	
Change to Outline view	View, Outline	

Your selection of a view depends upon the type of work that you are performing, as described in the following guidelines:

- *Perform most of your work using the Normal view.*
  The Normal view displays text with character and paragraph formatting, but does not show headers, footers, or newspaper-style text columns. The Normal view separates pages in a document with a dotted line, dividing the last line of one page from the first line of the next. Figure 4.1 shows a sample document in the Normal view.

- *Edit the final document before printing in the Page Layout view.*
  The Page Layout view displays a document in almost full WYSIWYG preview mode. All character, paragraph, and document formatting options are displayed, along with headers, footers, and newspaper-style text columns. The document is separated on-screen into what appear to be real pages. Figure 4.2 shows a document in the Page Layout view.

- *Organize and plan your document using the Outline view.*
  The Outline view displays a document as an outline with expandable and collapsible heading levels. This view is used for rearranging entire sections of a document or for moving to a specific section in a long document quickly. Figure 4.3 shows a document in the Outline view, collapsed to show only the major headings.

FIGURE 4.1 A DOCUMENT DISPLAYED IN NORMAL VIEW

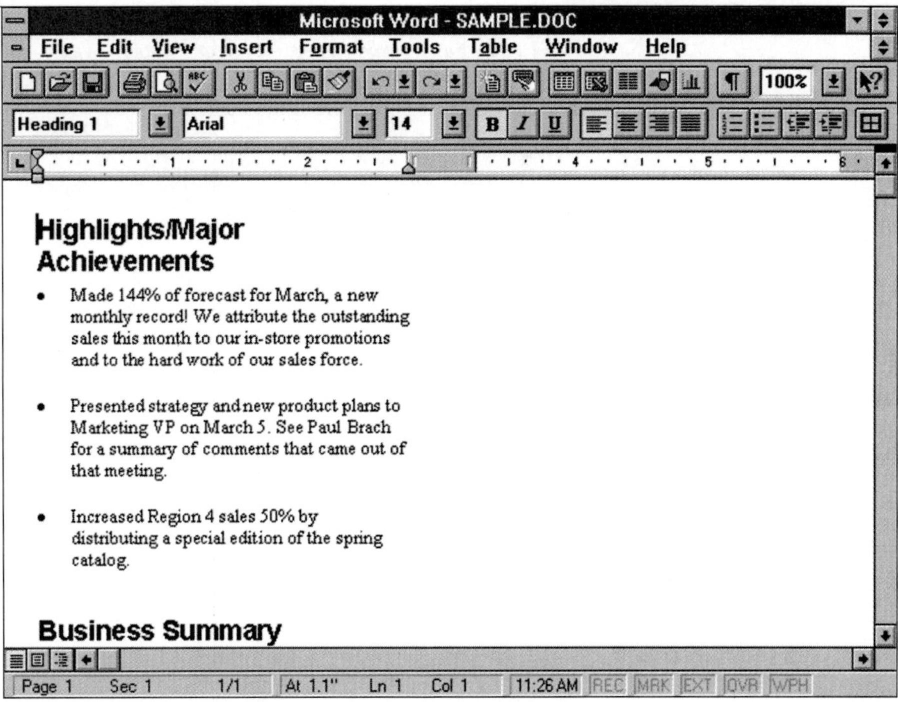

FIGURE 4.2 A DOCUMENT DISPLAYED IN PAGE LAYOUT VIEW

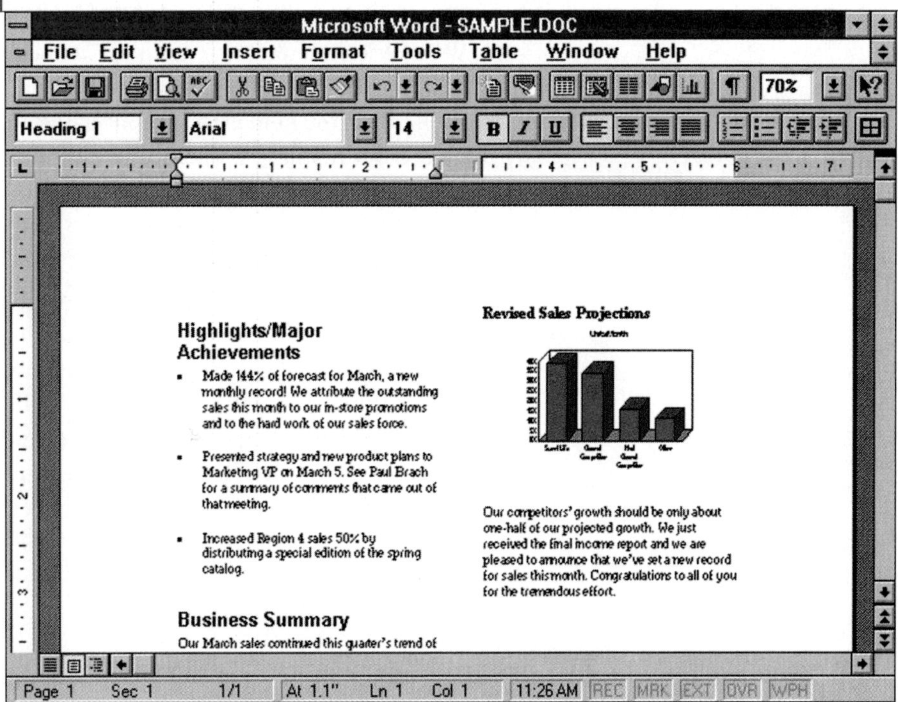

FIGURE 4.3 A DOCUMENT DISPLAYED IN OUTLINE VIEW

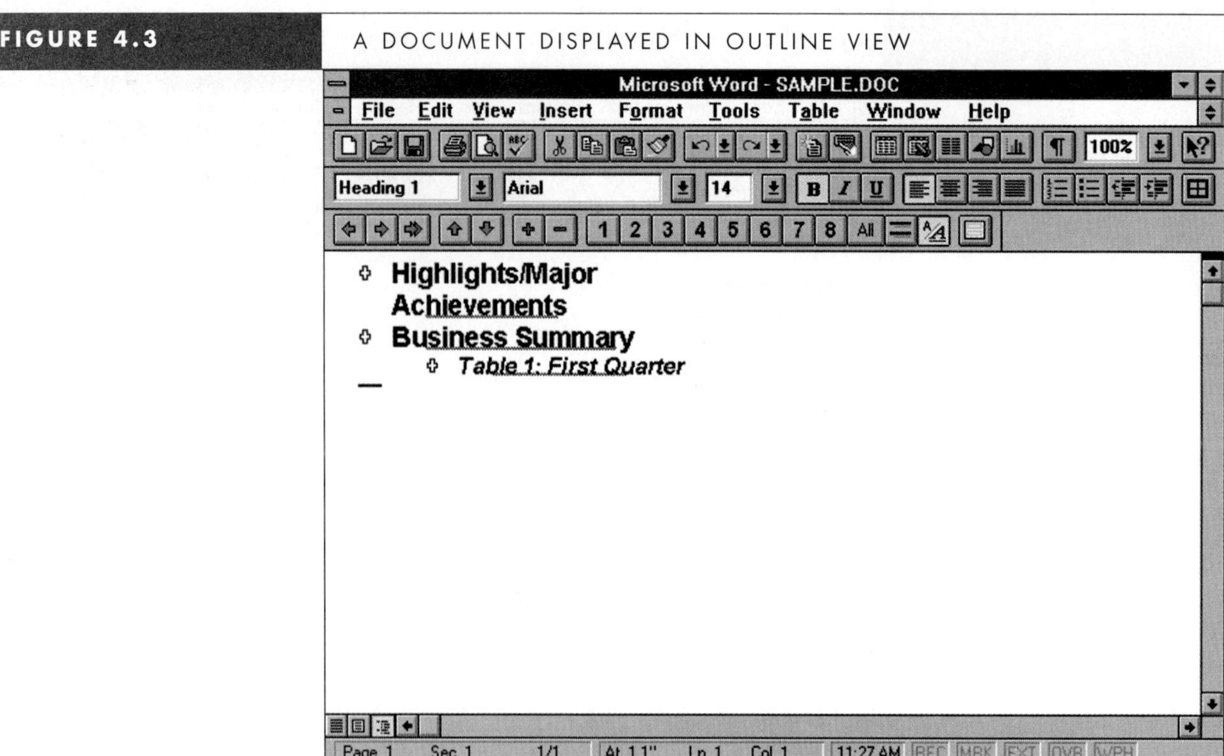

- *Enter large amounts of text quickly using the Draft Font.*
  The Draft Font speeds up the display of a document by not showing WYSIWYG character formatting. Although you continue to select the desired formatting, the formatted text only appears underlined in the document. You select Draft Font using the Tools, Options command. Figure 4.4 displays a document in Normal view and Draft Font.

- *Work with the largest text area possible using Full Screen mode.*
  The Full Screen mode lets you work on a document without the clutter of Word's Menu bar, toolbars, or Ruler. Indeed, the only indication that you are still using Word is the Full Screen button (shown at the right) that appears in the bottom right-hand corner. To change to Full Screen mode, choose View, Full Screen from the menu. To return to the regular Word workspace once you are in Full Screen mode, click the Full Screen button once or press ESC.

FIGURE 4.4 A DOCUMENT DISPLAYED IN NORMAL VIEW AND DRAFT FONT

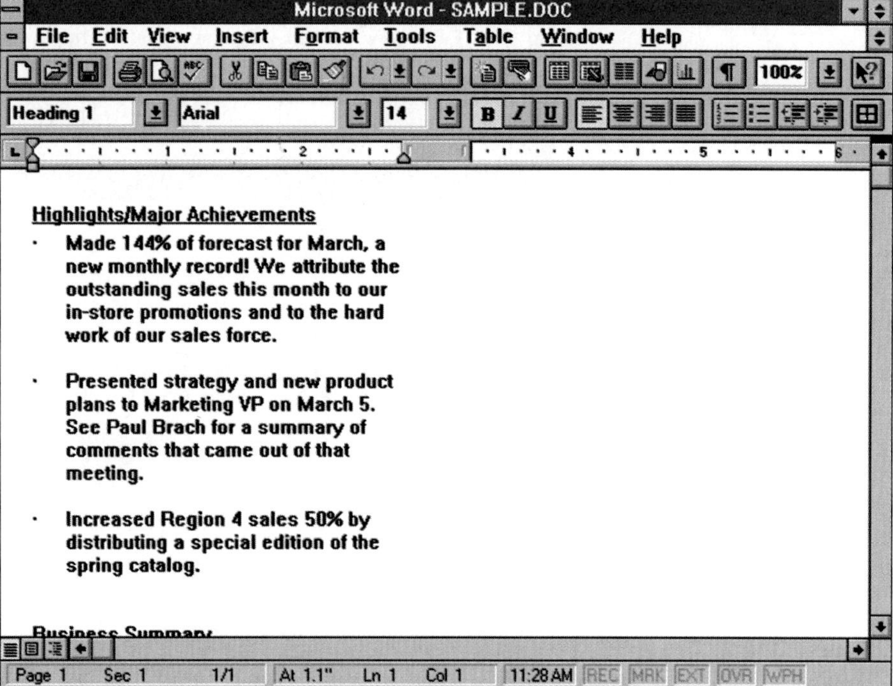

Perform the following steps to select different views.

1. Make sure that you've loaded Word 6.0 and the Advantage Diskette is inserted into drive A: or drive B:.

2. Retrieve the NEWSLETR document from the Advantage Diskette.

3. To change to a Page Layout view:
   CHOOSE: View, Page Layout
   Your document should look similar to Figure 4.5.

4. To change to Full Screen mode:
   CHOOSE: View, Full Screen
   You may be asking, "How do I choose commands if Word removes the Menu bar and toolbars?" In Full Screen mode, you must use the keyboard shortcut keys and shortcut (right-click) menus. (*Tip*: You can sometimes access the Menu bar by pointing to the very top of the screen and clicking the left mouse button.)

5. To return to the regular Word workspace:
   PRESS: ESC or CLICK: Full Screen button ( )

6. To change back to the Normal view:
   CLICK: Normal button ( ) on the horizontal scroll bar

FIGURE 4.5 THE NEWSLETR DOCUMENT IN PAGE LAYOUT VIEW

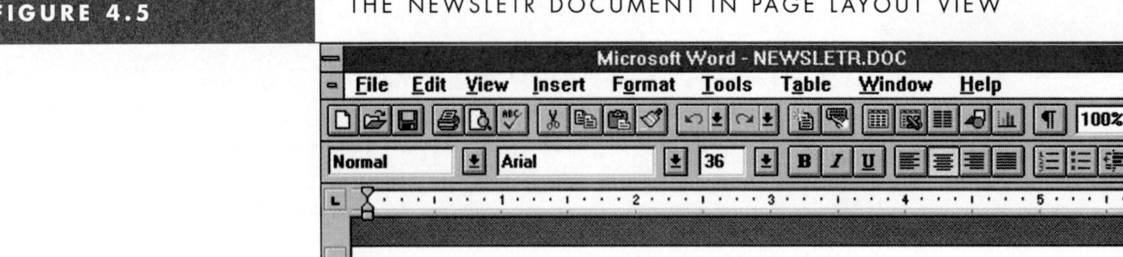

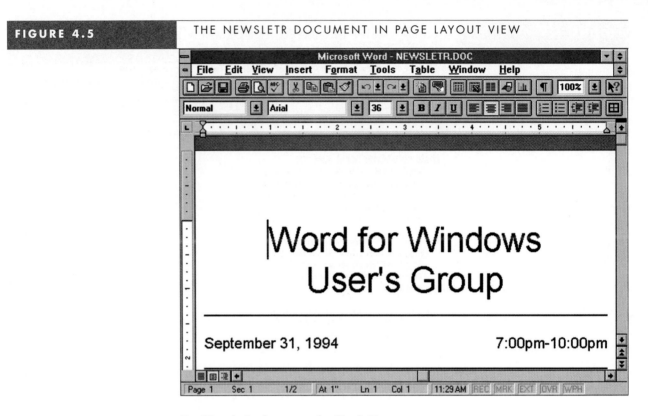

7. Now let's change to the Draft Font:
   CHOOSE: Tools, Options
   SELECT: View tab
   SELECT: Draft Font check box in the Show group
   Your dialog box should appear similar to Figure 4.6.

FIGURE 4.6 OPTIONS DIALOG BOX WITH DRAFT FONT SELECTED

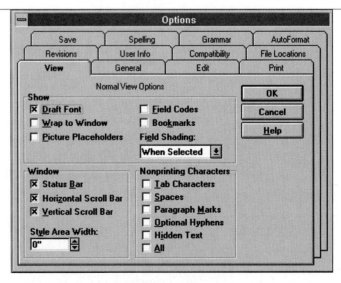

8. To return to the document:
   PRESS: ENTER or CLICK: OK
   You should notice that the document changes to an almost character-based display.

9. To remove the Draft display mode:
   CHOOSE: Tools, Options
   SELECT: Draft Font until no "×" appears in the check box
   PRESS: ENTER or CLICK: OK

QUICK REFERENCE
Selecting a View

- **For a normal WYSIWYG view:**
  CLICK: Normal button ( )
- **For a full WYSIWYG display:**
  CLICK: Page Layout button ( )
- **For a collapsible outline view:**
  CLICK: Outline button ( )

ZOOMING THE DISPLAY

Regardless of the view you select, Word lets you zoom in and out on a document, increasing and decreasing its display size. For example, you may want to enlarge Word's normal view to 200% of its original size when working with detailed graphics. To modify Word's zoom setting, you choose the View, Zoom command or select the Zoom Control box (120%) on the Standard toolbar.

Perform the following steps.

1. To zoom the NEWSLETR document by 200% its original size:
   CLICK: down arrow adjacent to the Zoom Control box (120%)

2. From the resulting drop-down list:
   SELECT: 200%
   The document is immediately magnified twice its original size.

3. To find the best-fit magnification:
   CLICK: down arrow adjacent to the Zoom Control box (120%)
   Your screen should now appear similar to Figure 4.7.

FIGURE 4.7 ZOOMING THE DISPLAY USING THE ZOOM CONTROL BOX

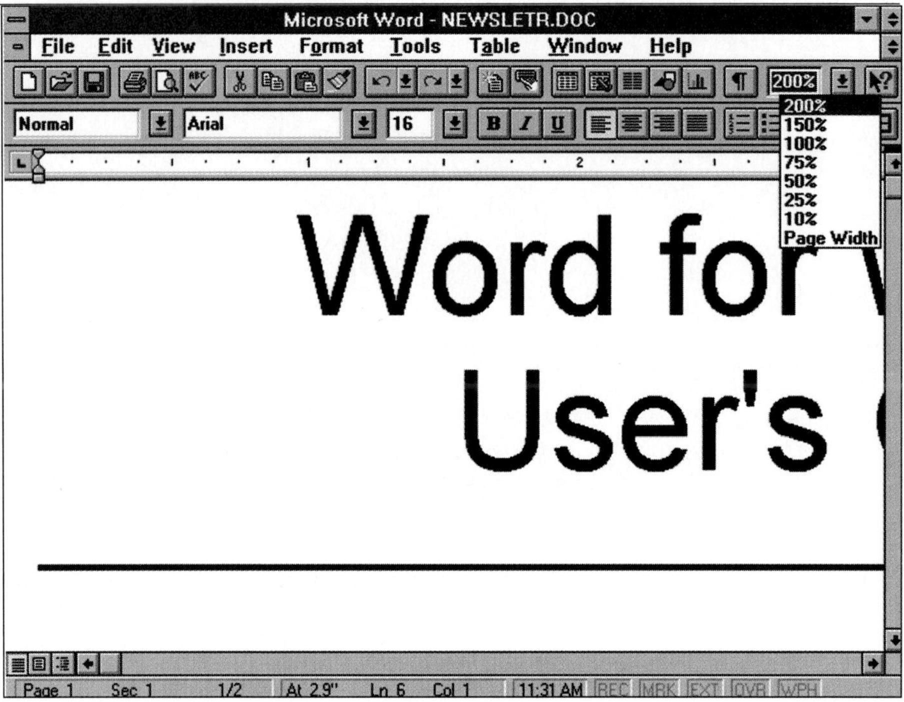

4. SELECT: Page Width from the drop-down list
   The view is zoomed to the best fit for your screen's resolution.

5. In addition to using the Zoom Control box (120%) to select a magnification factor, you can use the Zoom dialog box:
   CHOOSE: View, Zoom
   A dialog box similar to the one in Figure 4.8 appears.

6. SELECT: *the magnification options in the "Zoom To" area*
   Notice that the text displayed on the monitor in the Preview area is updated after each selection.

7. Before you proceed to the next section:
   SELECT: Page Width
   PRESS: ENTER or CLICK: OK

FIGURE 4.8

ZOOM DIALOG BOX

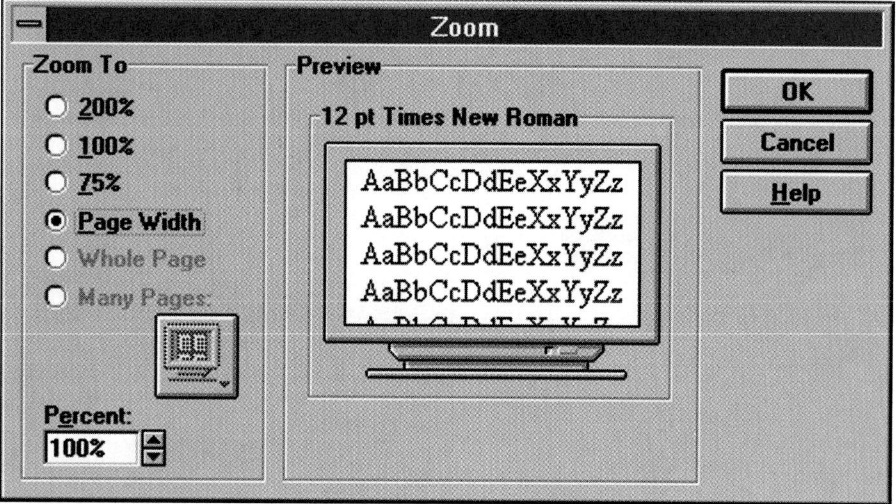

DISPLAYING AND HIDING TOOLBARS

Another method for customizing the work area involves manipulating the eight toolbars in Word. Most people work with only the Standard and Formatting toolbars displayed. However, you can open the additional six toolbars (Borders, Database, Drawing, Forms, Microsoft, and Word for Windows 2.0) and move them anywhere within the application window. Don't get carried away and display all of the toolbars on the screen at all times. You should attempt to keep your screen as clear as possible to maximize your document's work area.

Let's demonstrate some of the features that are available for manipulating toolbars. Perform the following steps.

1. To display the shortcut or pop-up menu for accessing toolbars, position the mouse pointer on any button in the Standard toolbar and click the right mouse button once. The shortcut menu at the right should appear.

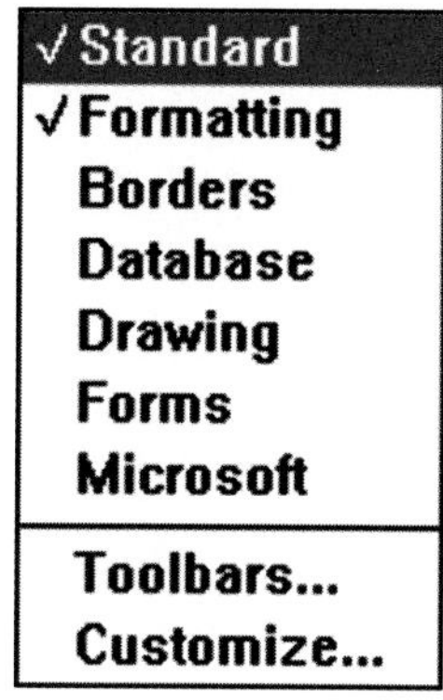

2. To display the Drawing toolbar:
   CHOOSE: Drawing
   Remember to click the command using the left mouse button. You should see the Drawing toolbar appear, usually positioned at the bottom of the screen.

3. To display the Borders toolbar using the Toolbars dialog box:
   CHOOSE: View, Toolbars
   SELECT: Borders check box
   (*Note:* You can also choose the Toolbars option on the shortcut menu to display the Toolbars dialog box.) Your screen should appear similar to Figure 4.9.

FIGURE 4.9 TOOLBARS DIALOG BOX

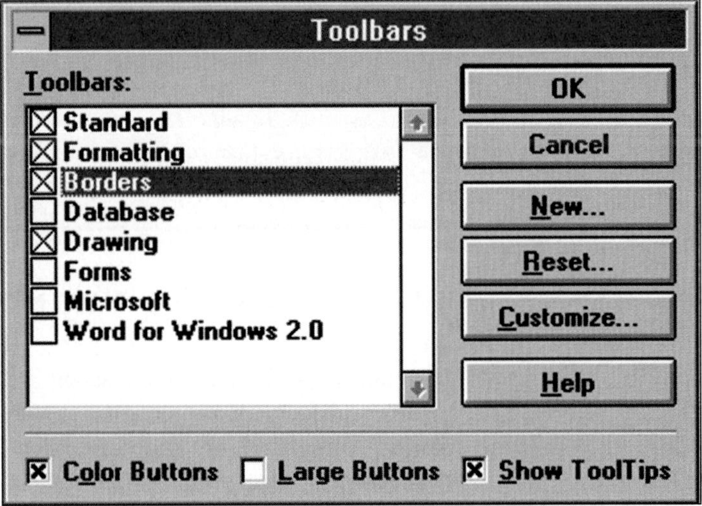

4. To accept your selections in the dialog box and proceed:
   PRESS: ENTER or CLICK: OK
   The Borders toolbar will usually appear below the Formatting toolbar.

5. You'll notice that we have mentioned that the Drawing and Borders toolbars *usually* appear somewhere on the screen. This statement is necessary because you can easily move these toolbars. To practice floating a toolbar away from its docked position, position your mouse pointer over the Borders toolbar, on the gray area between the No Border button ( ) and the Shadings box (Clear).

6. CLICK: left mouse button and hold it down
   DRAG: the toolbar into the document area
   You should notice that the shadowed frame changes from an elongated rectangle or horizontal bar to a more compact rectangle.

7. Release the mouse button to float the Borders toolbar. The toolbar should appear similar to the following example:

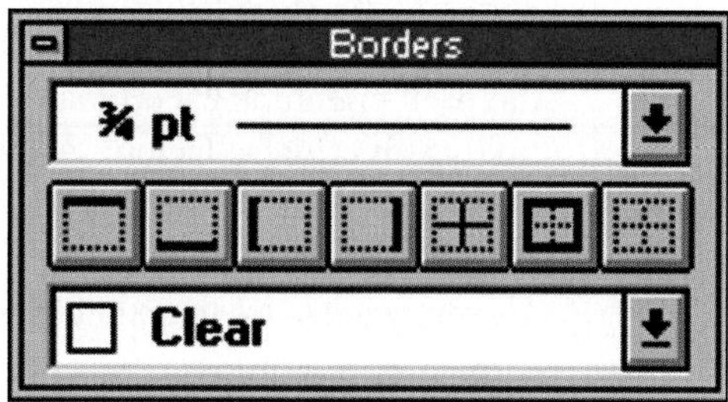

8. To replace the Borders toolbar underneath the Formatting toolbar, drag the floating toolbar up by its Title bar until the shadowed rectangle changes to a horizontal bar. Position the left edge of the shadowed horizontal bar against the left edge of the application window, immediately beneath the Formatting toolbar.

9. Release the left mouse button. If the toolbar doesn't return to its original position, drag it away from its docked location and try again.

10. Using the shortcut menu, remove the Drawing and Borders toolbars from the screen.

11. One last item for customizing your work area—you can hide the Ruler to create more screen real estate using the following command:
CHOOSE: View, Ruler

12. To re-display the Ruler:
CHOOSE: View, Ruler

QUICK REFERENCE
Customizing Your Work Area

- **To zoom in or out on your document:**
  CHOOSE: View, Zoom, or click the Zoom Control box (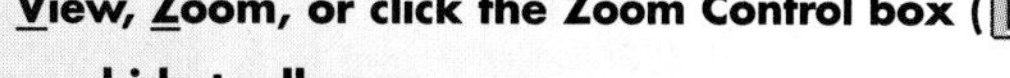)
- **To display or hide toolbars:**
  CHOOSE: View, Toolbars, or right-click a toolbar to display a menu
- **To display or hide the Ruler:**
  CHOOSE: View, Ruler

DOCUMENT FORMATTING COMMANDS

Simply stated, document formatting involves preparing a document for the printer. This section provides lessons on setting margins, specifying paper sizes and orientation, preventing widows and orphans, inserting page numbers, and lastly, creating headers and footers in a document.

SPECIFYING YOUR PAGE LAYOUT

Your document's page layout is affected by many factors, including the margins or white space desired around the edges of the page, the size of paper you are using, and the print orientation. Fortunately for us, Word provides a single dialog box for controlling all of these factors. Accessed by choosing File, Page Setup from the menu, the Page Setup dialog box provides four tabs: Margins, Paper Size, Paper Source, and Layout. Figure 4.10 shows the Page Setup dialog box with the Margins tab selected. The entry areas for the other three tabs are provided below the dialog box.

FIGURE 4.10 PAGE SETUP DIALOG BOX

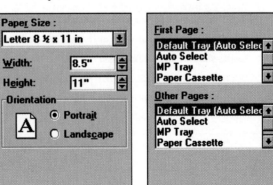

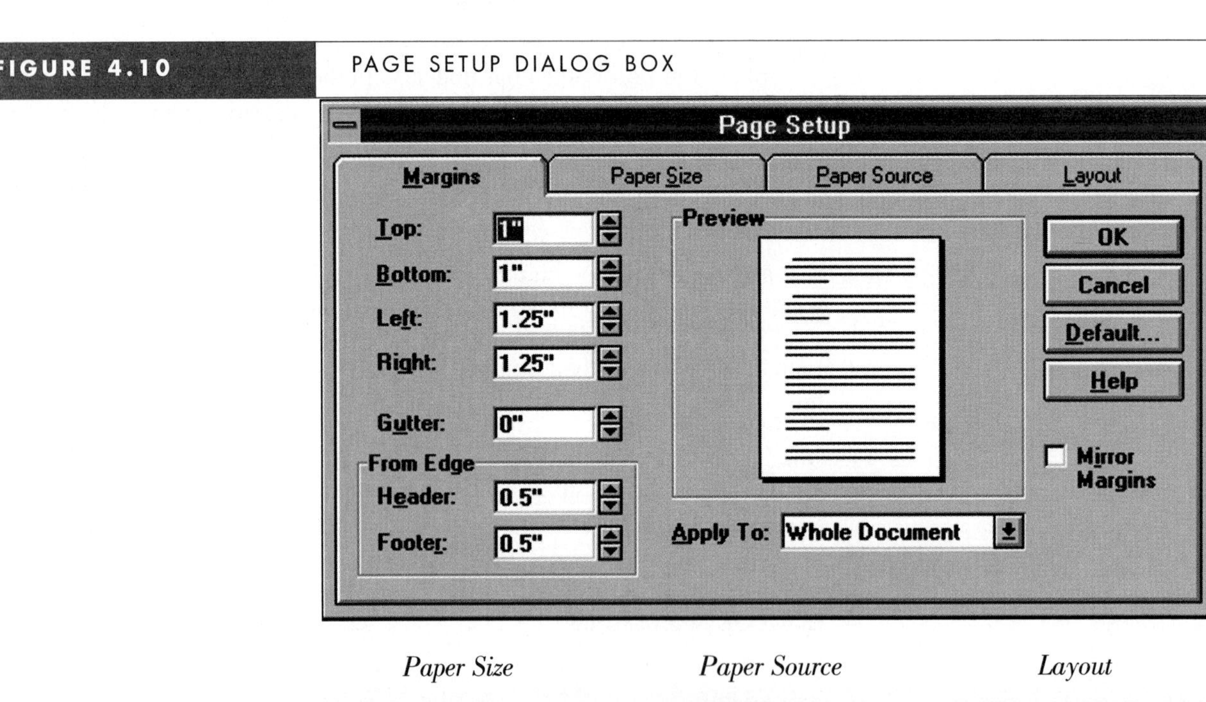

Paper Size

Paper Size :
Letter 8 ½ x 11 in
Width: 8.5"
Height: 11"
Orientation
Portrait
Landscape

Paper Source

First Page :
Default Tray (Auto Selec
Auto Select
MP Tray
Paper Cassette
Other Pages :
Default Tray (Auto Selec
Auto Select
MP Tray
Paper Cassette

Layout

Section Start:
New Page
Headers and Footers
Different Odd and Even
Different First Page
Vertical Alignment:
Top
Line Numbers...

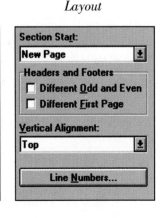

Not surprisingly, Word allows you to set the top, bottom, left, and right margins for a page. In addition, you can set a gutter margin to reserve space for binding a document. The **gutter** is where pages are joined in the center of the binding or hole-punched for a ring binder. Word provides default settings of 1.25 inches for the left and right margins and 1 inch for the top and bottom margins. The gutter margin is initially set at 0 inches, as most documents are not bound. With respect to paper size, your typical options include using letter- or legal-sized paper with a **portrait orientation** (8.5-inches wide by 11-inches tall) or a **landscape orientation** (11-inches wide by 8.5-inches tall). For the purposes of this section, you will not modify the paper source or section layout options.

Let's practice changing the page layout settings in the following steps.

1. Make sure that the Advantage Diskette is inserted in the disk drive.

2. Close all the open documents in the document area.

3. Retrieve the MEDIA document from the Advantage Diskette.

4. To change the margins from the default settings to an even 1 inch around the entire page:
   CHOOSE: File, Page Setup

5. Ensure that you are viewing the margin settings:
   SELECT: Margins tab at the top of the dialog box

6. To change the left and right margins to 1 inch:
   CLICK: down triangle adjacent to the Left margin text box repeatedly, until the value decreases to 1 inch
   CLICK: down triangle adjacent to the Right margin text box repeatedly, until the value decreases to 1 inch
   (*Note:* As you click the symbols, the Preview area at the right-hand side shows the effect of the change on your document.)

7. To illustrate the use of a gutter, you will increase the counter in the Gutter text box to 0.5 inches:
   CLICK: up triangle adjacent to the Gutter text box repeatedly, until the value increases to 0.5 inches
   (*Note:* The shaded area in the Preview area represents the binding.)

8. Reset the Gutter margin to 0 inches.

9. To select legal-size paper with a landscape orientation for this document, first display the paper size and orientation information:
   SELECT: Paper Size tab at the top of the dialog box

10. SELECT: Legal 8½ × 14-in from the Paper Size drop-down list

11. SELECT: Landscape option button from the Orientation group
    Notice that the Preview area changes with each selection.

12. PRESS: ENTER or CLICK: OK

13. When you return to the document, the page may be too wide to fit in the current view. To remedy this problem:
    CLICK: Page Layout button
    CLICK: Zoom Control box (120%)
    CHOOSE: Page Width
    Your document should now appear similar to Figure 4.11.

FIGURE 4.11 PAGE LAYOUT VIEW OF MEDIA WITH A LANDSCAPE ORIENTATION

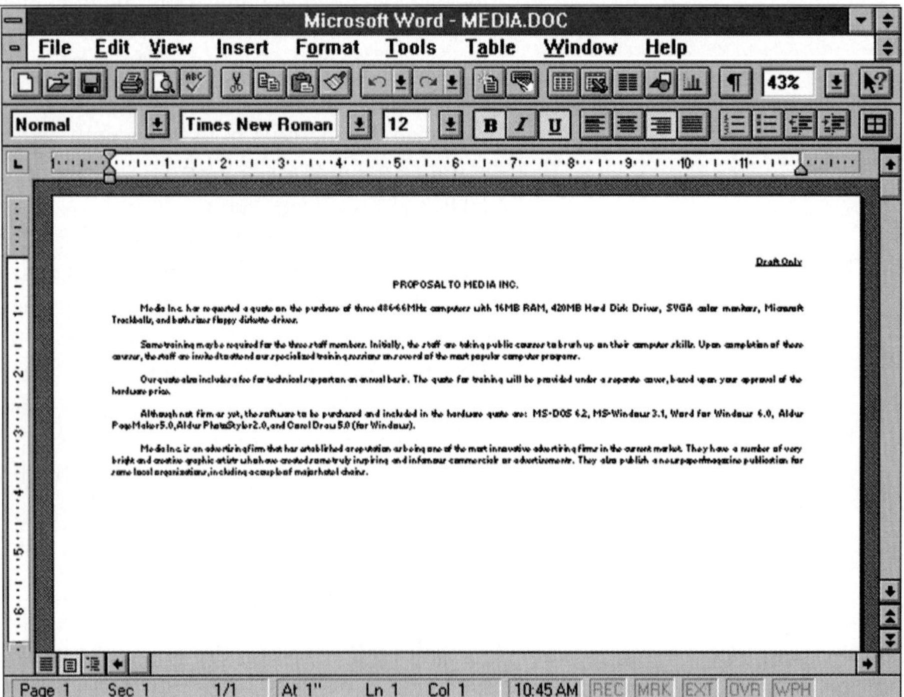

14. To return the document to letter-size paper with a portrait orientation, you will call up the Page Setup dialog box using a shortcut method:
    DOUBLE-CLICK: gray area in the Ruler (see diagram below)

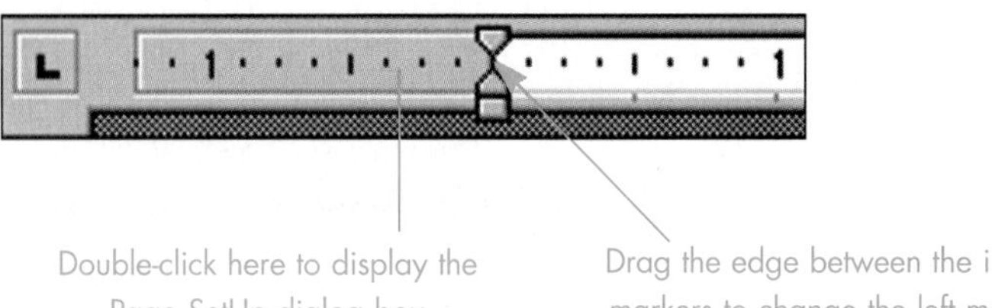

15. When the Page Setup dialog box appears:
    SELECT: Paper Size tab
    SELECT: Letter 8½ x 11-in from the Paper Size drop-down list
    SELECT: Portrait option button from the Orientation group
    PRESS: ENTER or CLICK: OK
    The document is immediately redrawn in the Page Layout view.

16. To change a document's margins using the mouse, you position the mouse pointer over the margin boundary (the line between the gray area and the white area on the Ruler) and then drag the boundary to increase and decrease the margin setting. (See the diagram in step 14.) If you've positioned your mouse pointer correctly, it changes from a white arrow to a black, two-headed arrow. To have Word display the margin measurements in the Ruler as you drag the margin boundary, you hold down the ALT key.

    Let's proceed—do the following:
    PRESS: ALT and hold it down
    DRAG: left margin boundary to the right until 1.25 appears as the measurement on the horizontal Ruler

    (*Note:* This sequence of steps works only in Page Layout and Print Preview modes.) Your document should appear similar to Figure 4.12.

17. Release the mouse button and the ALT key.

18. Using the same method as outlined in step 16, change the right margin to 1.25 inches. (*Note*: You can use this same method to change left, right, top, and bottom margins in a document.)

19. Save the document as MEDIA1 to the Advantage Diskette.

20. Close the document.

QUICK REFERENCE
Using the Page Setup Dialog Box

1. **CHOOSE: File, Page Setup**
2. **SELECT: Margins tab to display the settings page for margins**
3. **Specify a gutter margin if binding the document, as well as the top, bottom, left, and right margins.**
4. **SELECT: Paper Size tab**
5. **Specify the paper size and either portrait or landscape orientation.**

FIGURE 4.12

CHANGING MARGINS IN PAGE LAYOUT VIEW USING THE MOUSE AND ALT KEY

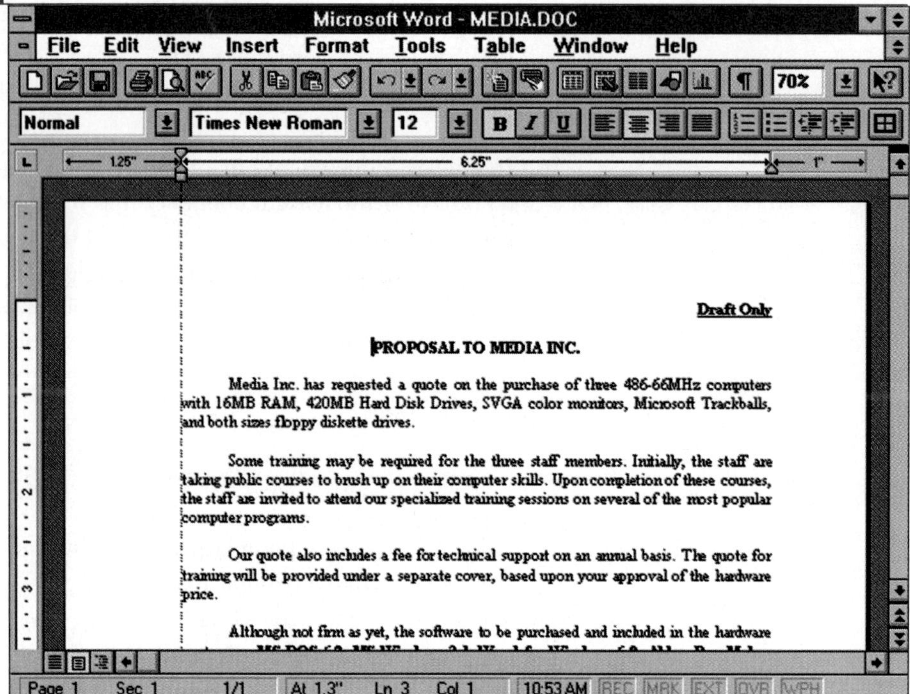

PREVENTING WIDOWS AND ORPHANS

Although the heading implies a plan for abolishing family suffering, this section deals with a much less serious topic—straggling sentences that are separated from their paragraphs by a page break. A **widow** is created when the last sentence in a paragraph flows to the top of the next page. An **orphan** is created when the first sentence of a paragraph begins on the last line of a page. When a single sentence is separated from a paragraph, the reader must work harder to keep up with the flow of the text. Fortunately, Word has a widow and orphan protection feature that automatically prevents these breaks from occurring.

Perform the following steps.

1. Retrieve the ETHICS document from the Advantage Diskette.

2. To ensure that the Widow and Orphan protection feature is turned on:
   CHOOSE: Format, Paragraph
   The Paragraph dialog box appears.

3. SELECT: Text Flow tab

4. Under the Pagination group, ensure that the Widow/Orphan Control check box is selected:
   SELECT: Widow/Orphan Control check box
   Remember, an "x" in the check box means that the option is selected.

5. PRESS: ENTER or CLICK: OK

QUICK REFERENCE
Protecting Against Widows and Orphans

1. **CHOOSE: Format, Paragraph**
2. **SELECT: Text Flow tab**
3. **SELECT: "Widow/Orphan Control" check box in the Pagination group**
4. **PRESS: ENTER or CLICK: OK**

INSERTING PAGE NUMBERS

Page numbers assist a reader in finding and referencing sections within a document. In Word, you can position page numbers at the top or bottom of a document and align the page number with the left, center, or right margins. Furthermore, you can select the format and starting page for the numbering scheme based on personal preference. For example, you can use standard numbers (1, 2, 3 ...), letters (a, b, c ... or A, B, C ...), or Roman numerals (i, ii, iii ...) for the numbering format and change the format for different sections in a document.

To add page numbers to a document, you choose the Insert, Page Numbers command. When the Page Numbers dialog box appears, you specify the position and alignment desired for the page numbers. Depending on your selections, Word creates a header or footer using the default numbering format (1, 2, 3 ...), starting at page 1.

Perform the following steps to insert page numbers.

1. CHOOSE: Insert, Page Numbers
   The dialog box shown in Figure 4.13 should appear on your screen. (*Note:* Figure 4.13 also shows the dialog box for changing the numbering format from standard numbers to letters or Roman numerals.)

2. To position the page number in the top right-hand corner of the page:
   SELECT: "Top of Page (Header)" in the Position drop-down list box
   SELECT: "Right" in the Alignment drop-down list box

3. PRESS: ENTER or CLICK: OK

4. Change to the Page Layout view:
   CLICK: Page Layout button ( )
   Notice the dimmed page number in the top right-hand corner.

FIGURE 4.13 PAGE NUMBERS DIALOG BOX

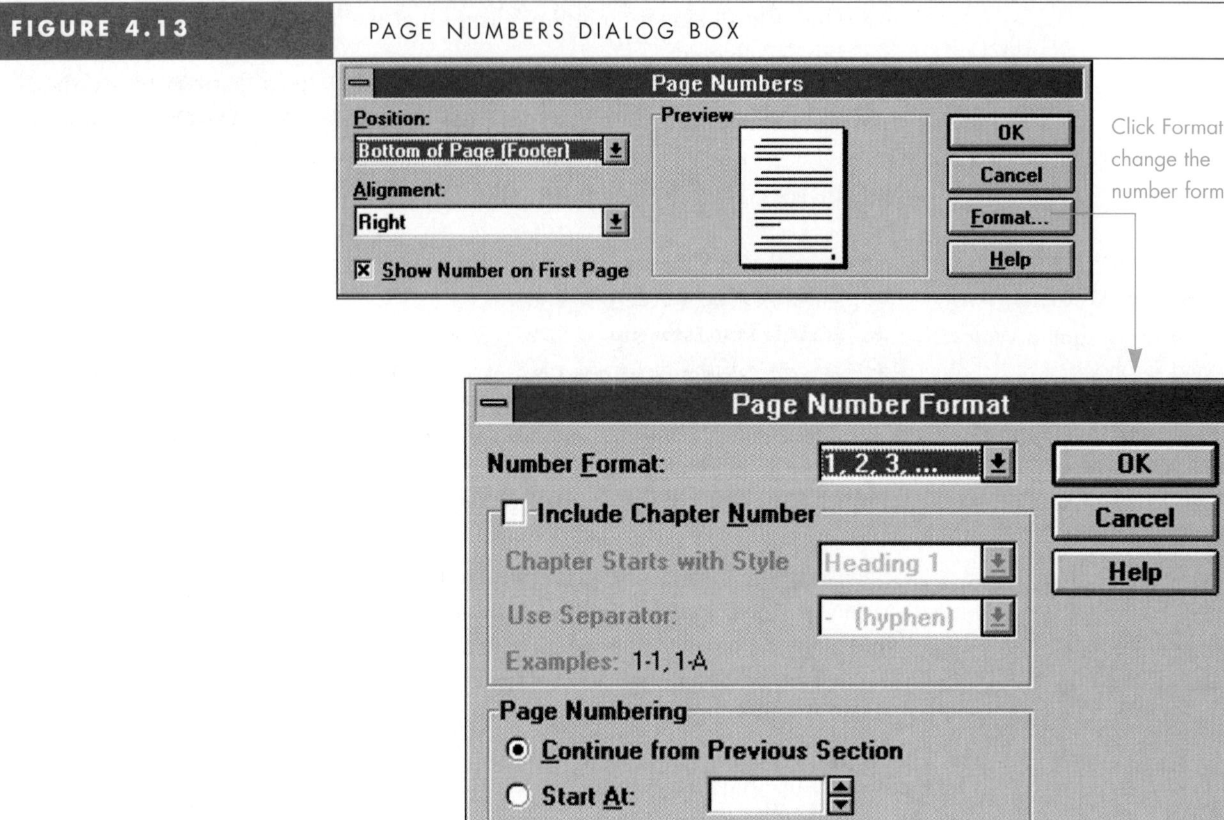

5. To move to the top of the second page:
   CLICK: Next page symbol (▼) at the bottom of the vertical scroll bar
   In the top right-hand corner, a "2" appears as the page number.

6. To change back to the Normal view:
   CLICK: Normal button (≣)

Because Word places the page numbering scheme into the header or footer of a document, you can further customize the page numbers by selecting a font and style for them.

QUICK REFERENCE
Inserting Page Numbers

1. **CHOOSE: Insert, Page Numbers**
2. **SELECT: an option from the Position drop-down list box**
3. **SELECT: an option from the Alignment drop-down list box**
4. **PRESS: ENTER or CLICK: OK**

CREATING HEADERS AND FOOTERS

A document **header** and **footer** can appear at the top and bottom of each page. The header often contains the title or section headings for a document while the footer might show the page numbers or copyright information. Adding a header or footer produces a more professional-looking document and makes longer documents easier to read.

In the last section, you inserted page numbers in the ETHICS document. When you specified that the numbering should appear at the top of the page, Word automatically created a header for the document. To view the page numbers, you switched to Page Layout view since headers and footers are not visible in Normal view. In the next exercise, you learn how to edit and format the header in Page Layout view.

Perform the following steps to create a header and a footer.

1. Make sure that the ETHICS document is open in the document area.

2. To edit the header and footer for the ETHICS document:
   CHOOSE: View, Header and Footer
   Upon selecting this command, Word switches you to Page Layout view, displays the Header and Footer toolbar, creates an editable text area for the header and footer, and dims the document's body text. Your screen should now look similar to Figure 4.14. Figure 4.15 identifies the buttons in the Header and Footer toolbar.

3. The page number, inserted in the last section, appears at the far right-hand side of the first line in the header area. Your insertion point should appear flashing at the left edge. To enter a title for the document:
   TYPE: `Ethics and Technology`

4. To format this new title, you must first highlight the text:
   SELECT: Ethics and Technology
   SELECT: Arial from the Fonts drop-down list (Times Roman)
   SELECT: 14 point from the Font Size drop-down list (10)
   CLICK: Bold button (**B**)

5. Similar to the previous step, you format the page number by first selecting the text. However, Word places the page number in a special box called a frame. To select text inside a frame, you must position the I-beam pointer carefully and drag across the text. Do not drag the mouse pointer when it appears as a pointer with a cross-shaped, four-headed arrow—this moves the entire frame.
   Now, do the following:
   DRAG: I-beam mouse pointer across the page number

The page number should appear highlighted and surrounded by a shaded box (see below):

FIGURE 4.14 VIEWING A DOCUMENT'S HEADER AND FOOTER IN PAGE LAYOUT VIEW

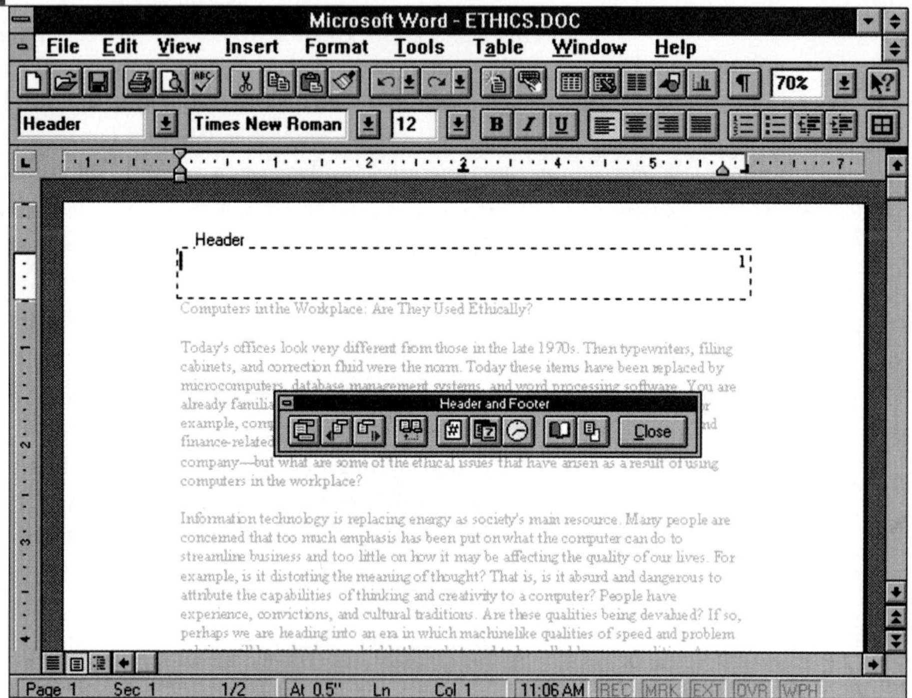

FIGURE 4.15 HEADER AND FOOTER TOOLBAR

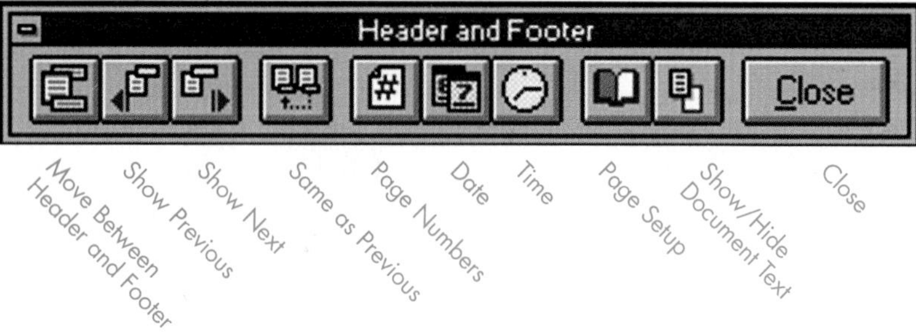

6. To format the page number with the same options as the title:
   SELECT: Arial from the Fonts drop-down list (Times Roman)
   SELECT: 14 point from the Font Size drop-down list (10)
   CLICK: Bold button (B)

7. Congratulations, you've finished formatting the header! Now, we'll turn our attention to the document footer. To view the footer:
   CLICK: Switch Between Header and Footer button () on the Header and Footer toolbar

8. To right-align the footer information:
   PRESS: TAB twice
   Notice that Word automatically sets a center-aligned tab and a right-aligned tab for headers and footers. The insertion point should appear flashing against the right edge.

9. TYPE: `Printed on`
   PRESS: Space Bar

10. To place the date and time in the footer and have them automatically updated when you print the document:
    CLICK: Date button () on the Header and Footer toolbar
    PRESS: Space Bar
    TYPE: `at`
    PRESS: Space Bar
    CLICK: Time button () on the Header and Footer toolbar

11. To format the footer to remain somewhat consistent with the header:
    SELECT: *the entire footer text*
    SELECT: Arial from the Fonts drop-down list (Times Roman)
    SELECT: 10 point from the Font Size drop down list (10)
    CLICK: Bold button (B)
    Your screen should appear similar to Figure 4.16 (with a different date and time in the footer, of course.)

12. To finish editing the header and footer and return to your document:
    CLICK: Close button (Close) on the Header and Footer toolbar
    You are returned to the view you were using prior to choosing the View, Header and Footer command.

    (*Tip*: You can double-click the dimmed body text in the Page Layout view to return to editing the document. To switch back to the header and footer in Page Layout view, you double-click its dimmed text.)

FIGURE 4.16 COMPLETED HEADER AND FOOTER FOR THE ETHICS DOCUMENT

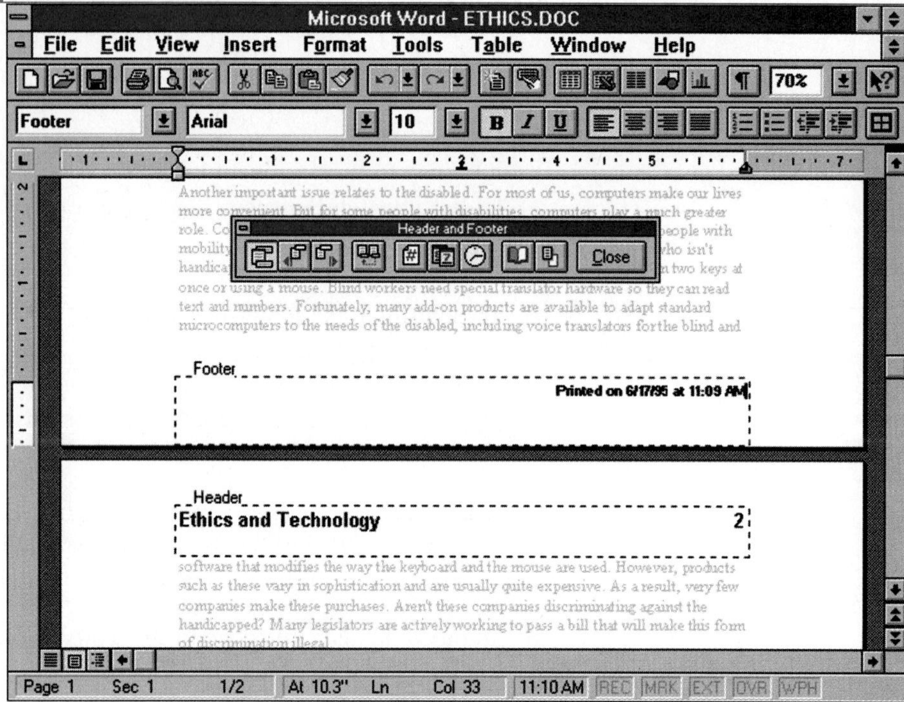

13. Ensure that you are viewing the document in Normal view:
    CLICK: Normal button (▤)

14. Save the document as HEADER to the Advantage Diskette.

QUICK REFERENCE
Creating a Header or Footer

1. **CHOOSE: View, Header and Footer**
2. **Edit and format the header and footer using the regular formatting commands and the buttons on the Header and Footer toolbar.**
3. **CLICK: Close button (Close)**

IN ADDITION WORKING WITH TEMPLATES

If your proposals, for example, all use the same margin settings, headers and footers, character formatting commands, and perhaps display the company logo on the top of the page, consider creating a template that stores all the elements that you typically include in a document proposal.

A *template* is a file that contains all the parts and features of a particular type of document. A template can contain text, headers, footers, graphics, page and paper layouts, and more.

To learn more about templates, choose Help, Search from the Menu bar. Then type "templates, creating" and click the Show Topics button.

PRINTING A DOCUMENT

This section introduces the printing commands for Word, including setting print options and previewing the output. Windows includes a program called the **Print Manager** to assist all applications in sharing and managing printer resources. Documents sent to the printer are actually intercepted by the Print Manager and placed in a **queue** for **batch processing.** A queue is a temporary holding area for documents that are waiting to print. This feature, coupled with Word's new background printing option, allows you to immediately return to your document after sending it to the printer. In other words, there is no waiting for the printer to complete its work before you can begin your own work.

PREVIEWING THE DOCUMENT

A primary benefit of working with today's sophisticated word processing programs, including Word, is the ability to preview documents in a full-page display before sending them to the printer. To access Word's Print Preview mode, you choose File, Print Preview from the menu or click the Print Preview button ( ) on the Standard toolbar. Some of the features of Print Preview include:

- View one page or multiple pages at the same time.
- Select Zoom mode to view your document or Edit mode to modify and format your document without leaving Print Preview.
- Make last-minute changes to margin settings by dragging the margin boundaries on the Ruler, similar to Page Layout view.

Perform the following steps.

1. Make sure that the HEADER document is open in the document area.

2. CLICK: Print Preview button ( )
   Upon selecting this command, Word switches you to Print Preview mode. Your screen should now look similar to Figure 4.17. Figure 4.18 identifies the buttons on the Print Preview toolbar.

3. To view both pages of this document side-by-side:
   CLICK: Multiple Pages button ( ) and hold down the mouse button
   DRAG: mouse pointer down to highlight the boxes that appear
   SELECT: 1 × 2 page display

4. To view a single page only:
   CLICK: One Page button ( )

FIGURE 4.17 PREVIEWING THE HEADER DOCUMENT

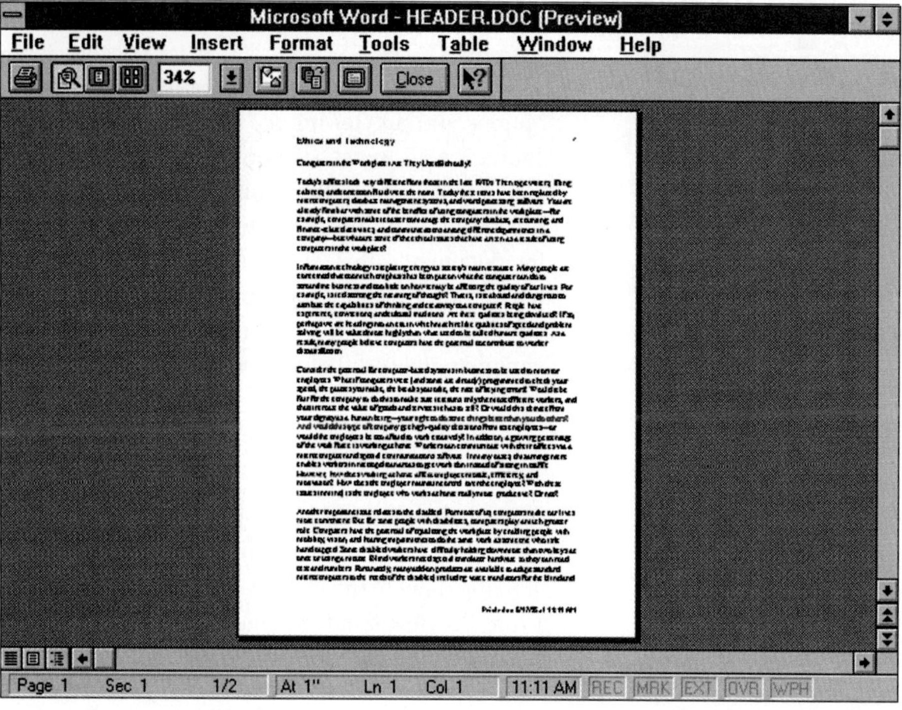

FIGURE 4.18 PRINT PREVIEW TOOLBAR

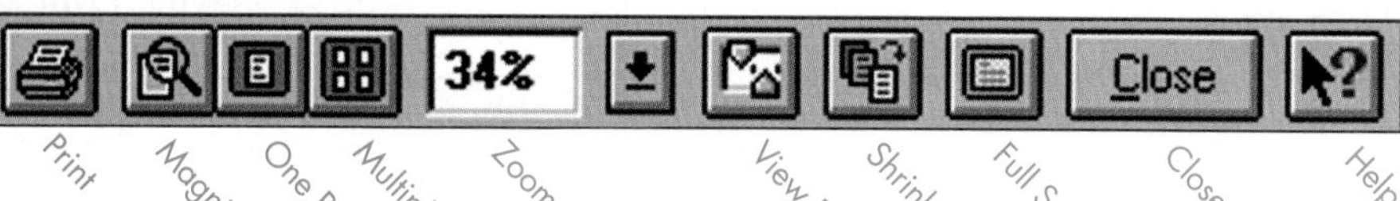

5. To zoom in on the document, move the mouse pointer over the first paragraph until it changes to a magnifying glass with a plus sign.

6. CLICK: left mouse button once to zoom the view to 100%
   Notice that the plus sign in the magnifying glass mouse pointer changes to a minus sign.

7. To switch Print Preview from Zoom mode to Edit mode:
   CLICK: Magnifier button ( )

8. Move the mouse pointer over the document. Notice that the mouse pointer becomes an I-beam, as opposed to a magnifying glass.

9. To format the title text:
   SELECT: Computers in the Workplace: Are They Used Ethically?

10. To display the shortcut menu for formatting text:
    RIGHT-CLICK: *the selected text*
    CHOOSE: Font

11. In the Font dialog box:
    SELECT: 14 point from the Size list box
    SELECT: Bold from the Font Style list box
    PRESS: ENTER or CLICK: OK

12. To change back to Zoom mode:
    CLICK: Magnifier button ( )

13. To zoom out, position the magnifying glass mouse pointer over the document and click the left mouse button once.

14. To exit Print Preview:
    CLICK: Close button (Close)

15. Save the HEADER document to the Advantage Diskette, replacing the original version.

QUICK REFERENCE
Previewing a Document

1. **CLICK: Print Preview button ( )**
2. **Use Zoom mode to view the document and Edit mode to change margin settings, edit text, and format your document.**
3. **CLICK: Close button (Close) to return to the document**

PRINTING THE DOCUMENT

If you are satisfied with your document after viewing it in Page Layout view and Print Preview, it's time to send it to the printer. The quickest and easiest method for printing a single copy of every page in a document is to click the Print button ( ) on the Standard toolbar. If you want to print specific pages only, or if you want multiple copies of a document, you must choose the File, Print command and make your selections in the Print dialog box (shown in Figure 4.19.)

Perform the following steps to print a document.

1. To print the HEADER document:
   CLICK: Print button ( )
   You will see a small printer icon appear in the Status bar as the document is sent to the printer. If you wanted to cancel the print job (which you don't in this exercise), you could double-click this printer icon or press ESC.

2. Close all the documents in the document area.

FIGURE 4.19 PRINT DIALOG BOX

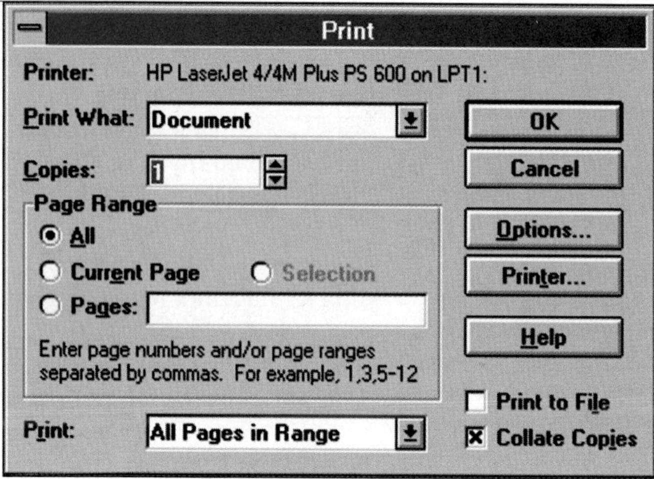

QUICK REFERENCE
Printing a Document

1. **CLICK: Print button ( )**
2. **Select the number of copies to print, and specify whether to print certain pages or the entire document.**
3. **PRESS: ENTER or CLICK: OK**

FILE MANAGEMENT COMMANDS

While creating, formatting, and printing documents are definitely major topics in this guide, the importance of file management should not be understated. Without file management commands, you could not back up your work, free up disk space for more files, or organize your documents into a logical filing system. Specifically, file management refers to copying, deleting, renaming, and sorting documents that reside on your hard disk and floppy diskettes.

CREATING A DOCUMENT INVENTORY

Word's file management utilities are accessed through the File, Find File command. While primarily a document retrieval tool, the Find File utility can also open, print, copy, delete, and sort documents. In addition to listing file names, the Find File dialog box eases the task of searching for files by displaying document previews and statistical summary information. This section provides an example of how you can use the File, Find File command to locate documents.

Perform the following steps to find and open files.

1. Ensure that there are no open documents in the document area.

2. CHOOSE: File, Find File
   If this is the first time that you've chosen the Find File command, the Search dialog box shown in Figure 4.20 appears.

3. If the Find File dialog box appears on your screen (see Figure 4.21), do the following to display the Search dialog box:
   SELECT: Search command button
   Before you proceed to the next step, make sure that the Search dialog box is displayed on your screen.

FIGURE 4.20 FIND FILE'S SEARCH DIALOG BOX

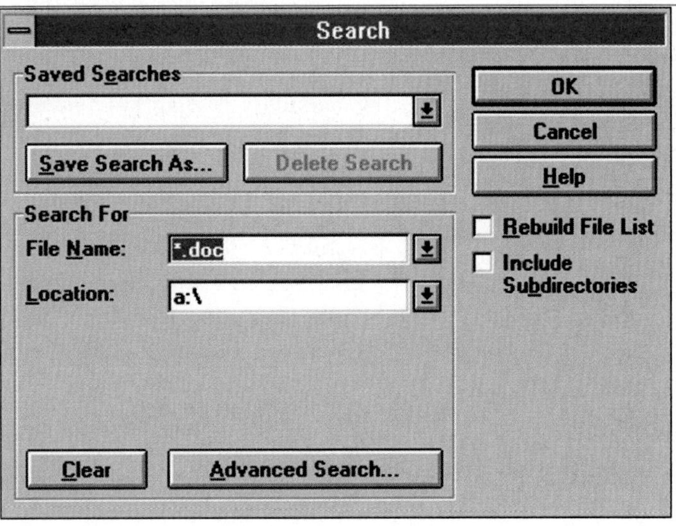

4. To clear the Search dialog box of the previous search criteria:
   SELECT: Clear command button
   SELECT: Rebuild File List check box

5. To display the types of files that you can search for using this utility:
   CLICK: down arrow adjacent to the File Name text box
   From this drop-down list, you can limit your search to Word Documents (*.doc), Document Templates (*.dot), Windows Bitmaps (*.bmp), Windows Metafiles (*.wmf), or perform a broad search for All Files (*.*). You can also type in your own file specification if you want to search for specific files not included in the drop-down list.

6. SELECT: Word Documents (*.doc) in the File Name drop-down list

7. To have Word search the Advantage Diskette only:
   CLICK: down arrow adjacent to the Location text box
   SELECT: a:

8. To execute the search:
   PRESS: ENTER or CLICK: OK
   After several seconds, the Find File dialog box appears with a list of all Word documents found on the Advantage Diskette.

9. There are three views available in the Find File dialog box:

   - Preview — Displays a preview of the highlighted file in the list.
   - File Info — Displays standard file information, including the document's title, size, author's name, and the date it was last saved.
   - Summary — Displays a summary screen for each file, containing document statistics, comments, and other useful information.

   To display a preview of a document file:
   SELECT: AUTOTEXT.DOC in the list box
   CLICK: down arrow adjacent to the View text box
   SELECT: Preview from the drop-down list
   Your screen should now appear similar to Figure 4.21.

10. SELECT: File Info view

11. To sort the list by file size, you use the Commands pop-up menu:
    SELECT: Commands pop-up menu
    CHOOSE: Sorting
    The following dialog box appears:

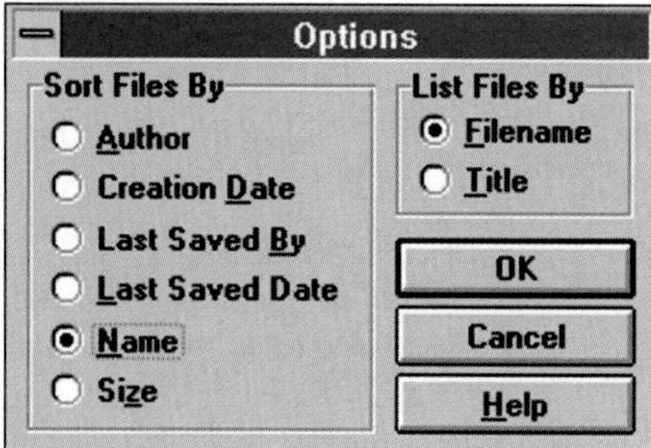

12. SELECT: Size option button in the Sort Files By group
    PRESS: ENTER or CLICK: OK
    The list is sorted in ascending order by file size.

13. After you've settled on a view and sort order for browsing the list of files, you can open a file by double-clicking its file name or by highlighting the file and selecting the Open command button. Let's open the MEDIA document:
    DOUBLE-CLICK: MEDIA.DOC in the list box
    The Find File dialog box disappears and the MEDIA document is opened in the document area.

14. Close the document.

FIGURE 4.21 FIND FILE'S DIALOG BOX

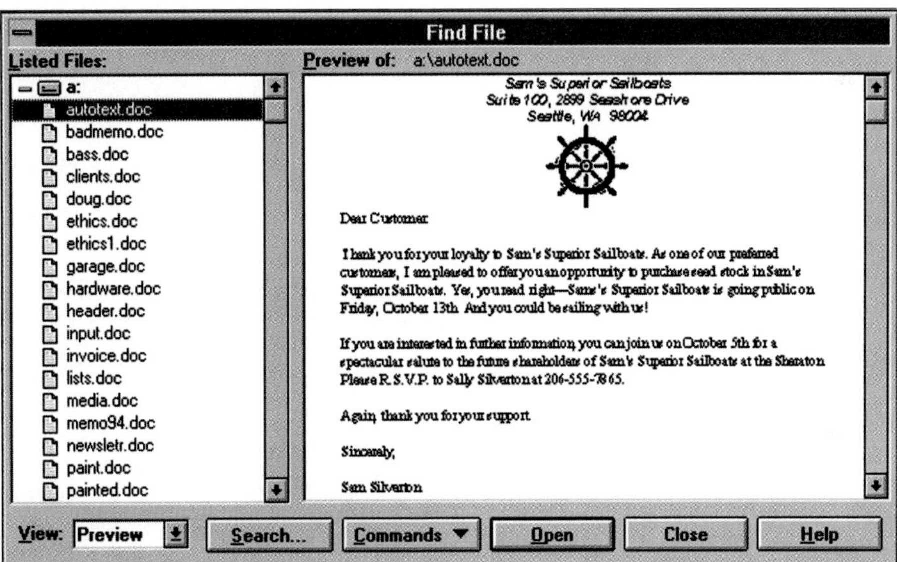

> **QUICK REFERENCE**
> Finding and Opening Files
>
> 1. **CHOOSE: File, Find File**
> 2. **Specify search options using the Search dialog box.**
> 3. **Specify a sort order and view for displaying the files.**
> 4. **Open a file by double-clicking its file name.**

COPYING AND DELETING FILES

Besides displaying and opening files, the Find File utility provides two commands for copying and deleting files. These file management tasks are among the most common performed in word processing. The Copy command enables you to copy a file to a new drive or directory. The Delete command removes the file from the current drive or directory.

Another useful feature of the Find File utility is the ability to select more than one file at a time for copying, deleting, and printing documents. There are two methods for selecting a group of documents from the list box. First, to select a group of contiguous files (all files are next to each other in the list box), you select the first file, hold down the SHIFT key, and then click the last file. All the documents between the first and last files are automatically highlighted. Second, to select a group of noncontiguous files, you select the first file and then hold down the CTRL key while clicking on each additional file. Once the files are highlighted, you issue a file management command from the Commands pop-up menu.

Perform the following steps to copy and delete a file.

1. CHOOSE: File, Find File

2. To place a copy of the ETHICS document on the hard disk:
   SELECT: ETHICS.DOC in the list box
   SELECT: Commands pop-up menu
   CHOOSE: Copy
   The Copy dialog box appears similar, but not identical, to the graphic presented below.

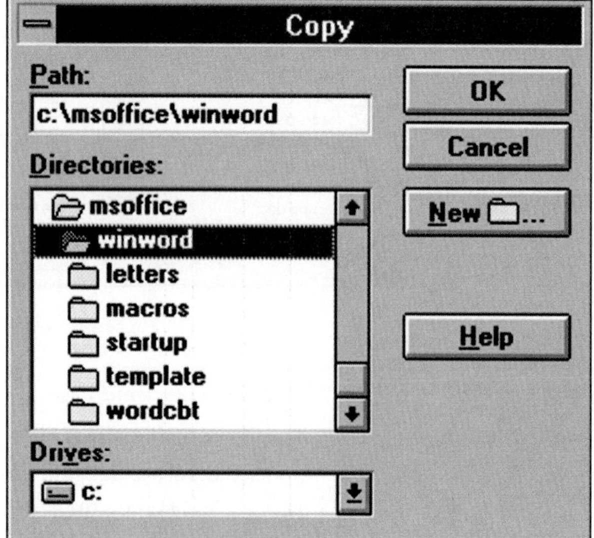

3. You will copy the ETHICS file to the root directory of the hard disk and then delete it later. To specify the root directory:
   TYPE: **c:**
   PRESS: ENTER or CLICK: OK
   A dialog box appears briefly informing you that the file is being copied. Although this example teaches you how to copy files from drive A: to drive C:, you are more likely to copy files from your hard disk to a diskette in order to back up your documents.

4. Let's change the search path to view the documents on drive C:.
   SELECT: Search command button
   The Search dialog box appears.

5. To limit the search to Word documents in the root directory:
   SELECT: Word Documents (*.doc) in the File Name text box
   SELECT: c: in the Location text box
   PRESS: ENTER or CLICK: OK
   Once it has completed the search, you will see the ETHICS document displayed in the Find File dialog box.

6. To delete the ETHICS.DOC file from drive C:, do the following:
   SELECT: ETHICS.DOC in the list box
   SELECT: Commands pop-up menu
   CHOOSE: Delete
   SELECT: Yes when asked to confirm the deletion (see below)

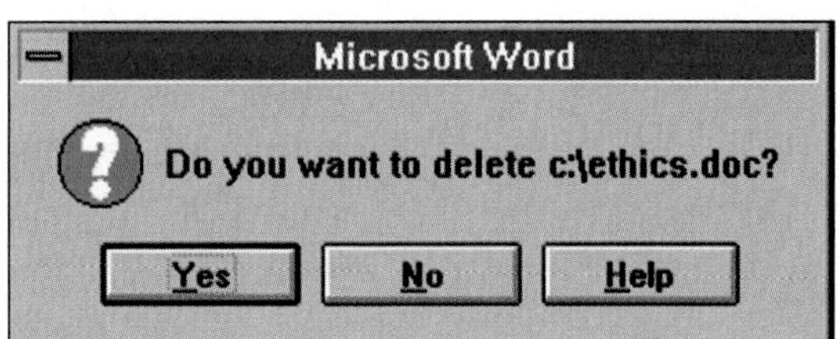

7. Before proceeding, change the search path back to the Advantage Diskette:
   SELECT: Search command button
   SELECT: a: in the Location text box
   PRESS: ENTER or CLICK: OK

QUICK REFERENCE
Copying and Deleting Files

1. **CHOOSE: File, Find File**
2. **Copy or delete a file by highlighting it, selecting the Commands pop-up menu, and then choosing the appropriate command.**

PRINTING FILES

Word allows you to print one document or multiple documents directly from the Find File utility. As in the process for copying and deleting files, you highlight the desired file or files, select the Commands pop-up menu, and then choose the Print command. When the Print dialog box appears, you specify the number of copies you want printed and then press ENTER or click OK.

Perform the following steps.

1. To print both the ETHICS and HARDWARE documents using the Find File utility, first select the files from the list box:
   SELECT: ETHICS.DOC in the list box

2. Position the mouse pointer over the HARDWARE document.

3. PRESS: CTRL and hold it down
   CLICK: left mouse button once
   Both files should now be highlighted.

4. Release the CTRL key.

5. SELECT: Commands pop-up menu
   CHOOSE: Print
   The Print dialog box appears.

6. PRESS: ENTER or CLICK: OK
   Both documents are sent to the printer and you are returned to the document screen.

7. Exit Word.

QUICK REFERENCE
Printing Documents

1. **CHOOSE: File, Find File**
2. **Print a file by highlighting it, selecting the Commands pop-up menu, and then choosing the Print command.**

SUMMARY

This session introduced the document formatting commands for preparing a document to send to the printer. The majority of page layout options are selected from the Page Setup dialog box, including margins, paper size, print orientation, and paper source. Other formatting topics covered this session included preventing widows and orphans, inserting page numbers, and creating headers and footers. Because the WYSIWYG capabilities of Word can sometimes slow the text entry process, Word provides several alternative views for a document. Whereas the Normal view is used for the majority of your work, you'll find that the Page Layout and Outline views provide additional features for finalizing and managing documents.

The last half of the session examined printing options and file management commands. Topics included using the Zoom and Edit modes in Word's Print Preview and using the Find File utility to find, copy, delete, and print documents. Table 4.2 provides a list of the commands and procedures covered in this session.

TABLE 4.2

Command Summary

Task Description	*Menu Command*	*Toolbar Button*	*Keyboard Shortcut*
Display text with character and paragraph formatting only	View, Normal		
Display a document as a collapsible outline	View, Outline		
Display text with all formatting (headers, footers, and columns)	View, Page Layout		
Access the Zoom dialog box	View, Zoom	120%	
Display or hide Word's toolbars	View, Toolbars		
Display or hide the Ruler line	View, Ruler		
Set page layout options	File, Page Setup		
Set paragraph pagination options (widows and orphans)	Format, Paragraph, and Text Flow tab		
Insert page numbers in the header or footer of a document	Insert, Page Numbers		

continues

TABLE 4.2 *concluded*

Command Summary

Task Description	Menu Command	Toolbar Button	Keyboard Shortcut
Change to Page Layout view for editing the header and footer	View, Header and Footer		
Display a document in Print Preview mode	File, Print Preview		
Send a document to the printer	File, Print		CTRL+p
Perform file management functions	File, Find File		

KEY TERMS

batch processing
The saving up of jobs, activities, or transactions in order to perform them together at a later time. The Print Manager uses a queue for batch processing documents sent to the printer.

footer
Descriptive text that appears at the bottom of each page in a document. The footer usually contains page numbers or copyright information.

gutter
The gutter is where pages are joined together in a bound document.

header
Descriptive text that appears at the top of each page in a document. The header usually contains titles or section headings.

landscape orientation
Describes how a page is printed. Letter-size paper with a landscape orientation measures 11-inches wide by 8.5-inches high. Legal-size paper with a landscape orientation measures 14-inches wide by 8.5-inches high.

orphan
In printing, a single sentence that appears at the bottom of a page, separated from the rest of its paragraph on the next page.

portrait orientation

Describes how a page is printed. Letter-size paper with a portrait orientation measures 8.5-inches wide by 11-inches high. Legal-size paper with a portrait orientation measures 8.5-inches wide by 14-inches high.

Print Manager

A Windows program that intercepts print instructions from applications and processes the instructions based on application priority and printer selection. The Print Manager uses a queue to line up documents waiting for printer time.

queue

In printing, a program that uses memory and the disk to line up and prioritize documents waiting for printer time.

widow

In printing, a single sentence that appears at the top of a page, separated from the rest of its paragraph on the previous page.

EXERCISES

SHORT ANSWER

1. Name three different views you can access by clicking buttons on the horizontal scroll bar.
2. When would you use the Draft Font?
3. How do you return to Word's application window when you are in Full Screen mode?
4. Name the four tabs in the Page Setup dialog box.
5. How do you prevent widows and orphans in a document?
6. What are two methods for inserting page numbers?
7. What are two methods for changing the margins in a document?
8. How do you preview a document before sending it to the printer?
9. What are the two modes available in Print Preview?
10. Name two methods for selecting multiple files in the Find File dialog box.

HANDS-ON

(*Note:* In the following exercises, save your documents onto and retrieve files from the Advantage Diskette.)

1. This exercise uses some character and paragraph formatting commands, as well as document formatting commands. Open SOFTWARE from the Advantage Diskette and then perform the following steps:

    a. Include a header that displays the current date in the flush-right position.

    b. Protect against widows and orphans.

    c. Left-justify the entire document.

    d. Include your name and the current page number in a footer.

    e. Spell-check the document.

    f. Save the file as SOFTWARE onto the Advantage Diskette.

    g. Print SOFTWARE.

    h. Close the document.

2. The following exercise retrieves an existing file from the Advantage Diskette and modifies its page layout settings.

    a. Retrieve DOUG.DOC from the Advantage Diskette.

    b. Change to a Page Layout view.

    c. Using the Zoom Control box, shrink the display until you can see the entire page on the screen.

    d. Access the Page Setup dialog box by double-clicking the Ruler.

    e. Change the top, bottom, left, and right margins to 1.5 inches.

    f. Using the mouse, change all the margins to 1.25 inches by dragging the margin boundaries.

g. Add a footer to the letter that centers the following phrase: "From the Desk of *your name*." Substitute your own name for the italicized words.

h. Format the footer with an Arial typeface and a 10 point font size.

i. Close the footer area and return to the Normal view.

j. View the document using Print Preview.

k. Using the mouse in Print Preview, change the top and bottom margins to 1 inch.

l. Send the document to the printer from the Print Preview screen.

m. Save the document as DOUGREF onto the Advantage Diskette.

n. Close the document.

3. This exercise creates a document with headers and footers.

a. Open a new document.

b. Center the title "Budget Forecast - 1995" at the top of the page.

c. Center the subtitle "ABC Realty Inc." on the next line immediately below the title.

d. Enhance the title with an Arial, 18 point font and make it bold.

e. Enhance the subtitle with an Arial, 14 point font and make it bold and italic.

f. Enter four blank lines and left-justify the new paragraph.

g. Make sure that the font is Times New Roman, 12 point, before proceeding.

h. Type the text appearing in Figure 4.22.

FIGURE 4.22 BUDGET95 DOCUMENT

```
Introduction

Now that we are in the first quarter of 1995, it
is time we stopped to review our direction for
the remainder of the year. We had a tough year in
1994, but it seems that the economy is well on
its way to recovery. We are anticipating a good
year for all the staff.

This report is confidential and should not be
circulated outside of this office. It is intended
to be a planning document for the Sales Team in
1995. Any questions or suggestions can be directed
to your immediate supervisor.
```

i. Return to the top of the document.

j. Create a header and footer for the document. Center-align the text "ABC Realty Inc." in the header. Left-align the text "Prepared by *your name*" in the footer, along with a right-aligned page number. Substitute your name for the italicized text in the footer.

k. View the document using Print Preview.

l. Print the document.

m. Save the document as BUDGET95 onto the Advantage Diskette. Keep the document open for use in the next exercise.

4. This exercise practices using some commands from previous sessions as well as document formatting commands.

a. Ensure that BUDGET95.DOC appears in the document area.

b. Change to a Normal view.

c. Set the following page dimensions:

Paper Size:	Letter
Paper Orientation:	Portrait
Top Margin:	1 inch
Bottom Margin:	1 inch
Left Margin:	1 inch
Right Margin:	1 inch

d. Enter the information in Figure 4.23. (*Hint:* Use tabs.)

FIGURE 4.23 BUDGET95 DOCUMENT

ABC REALTY INC.

	1995
Revenue	
Commercial Properties	$125,500,000
Residential Properties	35,000,000
Leased Properties	875,000
Total Revenue	**$161,375,000**
Expenses	
Insurance	$50,000
Salaries	750,000
Commissions	15,500,000
Office Supplies	25,000
Office Equipment	20,000
Utilities	15,000
Leased Automobiles	50,000
Travel	250,000
Advertising & Promotion	25,000,000
Total Expenses	**41,660,000**
Net Income	**$119,715,000**

e. Preview the document.

f. Print the document.

g. Save the document to the Advantage Diskette, replacing the original version.

h. Close the document.

CASE PROBLEMS

GINO'S PIZZA KITCHEN

(*Note*: In the following case problems, assume the role of the primary characters and perform the same steps that they identify. You may want to re-read the session opening.)

1. After a relaxing Christmas holiday, Larry arrives at the office to find the following note on his desk: *Larry, I trust you had a wonderful time on Nantucket Island. Sorry to be a pain, but I'd like to see the monthly restaurant report ASAP. This time, please include the current page number and date at the bottom of each page. Also, could you leave some room on the left side of each page so that I have a place to take notes? Thanks. Gino.*

With his favorite mug in tow, Larry heads directly for the coffee machine, planning his strategy along the way. When he returns to his desk, Larry turns on the computer, launches Word, and then locates the four manager's reports that are stored on the Advantage Diskette. These files are named R-NORTH, R-SOUTH, R-EAST, and R-WEST. He loads the four documents into separate windows. He then moves the cursor to the end of the R-NORTH document. After switching to the R-SOUTH document, Larry copies all the text in this document to the Clipboard. He then switches back to the R-NORTH document, pastes the text into the document, and then performs this same procedure for the R-EAST and R-WEST documents. When finished, the R-NORTH window contains the four summary reports. He saves this document as DECEMBER onto the Advantage Diskette.

Now that he has a single document to work with, he begins by inserting a formatted title on the first page of the report that reads:

Gino's Pizza Kitchen
Monthly Summary: December

Using character formatting commands, Larry makes the text in the long document easier to read. He selects a 1.5-inch gutter so that Gino has a place to take notes and then creates a footer displaying the current date and page number. To ensure that the document is easy to read when printed, Larry uses a command to make sure that widows and orphans are suppressed. He then saves the document back to the Advantage Diskette, prints the document, and places a copy on Gino's desk.

2. Now that Larry has created the DECEMBER document (in the last exercise), he no longer needs the individual R-NORTH, R-SOUTH, R-EAST, and R-WEST restaurant reports. Having just learned how to manage the files on his disk, he deletes them from the Advantage Diskette.

   Larry wants additional practice working with headers, footers, and other document formatting commands. He decides to make a copy of the DECEMBER document. He names the copy LARRY, which he will easily recognize as a practice file.

3. Before giving Gino the yearly summary report, Larry decides to format the document to improve its readability. It currently uses only a single font and doesn't incorporate headers, footers, or page numbers. The report is stored on the Advantage Diskette as R-1995. Larry also decides to include a title page for the report. When finished, he saves the document as R1-1995 and then prints it for Gino's review.

Microsoft Word 6.0

Increasing Your Productivity

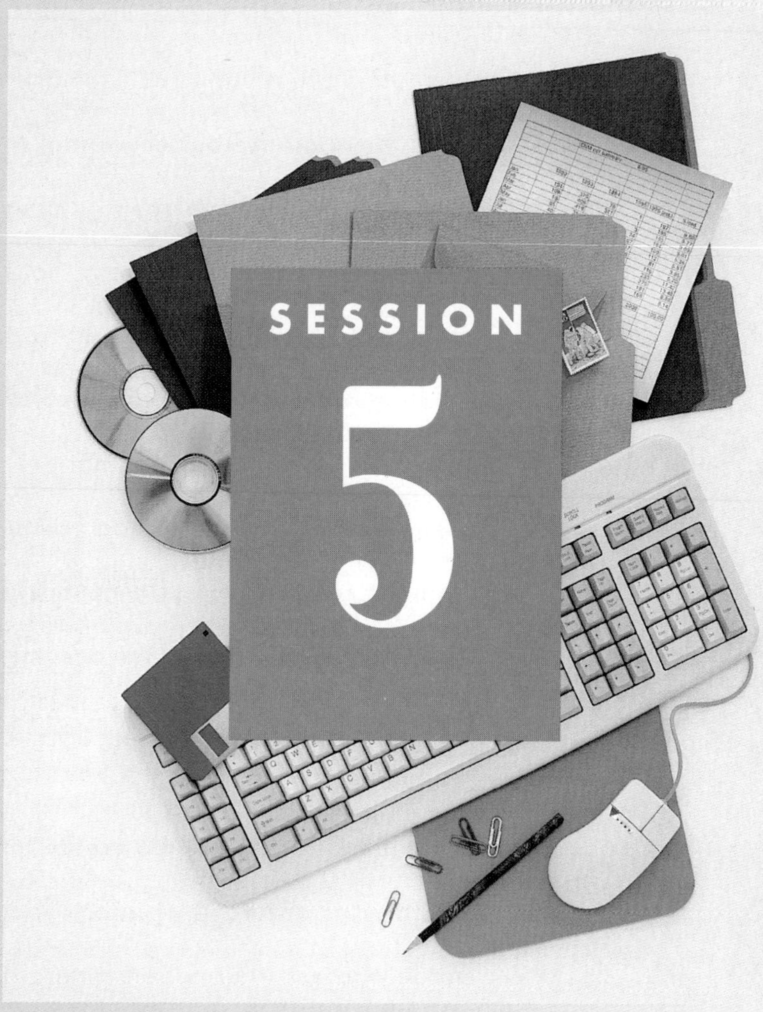

SESSION OUTLINE

INTRODUCTION

Computers are getting really smart! With the right tools, they balance our checkbooks, budget how much we're allowed to spend dining out per month, answer our phones when we're not home, and send faxes in the middle of the night to get the best long-distance rates. But what can a software company do to make a word processor smarter? Microsoft's answer: add Wizards to lead you step-by-step through creating professional-looking letters, reports, résumés, and other documents. In this session, you'll meet some of Word's most popular Wizards.

You will also learn how to create tables for organizing columns and rows of information and how to merge address information from a list of respondents into a standard form letter. The session concludes with a discussion on how to customize Word to best fit your working environment.

CASE STUDY THE UNION TENNIS CLUB

Jerry Garcia is the manager of the beautiful Union Tennis Club in Fort Lauderdale, Florida. He has worked at the club for three years and runs a very tight operation. The club's Board of Directors are pleased with his performance and he has a good relationship with most of his employees. Also, the ones who pay the bills, the members, find him approachable, capable, responsive, and friendly.

Jerry uses a computer to keep track of the club's finances and membership list. Although primarily self-taught on the computer, Jerry has received some help from a few computer-literate members. Jerry is now preparing to put the name of each member with an overdue account into a Microsoft Word document. He remembers his frustrations when performing this task the last time. First, he had trouble aligning the data for each member. And second, he was unable to use Word to send a reminder letter to each person in the table. Instead, he grudgingly used the standard "Overdue Account" form on which he wrote the name of the offending member. Jerry knows there's a better way—he just doesn't know where to begin.

In this session, you and Jerry will learn how to create tables for lining up information, merge data with a standard form letter, and customize Word to meet your particular needs.

USING WIZARDS TO CREATE DOCUMENTS

Wizards help you to do your work quicker and more efficiently. Whether you need to write a term paper or create an agenda for tomorrow's meeting, a **wizard** gets you started and headed in the right direction. It's not necessary to understand how a wizard works; but it is important to know that wizards are available and easily accessible.

You can select from nine wizards to create specialized documents, as summarized in Table 5.1. Because the documents created by wizards are based on standard document templates, you can easily edit and format them once they've been created. With a little more education and experience, you can also learn how to customize your own templates.

TABLE 5.1 Summary of Available Wizards

Name	*Description*
Agenda	Creates a meeting agenda; formatting options include Boxes, Modern, and Standard
Award	Creates an award certificate; formatting options include Formal, Modern, Decorative, and Jazzy
Calendar	Creates calendar pages; formatting options include Boxes and borders, Banner, and Jazzy
Fax	Creates a fax cover sheet; formatting options include Contemporary, Modern, and Jazzy
Letter	Creates a personal or business letter format, or provides a prewritten letter with "boilerplate" text
Memo	Creates a standard memo with an optional distribution list
Newslttr	Creates a multiple-text column newsletter; formatting options include Classic and Modern
Pleading	Creates a legal pleading paper, complete with line numbers
Résumé	Creates an entry-level, chronological, functional, or professional résumé

To access a wizard, you choose the File, New command and make a selection from the New dialog box. The selected wizard will then lead you through a series of pages in a dialog box, asking you questions about how you want the document formatted. On the last page, you click Finish and watch as the wizard creates the document right before your eyes.

The best way to learn about wizards is to practice selecting the different options. Although we cannot show you every wizard's creation, we will lead you through one example. Perform the following steps.

1. Ensure that you've loaded Microsoft Word 6.0 and the Advantage Diskette is in the drive. Also, open documents should be displaying in the document area.

2. To create a new document using a wizard:
   CHOOSE: File, New
   The New dialog box appears, as shown in Figure 5.1.

FIGURE 5.1 NEW DIALOG BOX

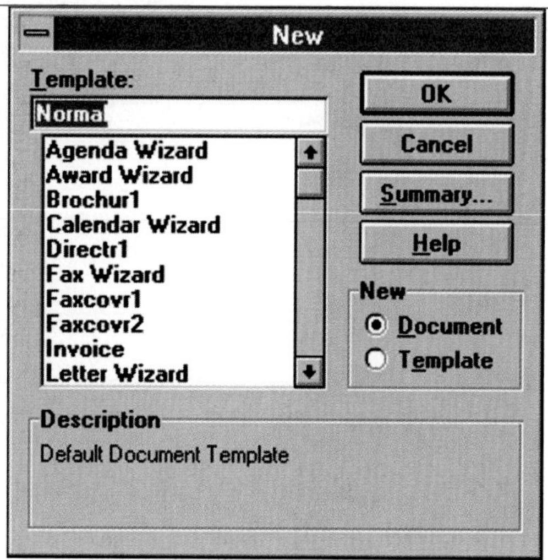

3. Let's start with a relatively simple wizard that is used quite frequently by business people:
   SELECT: "Fax Wizard" from the Template list box
   SELECT: Document option button in the New group
   PRESS: ENTER or CLICK: OK
   The Fax Wizard is launched and presents the first formatting question, as shown in Figure 5.2.

4. In response to the question regarding print orientation:
   SELECT: Portrait option button
   CLICK: Next >
   (*Note*: If you change your mind later, you can always review your selections.)

FIGURE 5.2 FAX WIZARD: INITIAL SCREEN

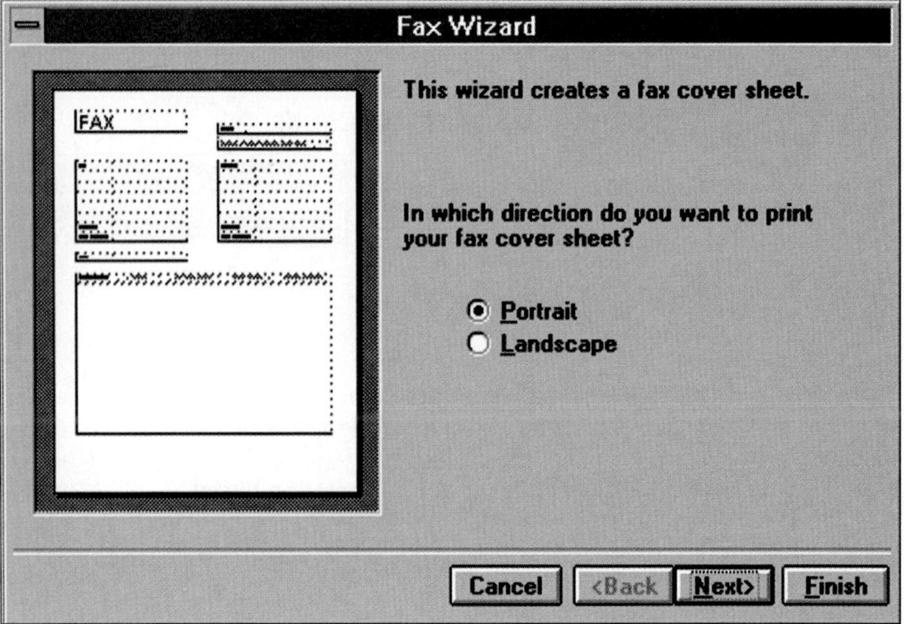

5. Now the Fax Wizard wants to know whether you prefer a Contemporary, Modern, or Jazzy format for your fax covers:
   SELECT: Jazzy option button (it's not really that jazzy!)
   CLICK: Next >
   The Fax Wizard proceeds to the next page of questions.

6. In this step, you specify the "From" address information to place on the fax cover. Complete your Fax Wizard's screen with your own name and address information. If you prefer, a fictitious entry is provided in Figure 5.3. (*Note*: You can press TAB or use the mouse to move the insertion point to the next text box.)

7. After you've finished entering your mailing address:
   CLICK: Next >

8. On this page of the Fax Wizard dialog box, you specify the phone and fax numbers to place in the "From" area:
   TYPE: `301-567-4960`
   PRESS: TAB
   TYPE: `301-567-5756`
   CLICK: Next >
   The dialog box shown in Figure 5.4 appears on your screen.

FIGURE 5.3 FAX WIZARD: ENTERING THE "FROM" INFORMATION

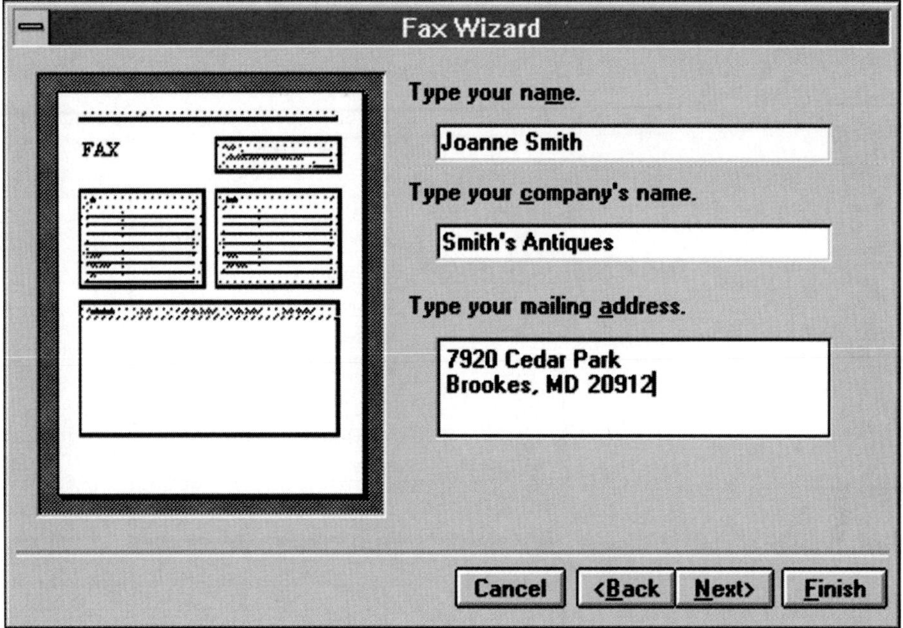

FIGURE 5.4 FAX WIZARD: FINAL SCREEN

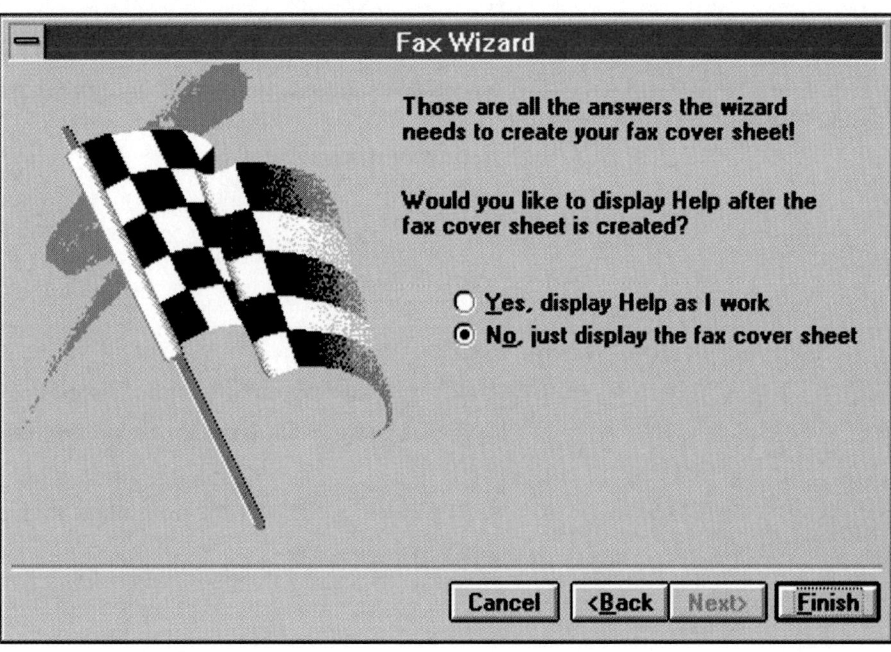

9. Congratulations, you've just created a fax cover sheet! Your last step is to tell the Fax Wizard to go ahead and create the new document:
   SELECT: No, just display the fax cover sheet
   CLICK: Finish

10. After several seconds (perhaps a minute on slower machines), the fax cover document appears in Page Layout view. Your next step is to complete the fax cover with the "To" information and add any additional comments. Using the mouse, or ⬆ and ⬇ keys, enter the "To" information as it appears in Figure 5.5.

FIGURE 5.5 PARTIAL VIEW OF THE COMPLETED FAX COVER SHEET

To:	
	Samantha Jones
	New Look Interiors
	2185 Spruce Park Lane
	Boston, MA 02116
Phone:	617-543-1090
Fax phone:	617-543-2437
CC:	

From:	
	Joanne Smith
Phone:	301-567-4960
Fax phone:	301-567-5756

REMARKS: ☒ Urgent ☐ For your review ☐ Reply ASAP ☒ Please comment

Hi Samantha,

This is a test of Microsoft Word's new Fax Wizard.

Please let me know what you think. Bye for now.

11. Save the document as MYFAX onto the Advantage Diskette.

12. To print the fax cover:
    CLICK: Print button (🖨)

13. Close the MYFAX document.

QUICK REFERENCE
Using Wizards

1. **CHOOSE: File, New**
2. **SELECT: a wizard from the Template list box**
3. **Make selections in the wizard's dialog box and then click [Next >] to proceed.**
4. **When you are satisfied with the options that you've chosen:**
   CLICK: [Finish]

TABLE FUNDAMENTALS

To organize information into a grid format, Word provides two options: tabs and tables. This session focuses on Word's table feature. You use a table to line up information into columns and rows. For example, a table works well for creating forms, phone lists, inventory lists, and even financial statements. Although Word provides a Table Wizard, you'll find that creating tables using the toolbar buttons and Word's AutoFormat feature is just as easy and more flexible.

CREATING A TABLE

To create a table in an existing document, you place the insertion point where you want the table to appear and then choose the Table, Insert Table command or click the Insert Table button (▦) on the Standard toolbar. Regardless of the method you choose to create the table, you need to then specify the desired number of columns and rows. Adding and deleting columns and rows is quite straightforward, so don't be concerned if you initially misjudge your requirements.

Perform the following steps to create an inventory tracking sheet using Word's table feature.

1. Open a new document using the New button (🗋). Ensure that you are viewing the document in Normal view.

2. TYPE: `Inventory List as of December 1994`
   PRESS: ENTER three times

3. To create a table that has 5 rows and 3 columns:
   CLICK: Insert Table button (▦) and hold it down
   DRAG: the mouse pointer downwards until a grid appears
   SELECT: 5 × 3 Table from the pop-up grid menu
   Your screen should appear similar to Figure 5.6.

FIGURE 5.6 CREATING A TABLE USING THE MOUSE

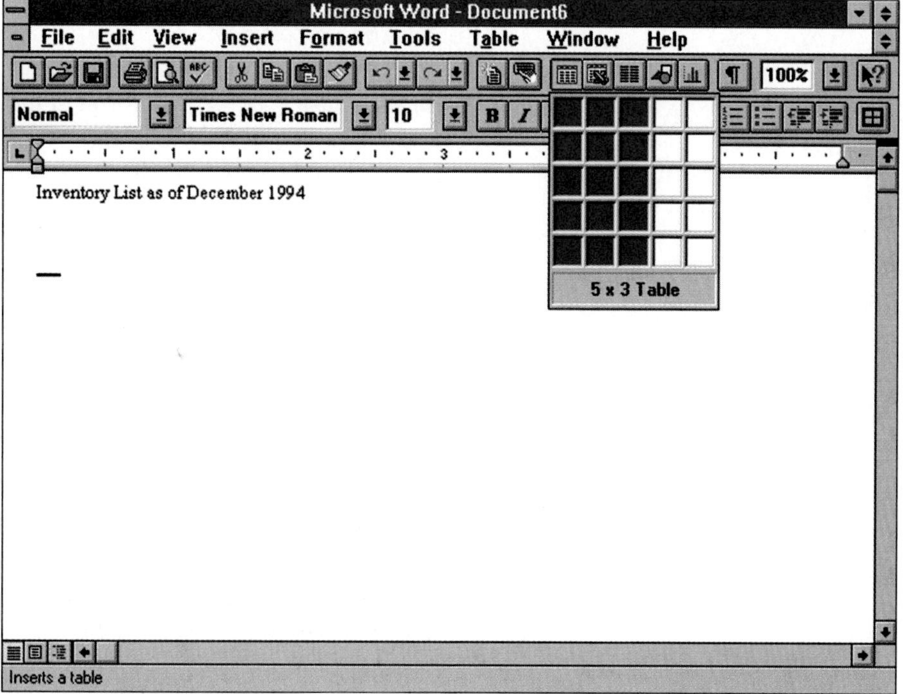

4. Release the mouse button. Word places a table with 5 rows and 3 columns at the insertion point. Notice the non-printing gridlines that appear in the document to help you line up information.

QUICK REFERENCE
Creating a Table Using the Mouse

1. **Position the insertion point where you want to insert the table.**
2. **CLICK: Insert Table button ( ) and hold it down**
3. **DRAG: to the desired grid pattern of rows and columns**
4. **Release the mouse button.**

ENTERING DATA INTO A TABLE

A table consists of rows and columns. You type information into a **cell**, which is the intersection of a row and column. To position the insertion point in a cell, you can use the I-beam mouse pointer, press the arrow keys (↑, ↓, ←, and →), or press TAB. If the insertion point is positioned in the rightmost cell of the last row, pressing TAB will automatically add another row to the bottom of the table. You format text within a cell like any other text in the document.

Perform the following steps to enter data.

1. With the insertion point in the first cell, let's enter some information into the table, starting with the headings:
   TYPE: `Inventory Code`
   PRESS: TAB
   TYPE: `Description`
   PRESS: TAB
   TYPE: `Quantity on Hand`
   PRESS: TAB
   Notice that the last TAB takes you to the next row in the table.

2. In the same manner as above, enter the following four items. You can press TAB to advance to the next cell, or you can try using the arrow keys and mouse pointer:

Inventory Code	*Description*	*Quantity on Hand*
VGA-cpd1304	VGA Monitor	12
CPU-intel486	486/33 MHz CPU	34
HDD-wd212	212MB Hard Disk	12
FDD-teac35	1.44MB Floppy Drive	118

3. With the insertion point in the last cell (118), press the TAB key to add another row to the table. (*Note*: If you already pressed TAB in the previous step and a new row appeared, move to step 4.)

4. Enter one more item into the table:
   TYPE: `VGA-nec4fg`
   PRESS: TAB
   TYPE: `VGA Monitor`
   PRESS: TAB
   TYPE: `15`
   PRESS: ↓
   Notice that the insertion point leaves the table with this last keystroke.

5. To add a blank line:
   PRESS: ENTER

6. To create a 2 × 2 table using the menu:
   CHOOSE: Table, Insert Table
   The dialog box in Figure 5.7 appears.

FIGURE 5.7 INSERT TABLE DIALOG BOX

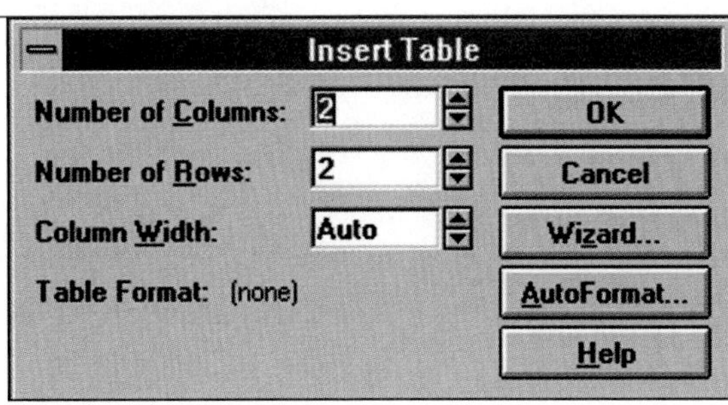

7. SELECT: 2 in the Number of Columns text box
   SELECT: 2 in the Number of Rows text box
   PRESS: ENTER or CLICK: OK
   A 2 × 2 table is placed at the insertion point.

8. Enter some information into this table:
   TYPE: `Inventory - Start of Period`
   PRESS: TAB
   TYPE: `$12,500`
   CLICK: Align Right button (≣) on the Standard toolbar
   PRESS: TAB
   TYPE: `Inventory - End of Period`
   PRESS: TAB
   TYPE: `$13,725`
   CLICK: Align Right button (≣) on the Standard toolbar

9. Save the document as INVENTRY onto the Advantage Diskette. Your screen should appear similar to Figure 5.8.

FIGURE 5.8 INVENTRY DOCUMENT

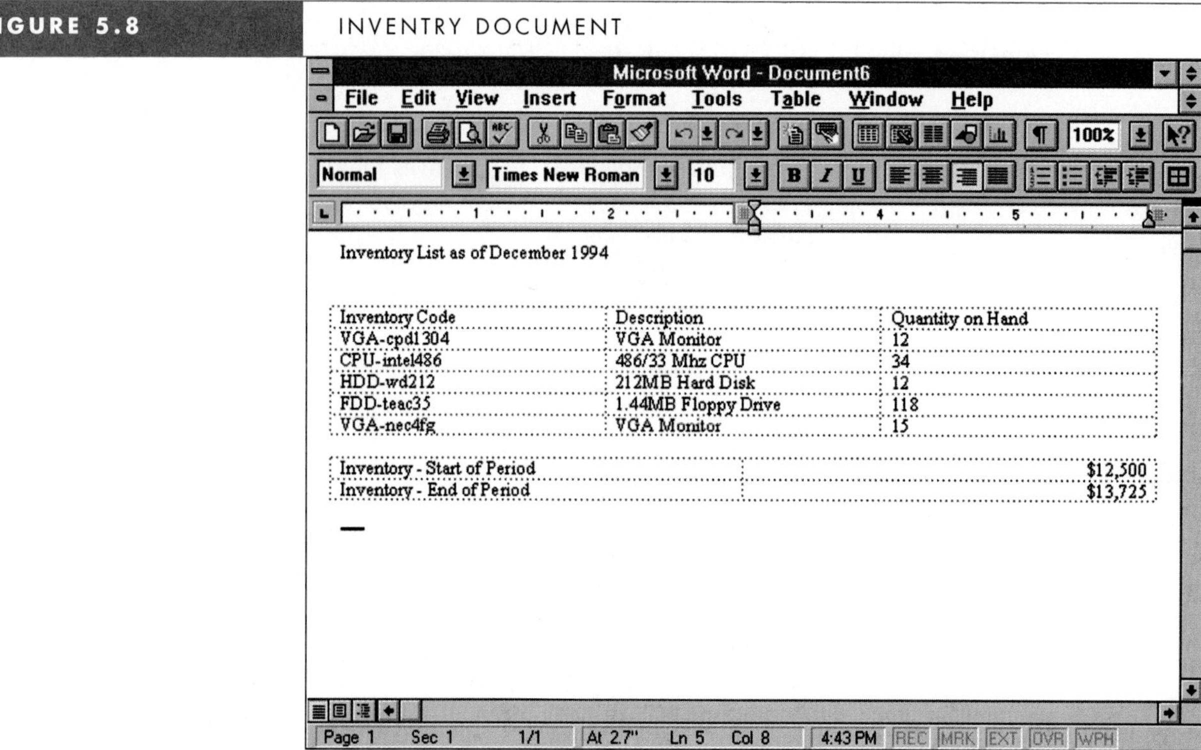

FORMATTING A TABLE

With Word's new Table AutoFormat command, you can format your tables in just a few keystrokes or mouse clicks. Using the menu, you must first place the insertion point in any cell of the table and then choose the Table, Table AutoFormat command. An easier method is to right-click the desired table and choose the Table AutoFormat command from its shortcut menu. Either way, the dialog box in Figure 5.9 appears, from which you can select one of over 30 professionally designed formats.

Perform the following steps to format a table.

1. Ensure that the insertion point appears in the 2 × 2 table. If not, move the insertion point into the table using the mouse or arrow keys.

2. To format the table:
   CHOOSE: Table, Table AutoFormat
   The dialog box in Figure 5.9 appears.

3. To view the formatting options:
   PRESS: ⬇ repeatedly, pausing between each press to view the formatting characteristics shown in the Preview area

FIGURE 5.9 TABLE AUTOFORMAT DIALOG BOX

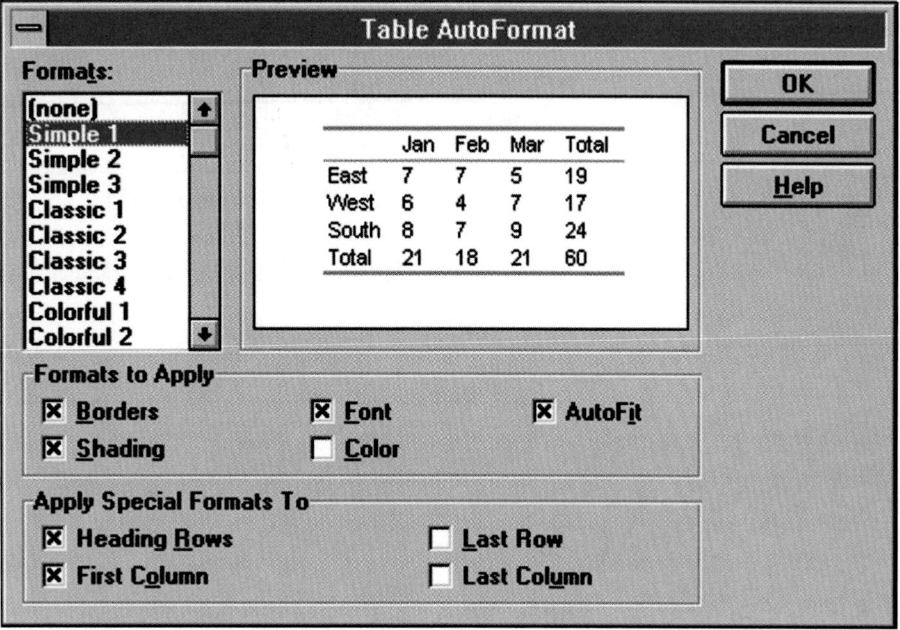

4. SELECT: "Grid 1" in the Formats list box
   PRESS: ENTER or CLICK: OK
   The table is immediately formatted using the Grid 1 options.

5. To format the first table you created:
   RIGHT-CLICK: the 5 × 3 table with the inventory items
   CHOOSE: "Table AutoFormat" from the shortcut menu

6. In the Table AutoFormat dialog box:
   SELECT: "Colorful 2" in the Formats list box
   PRESS: ENTER or CLICK: OK

7. Let's format the title at the top of the page before proceeding:
   SELECT: Inventory List as of December 1994
   SELECT: Arial from the Font drop-down list (Times Roman)
   SELECT: 14 point from the Font Size drop-down list (10)
   CLICK: Bold button (B)
   CLICK: *near the end of the document to remove the highlighting*
   Your screen should now appear similar to Figure 5.10.

8. Save the INVENTRY document to the Advantage Diskette, replacing the original version.

9. Close all the open documents in the document area.

FIGURE 5.10 INVENTRY DOCUMENT AFTER FORMATTING

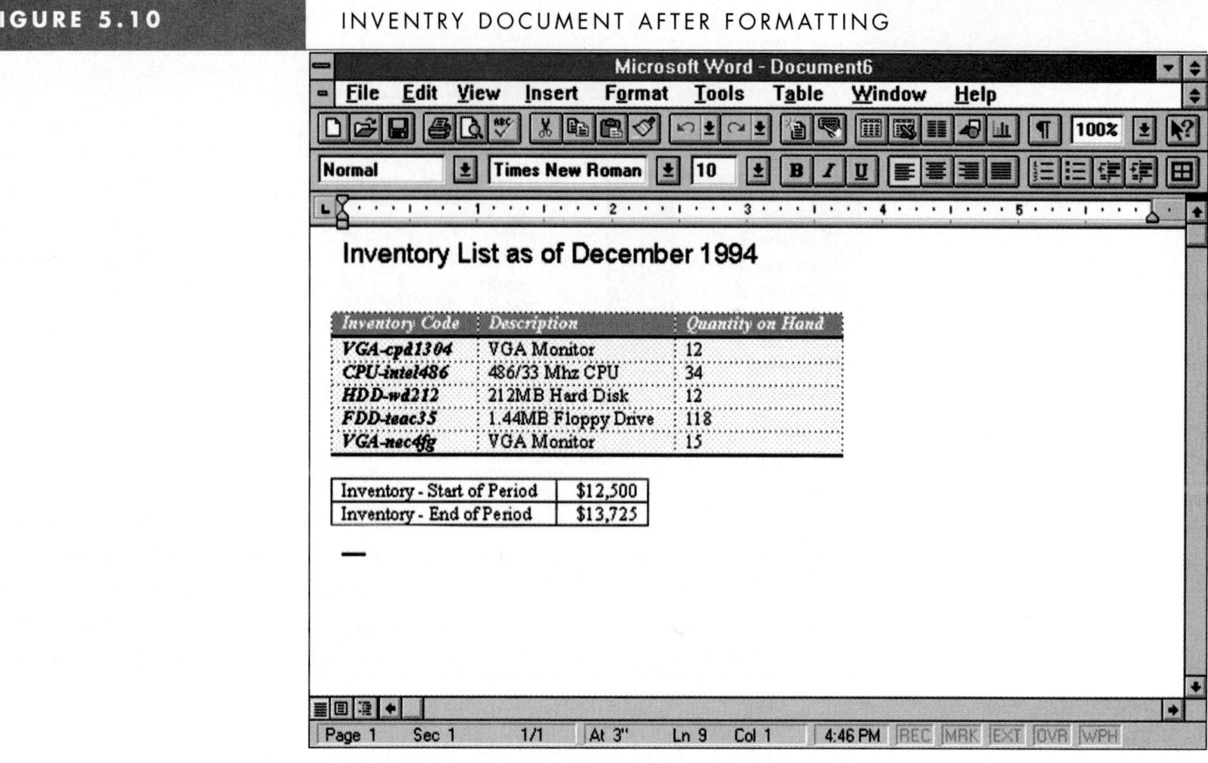

QUICK REFERENCE
Using Table AutoFormat

1. **Position the insertion point in the table you want to format.**
2. **CHOOSE: Table, Table AutoFormat**
3. **SELECT: a formatting option from the Formats list box**
4. **PRESS: ENTER or CLICK: OK**

IN ADDITION CREATING COLUMNS

Tables are best used for keeping text, numbers, or dates aligned in a grid format. Word also provides you with the capability to create *newspaper columns*, also known as *snaking columns*, whereby text wraps automatically to the top of the next column when it reaches the bottom of the current column.

To create columns, choose Format, Columns from the Menu bar. For more information, click the Help button in the Columns dialog box.

MERGING FUNDAMENTALS

Have you ever received a letter from a company or organization that you knew absolutely nothing about? Is your name typed in the salutation and perhaps mentioned in the body of the letter? This kind of document is called a form letter. Your name, along with thousands of others, is stored in a mailing list and placed into specific locations in a letter through a process called **merging**. Merging requires two files: the **data source** and the **main document**. The data source contains variable data, such as names and addresses, to be merged with the main document or form letter.

PREPARING A MERGE OPERATION

Similar to a wizard, Word provides a utility called the Mail Merge Helper that leads you through performing a mail merge from scratch. In addition to creating form letters, the Mail Merge Helper can assist you with printing mailing labels, envelopes, and catalogs. You start the Mail Merge Helper by choosing the Tools, Mail Merge command from the menu. In this section, you will perform a simple merge of an employee mailing list with an interoffice memo.

Perform the following steps to merge a list of names with a memo.

1. Open a new document using the New button (🗋). Ensure that you are viewing the document in Normal view.

2. To launch the Mail Merge Helper:
   CHOOSE: Tools, Mail Merge
   The Mail Merge Helper dialog box appears, as shown in Figure 5.11.

3. The Mail Merge Helper provides three steps as a checklist for performing a mail merge. The first step, according to the dialog box, is to create a main document file. To proceed:
   SELECT: Create command button
   A pop-up menu appears with four possible options: Form Letters, Mailing Labels, Envelopes, and Catalog.

4. To perform a merge for a letter or other such document (i.e., memo):
   CHOOSE: Form Letters from the pop-up menu

5. To use the active document for creating the main document file:
   SELECT: Active Window command button
   Notice that the information you selected appears below the Main Document area in the Mail Merge Helper dialog box.

FIGURE 5.11 MAIL MERGE HELPER

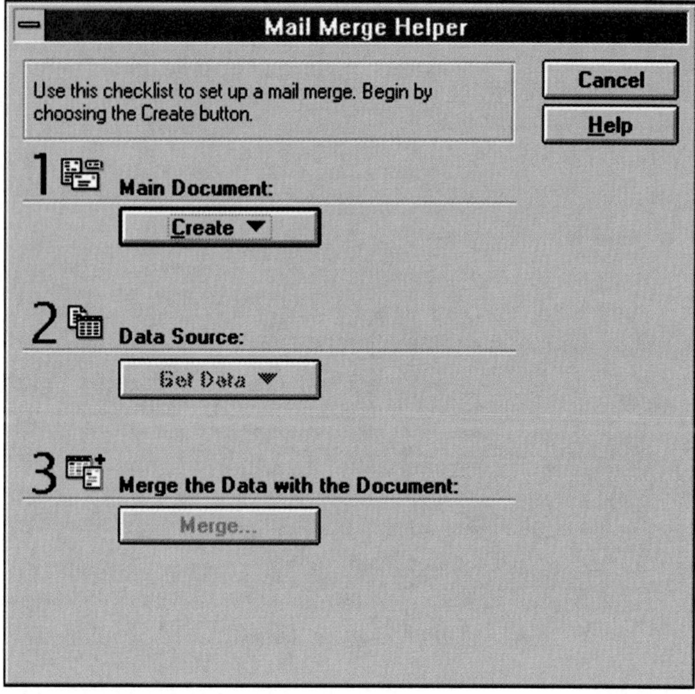

6. Because you are starting this mail merge operation from scratch, you must create a new data source file. To proceed:
   SELECT: Get Data command button
   CHOOSE: Create Data Source from the pop-up menu
   You should see the dialog box in Figure 5.12 appear on your screen.

FIGURE 5.12 CREATE DATA SOURCE DIALOG BOX

Create Data Source

A mail merge data source is composed of rows of data. The first row is called the header row. Each of the columns in the header row begins with a field name.

Word provides commonly used field names in the list below. You can add or remove field names to customize the header row.

Field Name:

Add Field Name >>

Remove Field Name

Field Names in Header Row:

Title
FirstName
LastName
JobTitle
Company
Address1
Address2

Move

OK | Cancel | MS Query... | Help

7. You use the Create Data Source dialog box to define the information you will be merging with the main document file. For the employee mailing list, you require entry blanks (also called **fields**) for their first name, last name, city, state, postal or zip code, and phone number. Fortunately, these fields are among the defaults provided in the Field Names in Header Row list box. To remove the other field names in the list box, you highlight a field name and then select the Remove Field Name command button. Do the following:
   SELECT: "Title" in the Field Names in Header Row list box
   SELECT: Remove Field Name command button

8. Using the procedure outlined in the previous step, remove all the field names in the Field Names in Header Row list box, except for FirstName, LastName, City, State, PostalCode, and WorkPhone.

9. To proceed to the next step:
   PRESS: ENTER or CLICK: OK

10. To save the data source file on the Advantage Diskette:
    TYPE: `a:maillist`
    PRESS: ENTER or CLICK: OK
    After Word finishes saving the file, it displays a dialog box giving you the choice of adding information to the data source or working in the main document.

11. To add the employee information to the MAILLIST data source file:
    SELECT: Edit Data Source command button
    The Data Form dialog box is displayed, as shown in Figure 5.13.

FIGURE 5.13 DATA FORM DIALOG BOX

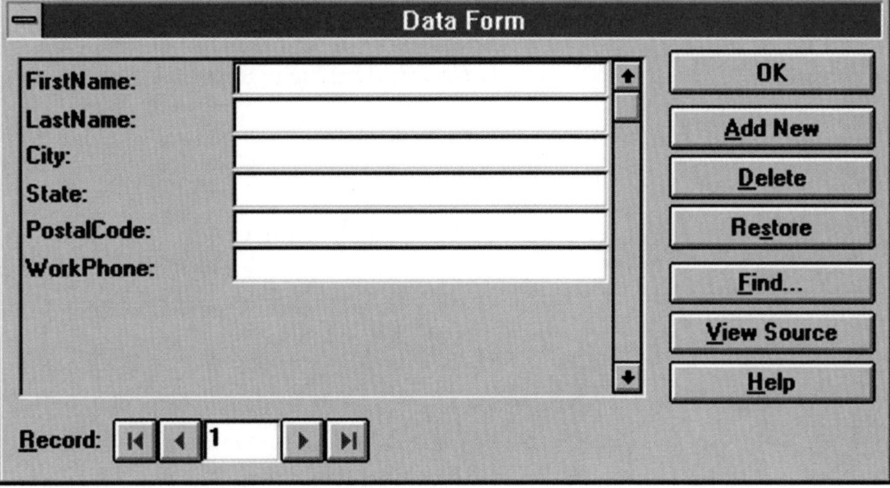

12. Enter the following information using the Data Form dialog box. To advance to the next field, you press TAB or use the mouse. When you reach the WorkPhone field, you press ENTER or click the Add New command button to add a new employee to the data file.

FirstName	*LastName*	*City*	*State*	*PostalCode*	*WorkPhone*
Janos	Sagi	Boston	MA	02116	617-552-4224
Becky	McFee	Chicago	IL	60637	312-654-9871
Sima	Veiner	Toronto	ON	M5B 2H1	416-599-1080
Jack	Yee	Seattle	WA	98004	206-787-3554

13. To finish adding information to the data source file:
    SELECT: OK command button
    You are placed in the main document file, where you will begin editing the form letter. Notice the Merge toolbar that appears below the Formatting toolbar.

14. Let's create a memo to the four employees in the data source file:
    TYPE: `DATE:`
    PRESS: TAB twice
    TYPE: *current date*
    PRESS: ENTER twice
    TYPE: `TO:`
    PRESS: TAB twice

15. To have Word automatically substitute the names of the employees into this memo, you need to specify the merge fields that contain the information:
    CLICK: Insert Merge Field button in the Merge toolbar
    CHOOSE: FirstName from the drop-down menu
    PRESS: Space Bar
    CLICK: Insert Merge Field button
    CHOOSE: LastName from the drop-down menu

16. Now let's add the merge field codes for address information:
    PRESS: ENTER to advance one line
    PRESS: TAB twice
    CLICK: Insert Merge Field button
    CHOOSE: City from the drop-down menu
    TYPE: `,` (a comma)
    PRESS: Space Bar
    CLICK: Insert Merge Field button
    CHOOSE: State from the drop-down menu
    PRESS: ENTER twice

17. TYPE: *FROM:*
    PRESS: TAB twice
    TYPE: *your name*
    PRESS: ENTER four times

18. Enter the body text of the memo:
    TYPE: `Please be advised that the meeting has been postponed until the 4th of January.`

19. Save the document as MAILMEMO onto the Advantage Diskette. Your document should now appear similar to Figure 5.14.

FIGURE 5.14 MAILMEMO DOCUMENT

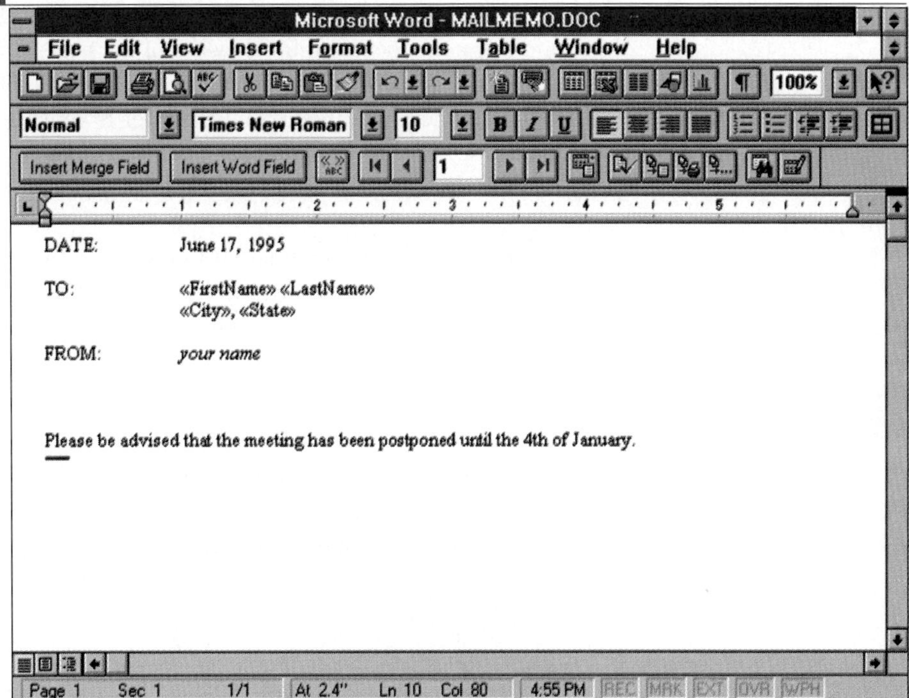

20. To return to the Mail Merge Helper dialog box:
    CHOOSE: Tools, Mail Merge
    (*Note*: You can also click the Mail Merge Helper button on the Merge toolbar.) The file names of the main document and the data source file should appear below their respective steps in the dialog box.

QUICK REFERENCE
Preparing a Mail Merge Operation

1. **CHOOSE: Tools, Mail Merge**
2. **Specify a main document file.**
3. **Specify an existing data source file or create a new data source file.**
4. **If necessary, add information to the data source file.**
5. **Edit the main document, inserting merge fields as desired.**

PERFORMING THE MERGE

Once the data source file and the main document file have been created, you are ready to perform the merge. The output of the merge is typically sent to a new document or to the printer. If there are only a few records in the data source file, you may prefer to merge to a new document, save the document for review, and then print the document at a later time. If there are 2,500 records in the data source file, and the main document file consists of ten pages, then merging the two files would result in a 25,000 page document—an unacceptable length by most standards. In this case, merging directly to the printer is your best option.

Perform the merge in the following steps.

1. With the Mail Merge Helper dialog box displayed:
   SELECT: Merge command button
   The Merge dialog box appears, as shown in Figure 5.15.

FIGURE 5.15 MERGE DIALOG BOX

2. In the Merge To drop-down list box:
   SELECT: New Document

3. To perform the merge:
   SELECT: Merge command button
   The data source file is merged with the main document file and the result is displayed in a separate document.

4. Save the new document as MAILDONE to the Advantage Diskette.

5. Close all the open documents in the document area. When asked to save changes to your documents, respond yes to all dialog boxes.

QUICK REFERENCE
Performing the Merge

1. **In the Mail Merge Helper dialog box:**
   SELECT: Merge command button
2. **In the Merge dialog box:**
   SELECT: Merge command button

CUSTOMIZING WORD

This section introduces you to some of the basic customization options available in Word 6.0. This section is not intended to be an all-inclusive discussion.

IN ADDITION

FOR MORE INFORMATION

If you require further information, please consult Chapter 31, Customizing and Optimizing Word, in the *Microsoft Word User's Guide*.

CHANGING WORD'S DEFAULT SETTINGS

You modify Word's default settings in the Options dialog box, accessed by choosing the Tools, Options command. There are a variety of customization topics contained in this dialog box. For example, you can remove the Status bar and scroll bars from the application window, display the Paragraph symbol on-screen at all times, change Word's default mode to Overtype, and tell the Spell Checker to ignore words in uppercase. This section is a guided tour of only some of these topics, providing you with enough information to explore them on your own.

Perform the following steps to change default settings.

1. Open a new document.

2. To access the Options dialog box:
   CHOOSE: Tools, Options
   Notice the topical tabs that appear in this dialog box.

3. Let's review the View settings first:
   SELECT: View tab
   There are three primary groups on this page: Show, Window, and Nonprinting Characters. The Show group provides an option for viewing your document using a Draft Font. The Window group lets you remove the Status bar and scroll bars from the application window to increase your document viewing area. One of my favorite features is the ability to display just the Paragraph symbol on-screen without having to show all the other hidden characters and codes. You select this option from the Nonprinting Characters group.

4. SELECT: Save tab
   The most popular save options (shown in Figure 5.16) include:
   - Always Create Backup Copy
   - Allow Fast Saves
   - Automatic Save Every 10 Minutes

   Although relatively self-explanatory, you can find more information about each option by selecting the Help command button.

FIGURE 5.16 OPTIONS DIALOG BOX: SAVE

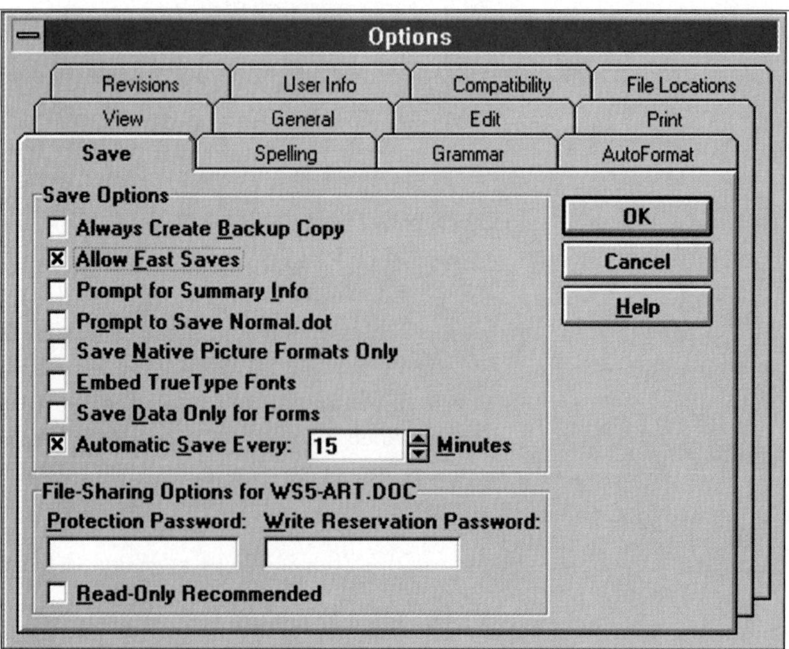

5. SELECT: File Locations tab
   To specify where on your disk you would like Word to look for documents, highlight the Documents option and then select the Modify command button. Word uses this information in the Open dialog box.

6. SELECT: Spelling tab
   If you work with technical terms, abbreviations, or figures, you will appreciate the two check boxes on this page for ignoring information during a spelling check. When the Words in UPPERCASE and Words with Numbers check boxes are selected, Word progresses through a spelling check without stopping on text like RAM, CPU, or 486. Figure 5.17 provides an example of the Spelling options.

FIGURE 5.17 OPTIONS DIALOG BOX: SPELLING

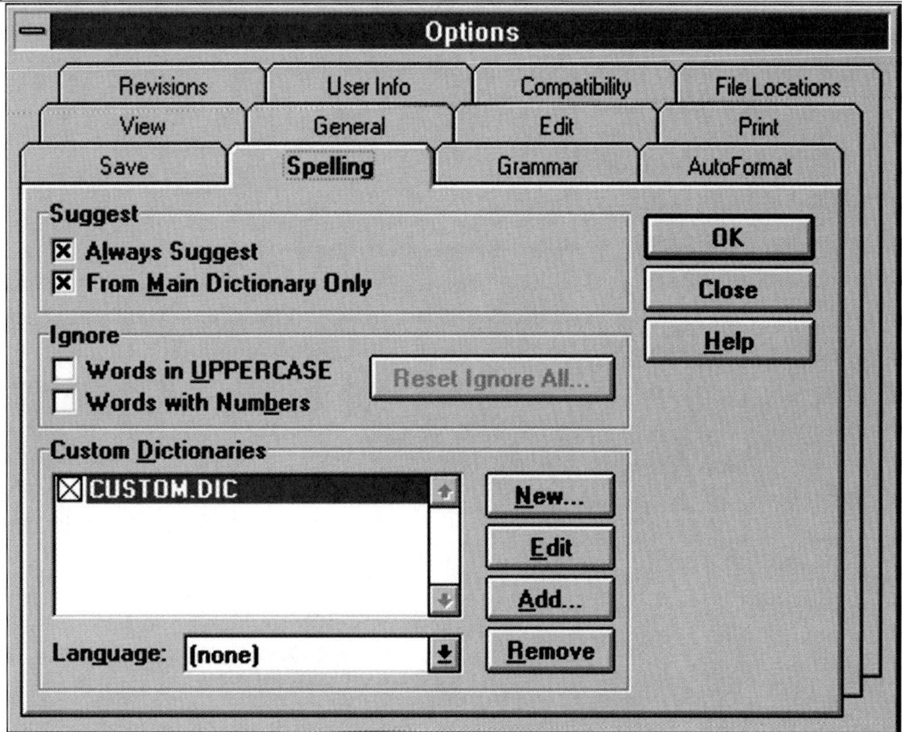

7. To cancel our whirlwind tour through the Options dialog box:
   PRESS: ESC or CLICK: Cancel

IN ADDITION FOR MORE INFORMATION

To find out more information about any setting in the Options dialog box, select the tab of the page you want to learn more about, and then click the Help button.

UNDERSTANDING MACROS

A **macro** is a collection of keystrokes that has been recorded in order to automate a particular sequence of tasks. Once recorded, the procedure or task may be executed again and again by simply selecting the macro from a list or by pressing a shortcut key combination. You can also assign macros to buttons on the toolbar or create new pull-down menu commands. Macros are usually created to cut down on the amount of time and effort required to perform repetitive tasks that are specific to your work.

IN ADDITION FOR MORE INFORMATION

Creating macros is beyond the scope of this session, but definitely not beyond your grasp to learn and use in your documents. To find out more about macros, choose Tools, Macro from the Menu bar and then click the Help button.

SUMMARY

This session introduced you to creating complex documents using wizards. Word 6.0 provides nine wizards for creating agendas, award certificates, calendars, fax covers, letters, memos, newsletters, legal pleading papers, and resumes. Using the Fax Wizard in this session, you produced an attractive fax cover sheet within minutes. You also created and formatted tables in this session for organizing information into rows and columns.

With Word's Mail Merge Helper, you can easily produce form letters. A form letter is a standard document where only the addressee or other variable information changes. With the variable information entered into a data source file, only a single form letter needs to be created. The process of merging takes the information from the data source file and inserts it into the correct locations in the form letter. In this session, you merged names and addresses into a standard memo.

The session concluded with a brief discussion on customizing Word's default settings. Table 5.2 provides a list of the commands and procedures covered in this session.

TABLE 5.2 Command Summary

Task Description	*Menu Command*	*Toolbar Button*
Access wizards for creating new documents	File, New	
Create or insert a table	Table, Insert Table	
Format a table based on predefined formatting guidelines	Table, Table AutoFormat	
Start the Mail Merge Helper to lead you through a mailmerge	Tools, Mail Merge	
Access Word's default settings	Tools, Options	

KEY TERMS

cell
The intersection of a column and row in a table.

data source
A document file that uses a table to capture and store variable information for the merge process.

fields
In a data source file, the entry blanks or individual pieces of information. In a table, rows are complete records for items or people and columns are fields or pieces of information in each record.

macro
A collection of keystrokes that is recorded for playback at a later date. A macro enables you to perform a series of operations by pressing a shortcut key combination or clicking a toolbar button.

main document
A type of form letter document used by Word in the merge process. The main document file contains codes to insert information from the data source file.

merging
The process of taking information from a data source file and inserting it into a form letter or main document file, one record at a time. The results from merging these two files can be sent to a file or the printer.

wizard
A Word 6.0 feature that provides step-by-step assistance through the document creation process.

EXERCISES

SHORT ANSWER

1. List the nine wizards that are available in Word 6.0.
2. How would you create a resume using a wizard?
3. When would you use a table in a document?
4. Name two methods for creating a table.
5. What is the quickest method for formatting a table?

6. Explain the merge process.

7. What is a data source file?

8. List two options for where the results of a print merge can be sent.

9. How do you tell Word to display the Paragraph symbol on-screen without displaying the other nonprinting characters and codes?

10. How do you create a macro?

HANDS-ON

(*Note*: In the following exercises, save your documents onto and retrieve files from the Advantage Diskette.)

1. In the following exercise, you create and format a table.

   a. Open a new document.

   b. Create the document appearing in Figure 5.18.

   c. Insert the following table between the first and second paragraph.

Client Initial	*Qty*	*Description*	*Total Price*
	5	Laser Printers	$10,250.00
	5	Printer Cables	76.00
	20	3.5" Diskettes	30.00
	5	Windows 3.1	450.00

   d. Make the headings in the table bold.

   e. Add a new row at the bottom of the table and enter the following:

		TOTAL COST	$10,806.00

   f. Apply a predefined format of your choice to the table using the Table, Table AutoFormat command.

   g. Save the document as ROLAND onto the Advantage Diskette.

FIGURE 5.18 ROLAND DOCUMENT

```
[current date]

Mr. Roland Garros
Clay Supplies Inc.
1091 Panorama Ridge
Waco, TX  76798

Dear Mr. Garros:

Per your request, I am providing a list of the
items that you ordered for your office last
Wednesday.

Please confirm the order by placing your initial
beside each item in the column provided, and then
fax this letter back to me at 817-747-1234.

Yours sincerely,
Grand Slam Computer Sales


[your name]
Account Representative
```

h. Print the document.

i. Close the document.

2. In this exercise, you create a main document file and a data source file, and then perform a merge of the two documents to create a third file.

   a. Open a new document.

   b. CHOOSE: Tools, Mail Merge

   c. Use the active window as the main document file.

   d. Create a new file for the data source.

   e. Use the following fields for the data file: FirstName, LastName, Address1, City, State, ZipCode.

   f. Save the data source as CUSTDATA onto the Advantage Diskette.

g. Enter the following information into the data source file.

FirstName	LastName	Address1	City	State	ZipCode
Elliot	Lepinski	898 Burrard Ave.	Louisville	KY	40205
Red	Robinson	235 Johnson St.	Washington	DC	20052
Elaine	Maynard	1005 West 9th St.	Baton Rouge	LA	70803
Ranjitt	Singh	122 Cordova Ave.	Tacoma	WA	98416
William	Delaney	36 Primore Road	Wichita	KS	67208
Francisco	Ortez	875 Broadway	Albuquerque	NM	87131
Alice	Chan	29 Redmond Road	San Francisco	CA	92182
Jessica	Thomas	909 West 18th St.	Brooklyn	NY	11225
Jimmy	Kazo	888 East 8th Ave.	Billings	MT	59101

h. Create the document appearing in Figure 5.19. Do not type the merge codes. Use the Insert Merge Field button to add each merge code, such as <<FirstName>>, to the document.

i. Save the main file as CUSTFORM onto the Advantage Diskette.

j. Perform the merge to a new document, using the Mail Merge Helper.

k. Save the new file as CUSTDONE onto the Advantage Diskette.

3. Guess what? You've just been given an award for "Accomplished Microsoft Word User" by Sarah Hutchinson and Glen Coulthard of Richard D. Irwin, Inc.

   a. Use a document wizard to create your award.

   b. Save the award onto the Advantage Diskette as AWARD.

   c. Print the AWARD document.

4. In this exercise you create a main document file and a data source file, and then perform the merge of the two documents to create a third file. Choose Tools, Mail Merge to begin.

   a. Create a data source that contains the names and addresses of five or more family members and/or friends.

   b. Save the data source as FRIENDS onto the Advantage Diskette.

FIGURE 5.19 CUSTFORM DOCUMENT

[*today's date*]

<<FirstName>> <<LastName>>
<<Address>>
<<City>>, <<State>> <<ZipCode>>

Dear **<<FirstName>>:**

We're Moving!

Please be informed that as of August 31, 1993 we are moving to new premises located at 8030 United Boulevard in Boston.

We are looking forward to this move with great anticipation. Because of your continued support, we are expanding our training facilities to accommodate two training rooms and a board room.

As a result of this move, we will be closed from the third week in August to the end of September. An invitation to the Open House will be forwarded to you, **<<FirstName>>**, as soon as we are settled.

Let us know if we can do anything for you!

Sincerely,

[*your name*]
President

c. Create a document that describes what you've been up to lately. Insert the merge codes you defined in step a using the Insert Merge Field button.

d. Save the main file as MYNEWS onto the Advantage Diskette.

e. Perform the merge to a new document, using the Mail Merge Helper.

f. Print the documents, but don't save them.

CASE PROBLEMS

THE UNION TENNIS CLUB

(*Note*: In the following case problems, assume the role of the primary characters and perform the same steps that they identify. You may want to re-read the session opening.)

1. Now that he knows how to create tables, Jerry isn't dreading the task at hand. Nine members of the Union Tennis Club have overdue accounts and he must put their names and addresses (see below) into a table. When finished, he saves the file as OVERDUE onto the Advantage Diskette. (*Note*: Include the table headings in the first row of the table.)

FirstName	LastName	Address1	City	State	PostalCode
Muriel	Britzky	3710 Bush Street	San Francisco	CA	94111
Myron	Drexler	1485 Sonoma Hwy	Sonoma	CA	96555
Julie	Davis	100 Bosley Lane	New York	NY	90000
Mitch	Kaplanoff	20 Cactus Lane	Palm Desert	CA	98888
Michael	Reynolds	17 Windy Way	Lincoln	MA	09111
Jacob	Raggio	P.O. Box 145	Evergreen	CO	89777
Mary	Timberlake	151 Greer Road	Evanston	IL	60201
Todd	Bowman	200 Union Street	San Francisco	CA	14441
Valli	Terris	1871 Orrinton Ave	Chicago	IL	87555

2. Since he has already created the table of overdue members, Jerry decides to create a reminder letter complete with merge codes. During the process, Jerry selects "Open Data Source" to tell Microsoft Word where to "get" the data and specifies his OVERDUE document on the Advantage Diskette. After creating the form letter, Jerry saves it onto the Advantage Diskette as UNION. He then performs the merge and prints out the form letters. Because he's concerned about disk space on his computer, he doesn't save the merged form letters as a document onto the Advantage Diskette.

3. Jerry wants to include a table in the upcoming newsletter that lists the sale items available in the club's tennis shop. These items include:

Item	*Description*	*Cost*
Tennis Racket	Wilson Hammer	$139.00
Tennis Shirts	UTC logo	$14.95
Tennis Shorts	Navy-Mens	$21.99
Visors	White	$7.50
Tennis Balls	Wilson	$2.00
Tennis Bag	Penn	$24.99

After creating the table, Jerry formats it for the newsletter. He then saves it onto the Advantage Diskette as UTC-SALE. With his desk clear, Jerry pokes his head out of his office and asks politely: "Tennis, anyone?"

Appendix

Microsoft Word 6.0: Toolbar Summary

STANDARD

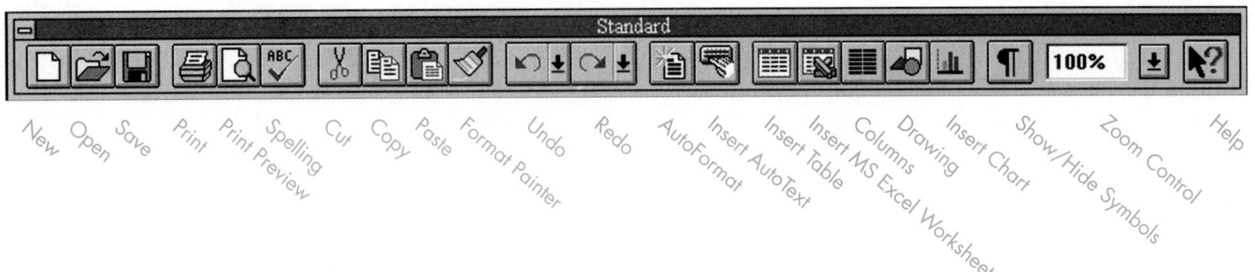

FORMATTING

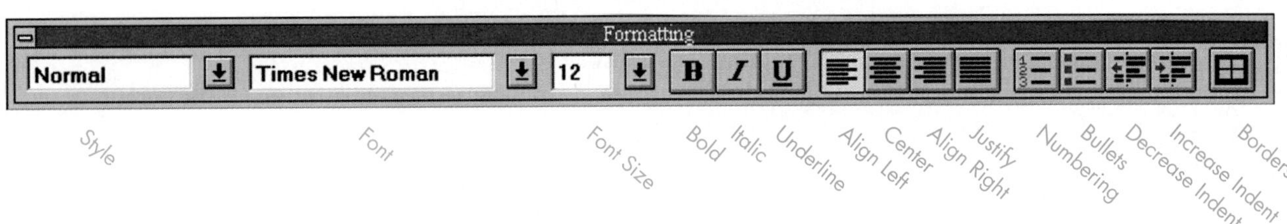

BORDERS

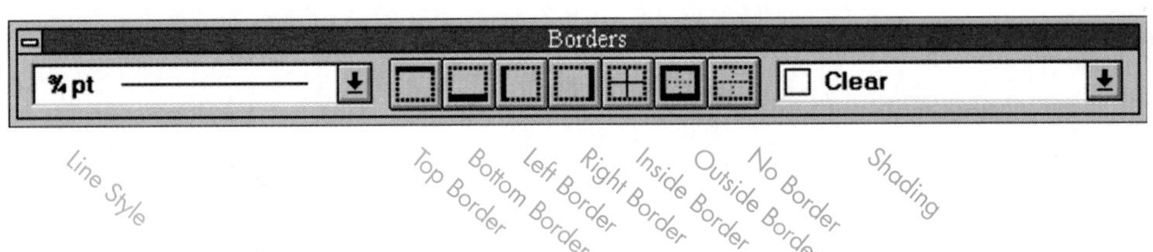

DATABASE

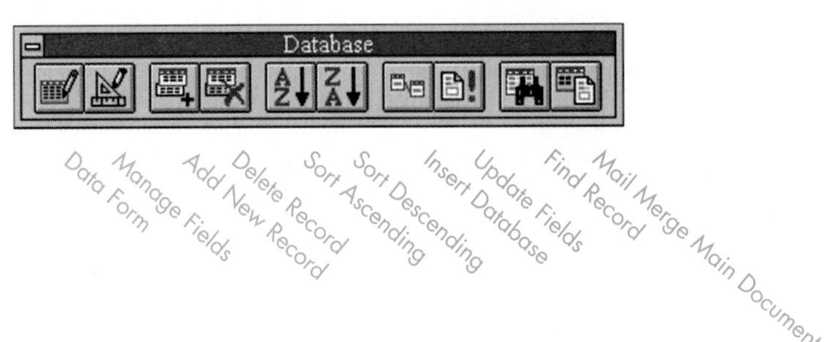

DRAWING

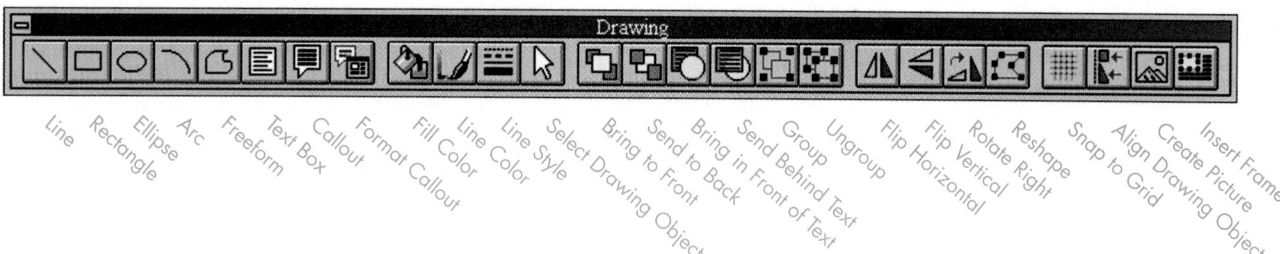
Drawing
Line
Rectangle
Ellipse
Arc
Freeform
Text Box
Callout
Format Callout
Fill Color
Line Color
Line Style
Select Drawing Objects
Bring to Front
Send to Back
Bring in Front of Text
Send Behind Text
Group
Ungroup
Flip Horizontal
Flip Vertical
Rotate Right
Reshape
Snap to Grid
Align Drawing Objects
Create Picture
Insert Frame

FORMS

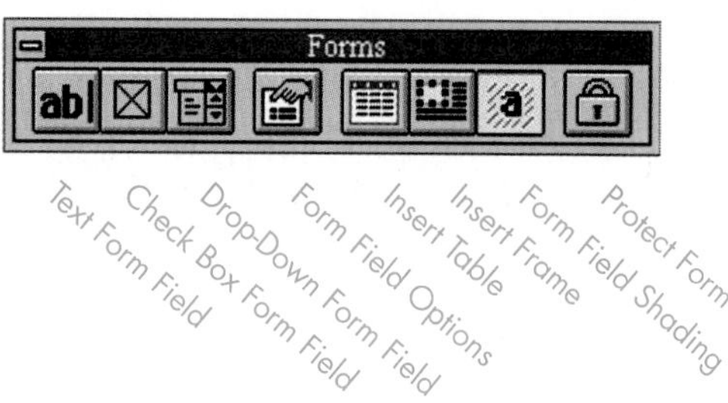
Forms
Text Form Field
Check Box Form Field
Drop-Down Form Field
Form Field Options
Insert Table
Insert Frame
Form Field Shading
Protect Form

MICROSOFT

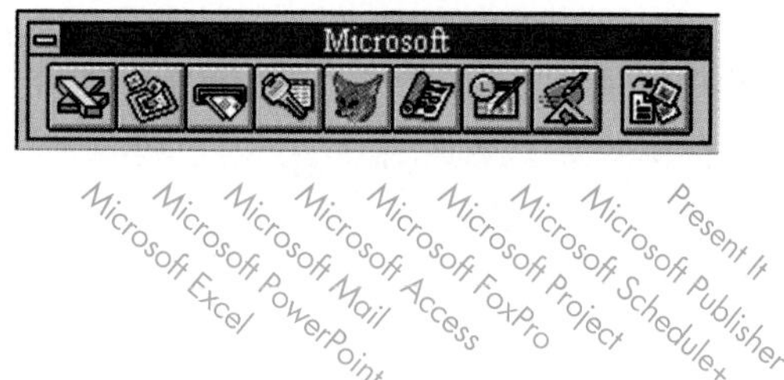
Microsoft
Microsoft Excel
Microsoft PowerPoint
Microsoft Mail
Microsoft Access
Microsoft FoxPro
Microsoft Project
Microsoft Schedule+
Microsoft Publisher
Present It

Index